Contents

City Centre Maps

Amsterdam	ii
Athens	ii
Bangkok	ii
Berlin	ii
Brussels	iii
Delhi	iii
Dublin	iii
Edinburgh	iii
Lisbon	iv
London	iv
Madrid	iv
Mexico City	v
Mumbai	v
New York	v
Paris	vi
Prague	vi
Rio de Janeiro	vi
Rome	vii
Singapore	vii
Sydney	vii
Tokyo	vii
World Cities: Distances	viii

World Maps

Time Zones and Key to Map Symbols	I
The World: Physical 1:95 000 000	2–3
The World: Political 1:95 000 000	4–5
Polar Regions 1:35 000 000	6
Scandinavia and the Baltic Lands 1:10 000 000	7
Iceland	
England and Wales 1:2 000 000	8–9
Scotland 1:2 000 000	10
Ireland 1:2 000 000	11

France 1:5 000 000	12
Spain and Portugal 1:5 000 000	13
Italy and the Balkan States 1:5 000 000	14–15
Germany and Central Europe 1:5 000 000	16
South-east Europe and Turkey 1:10 000 000	17
Russia and Central Asia 1:20 000 000	18–19
China and Korea 1:15 000 000	20–21
Hong Kong and Macau	
Japan 1:6 400 000	22
South-east Asia 1:20 000 000	23
Southern Asia and the Middle East 1:17 500 000	24–25
Northern Africa 1:15 000 000	26–27
Central and Southern Africa 1:15 000 000	28–29
Madagascar	
Australia and Oceania 1:20 000 000	30–31
South-east Australia 1:8 000 000	32
Tasmania	
New Zealand 1:6 000 000	33
Fiji, Tonga and Samoa Islands	
Pacific Ocean 1:54 000 000	34–35
Canada 1:15 000 000	36–37
Alaska	
Western United States 1:6 000 000	38–39
Hawaii	
Middle United States 1:6 000 000	40–41
Eastern United States 1:6 000 000	42–43
Mexico, Central America and the West Indies 1:15 000 000	44–45
Jamaica, Guadeloupe, Martinique,	
Puerto Rico, Virgin Islands, St Lucia and Barbados	
South America – North 1:16 000 000	46–47
Trinidad and Tobago	
South America – South 1:16 000 000	48
Index to World Maps	49–57

CITY CENTRE MAPS – KEY TO SYMBOLS

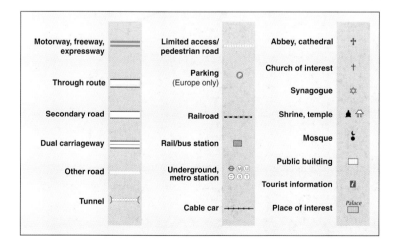

Philip's World Atlases are published in association with The Royal Geographical Society (with The Institute of British Geographers).

The Society was founded in 1830 and given a Royal Charter in 1859 for 'the advancement of geographical science'. It holds historical collections of national and international importance, many of which relate to the Society's association with and support for scientific exploration and research from the 19th century onwards. It was pivotal in establishing geography as a teaching and research discipline in British universities close to the turn of the century, and has played a key role in geographical and environmental education ever since.

Today the Society is a leading world centre for geographical learning – supporting education, teaching, research and expeditions, and promoting public understanding of the subject.

The Society welcomes those interested in geography as members. For further information, please visit the website at: www.rgs.org

CITY CENTRE MAPS – Cartography by Philip's
Page iii, Dublin: The town plan of Dublin is based on Ordnance Survey Ireland by permission of the Government Permit Number 7452. © Government of Ireland.

Ordnance Survey® Page iii, Edinburgh, and page iv, London: This product includes mapping licensed from Ordnance Survey® with the permission of the Controller of Her Majesty's Stationery Office. © Crown copyright 2002. All rights reserved. Licence number 100011710.

Vector data: Courtesy of Gräfe and Unser Verlag GmbH, München, Germany (city centre maps of Bangkok, Mexico City, Singapore, Sydney and Tokyo).

Published in Great Britain in 2002 by Philip's, a division of Octopus Publishing Group, 2–4 Heron Quays, London E14 4JP

Copyright © 2002 Philip's
Reprinted 2002
Cartography by Philip's

ISBN 0–540–08214–7

A CIP catalogue record for this book is available from the British Library.

Printed in Hong Kong

Details of other Philip's titles and services can be found on our website at: www.philips-maps.co.uk

Cover satellite images courtesy of NPA Group Limited, Edenbridge, Kent (www.satmaps.com)

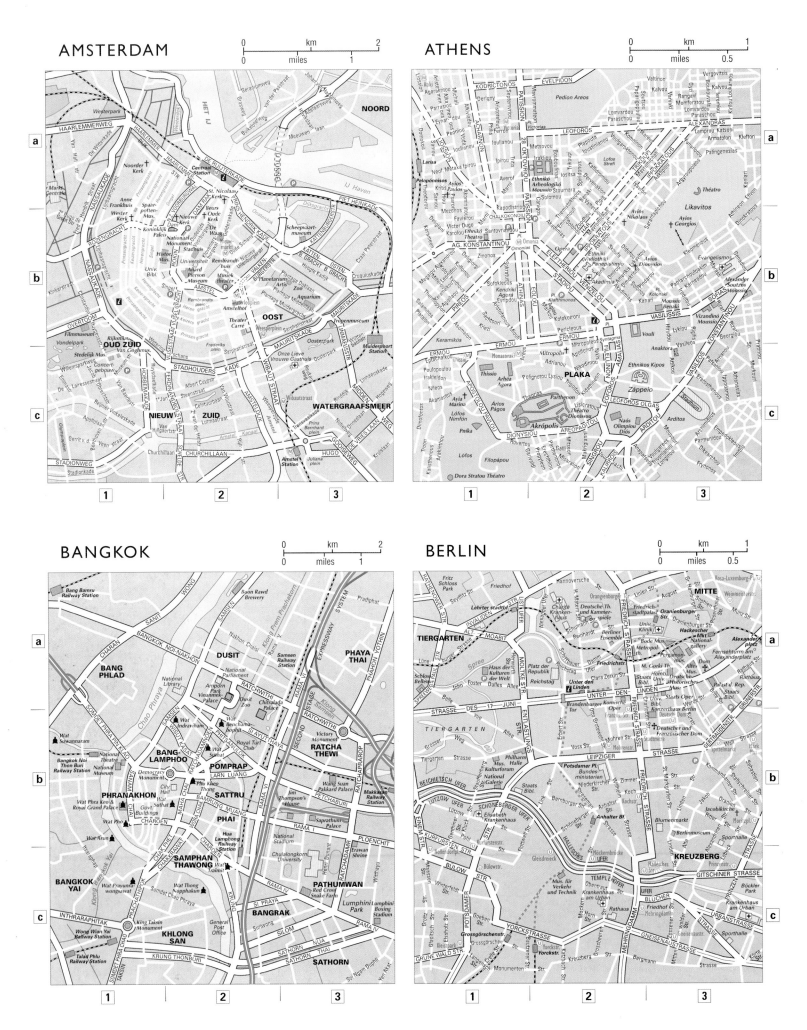

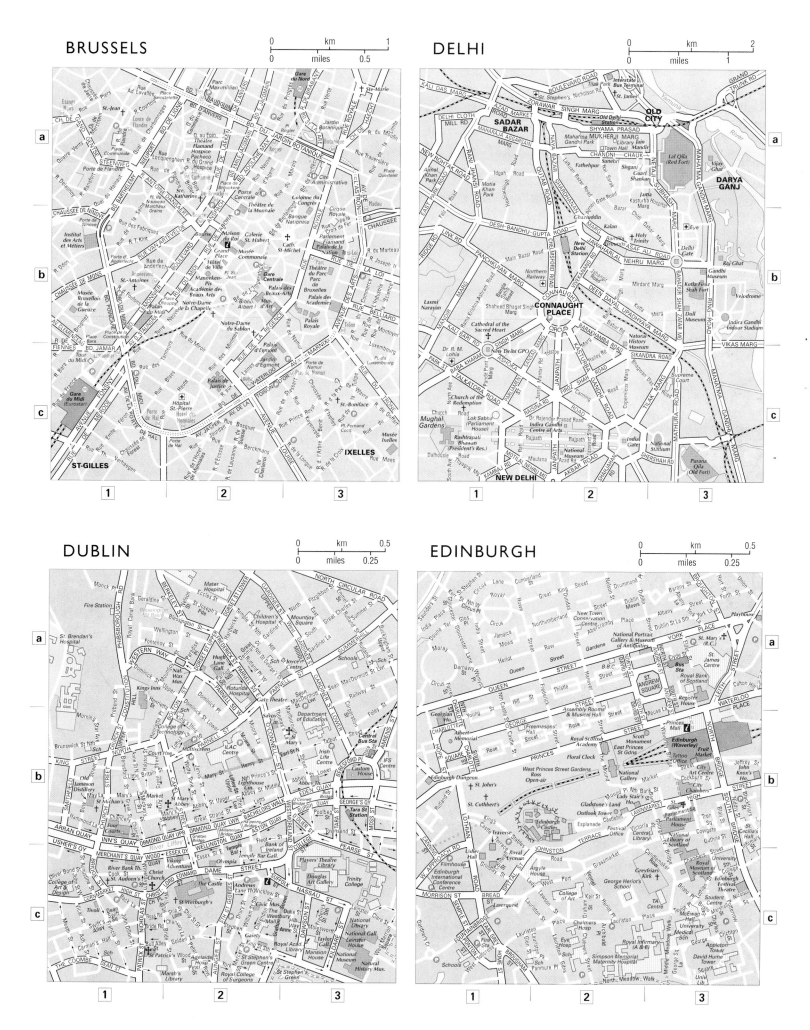

BRUSSELS

DELHI

DUBLIN

EDINBURGH

IV LONDON, LISBON, MADRID

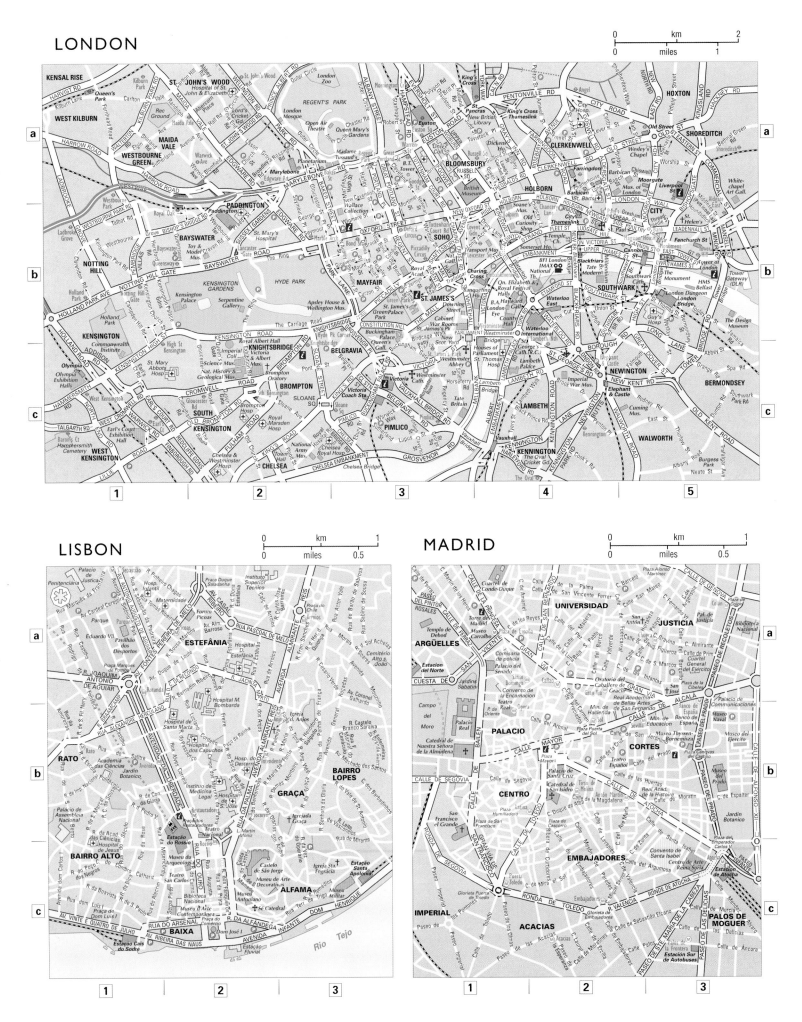

MEXICO CITY

MUMBAI

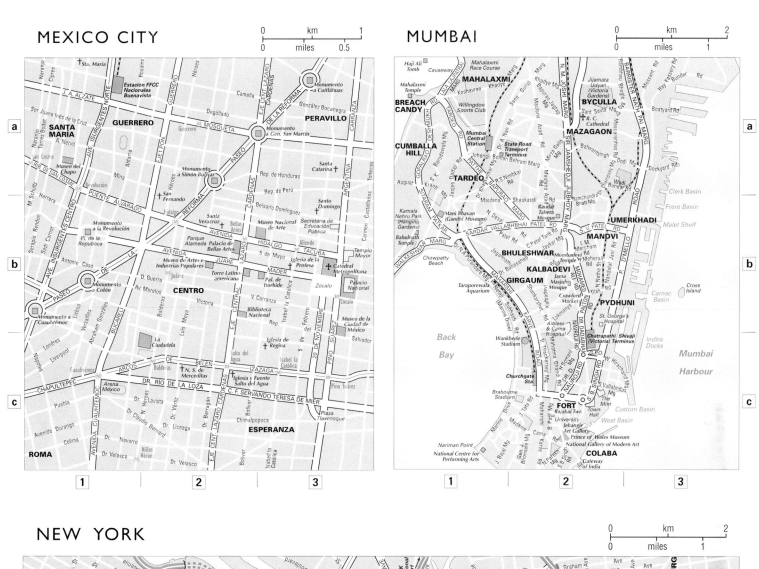

NEW YORK

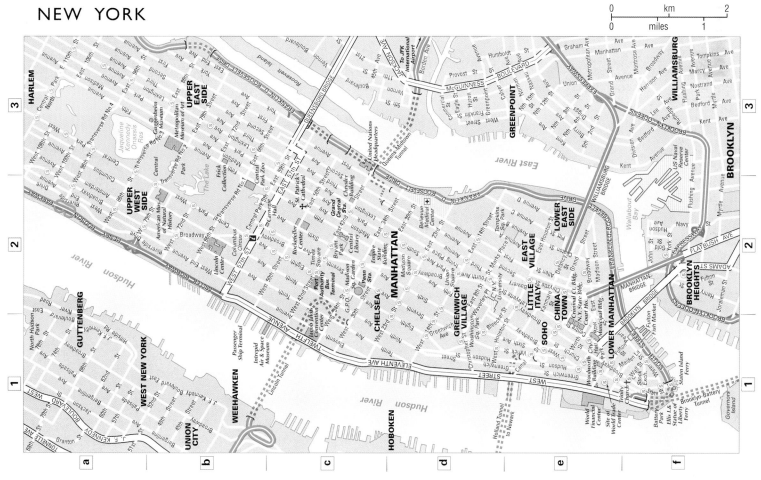

VI PARIS, PRAGUE, RIO DE JANEIRO

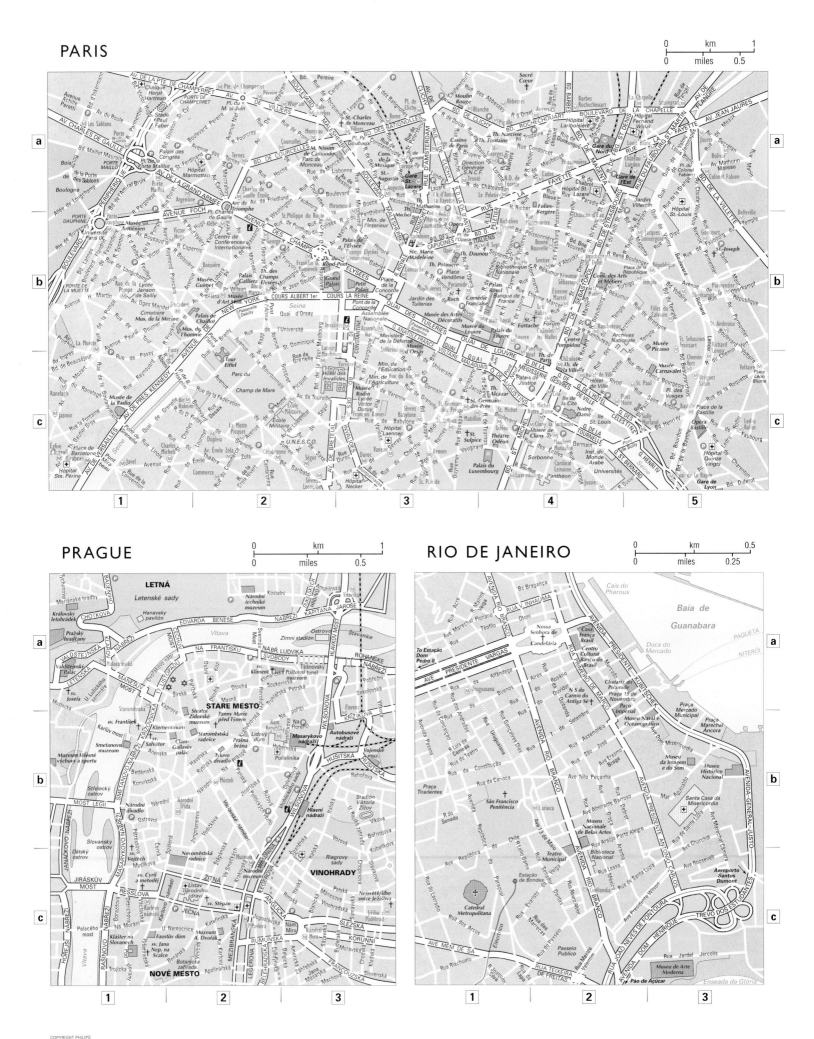

PARIS

PRAGUE

RIO DE JANEIRO

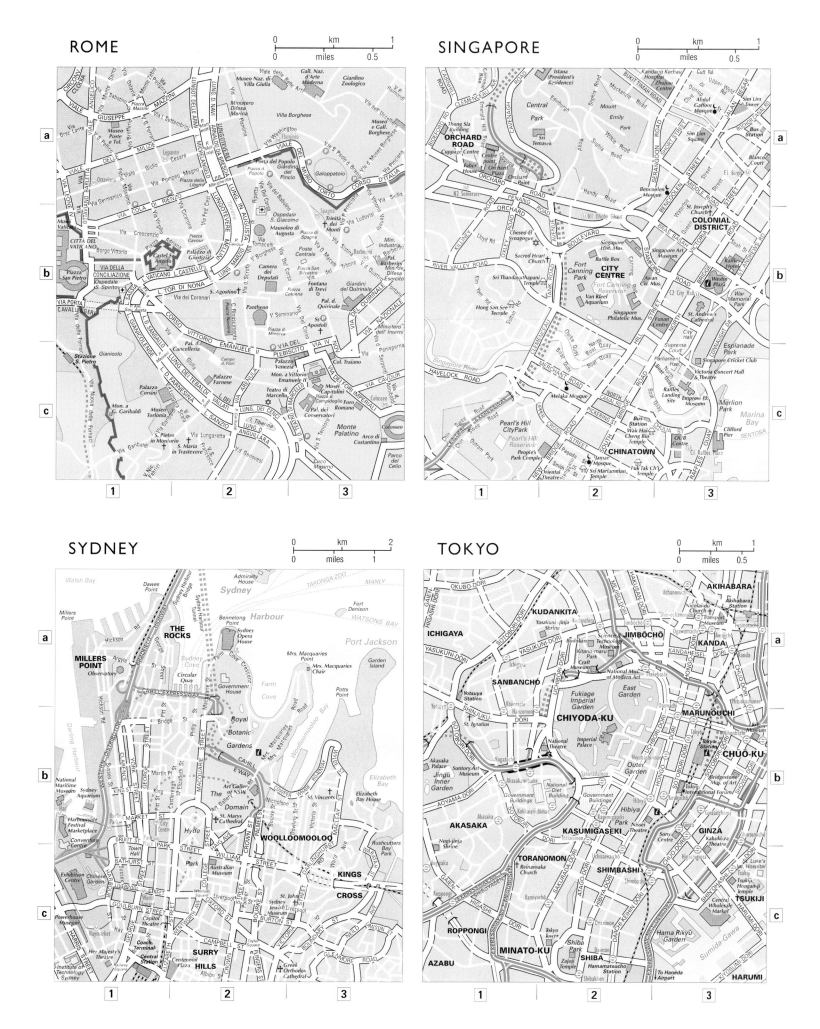

VIII WORLD CITIES: DISTANCES

The table shows air distances in miles and kilometres between 24 major cities. Known as 'Great Circle' distances, these measure the shortest routes between the cities, which aircraft use wherever possible. The maps show the world centred on six cities, and illustrate, for example, why direct flights from Japan to northern America and Europe are across the Arctic regions. The maps have been constructed on an Azimuthal Equidistant projection, on which all distances measured through the centre point are true to scale. The red lines are drawn at 5,000, 10,000 and 15,000 km from the central city.

The table gives distances in **Kms** (upper-right triangle) and **Miles** (lower-left triangle) between each pair of cities.

City	Beijing	Bombay (Mumbai)	Buenos Aires	Cairo	Calcutta (Kolkata)	Caracas	Chicago	Hong Kong	Honolulu	Johannesburg	Lagos	London	Los Angeles	Mexico City	Moscow	Nairobi	New York	Paris	Rio de Janeiro	Rome	Singapore	Sydney	Tokyo	Wellington
Beijing	—	2956	11972	4688	2031	8947	6588	1220	5070	7276	7119	5057	6251	7742	3600	5727	6828	5106	10773	5049	2783	5561	1304	6700
Bombay (Mumbai)	4757	—	9275	2706	1034	9024	8048	2683	8024	4334	4730	4467	8700	9728	3126	2816	7793	4356	8332	3837	2432	6313	4189	7686
Buenos Aires	19268	14925	—	7341	10268	3167	5599	11481	7558	5025	4919	6917	6122	4591	8374	6463	5298	6867	1214	6929	9867	7332	11410	6202
Cairo	7544	4355	11814	—	3541	6340	6127	5064	8838	3894	2432	2180	7580	7687	1803	2197	5605	1994	6149	1325	5137	8959	5947	10268
Calcutta (Kolkata)	3269	1664	16524	5699	—	9609	7978	1653	7048	5256	5727	4946	8152	9494	3438	3839	7921	4883	9366	4486	1800	5678	3195	7055
Caracas	14399	14522	5096	10203	15464	—	2502	10166	6009	6847	4810	4664	3612	2228	6175	7173	2131	4738	2825	5196	11407	9534	8801	8154
Chicago	10603	12953	9011	3206	12839	4027	—	7783	4247	8689	5973	3949	1742	1694	4971	8005	711	4132	5311	4809	9369	9243	6299	8358
Hong Kong	1963	4317	18478	8150	2659	16360	12526	—	5543	6669	7360	5980	7232	8775	4439	5453	8047	5984	11001	5769	1615	4582	1786	5857
Honolulu	8160	12914	12164	14223	11343	9670	6836	8921	—	11934	10133	7228	2558	3781	7036	10739	4958	7437	8290	8026	6721	5075	3854	4669
Johannesburg	11710	6974	8088	6267	8459	11019	13984	10732	19206	—	2799	5637	10362	9063	5692	1818	7979	5426	4420	4811	5381	6860	8418	7308
Lagos	11457	7612	7916	3915	9216	7741	9612	11845	16308	4505	—	3118	7713	6879	3886	2366	5268	2929	3750	2510	6925	9643	8376	9973
London	8138	7190	11131	3508	7961	7507	6356	9623	11632	9071	5017	—	5442	5552	1552	4237	3463	212	5778	889	6743	10558	5942	11691
Los Angeles	10060	14000	9852	12200	13120	5812	2804	11639	4117	16676	12414	8758	—	1549	6070	9659	2446	5645	6310	6331	8776	7502	5475	6719
Mexico City	12460	15656	7389	12372	15280	3586	2726	14122	6085	14585	11071	8936	2493	—	6664	9207	2090	5717	4780	6365	10321	8058	7024	6897
Moscow	5794	5031	13477	2902	5534	9938	8000	7144	11323	9161	6254	2498	9769	10724	—	3942	4666	1545	7184	1477	5237	9008	4651	10283
Nairobi	9216	4532	10402	3536	6179	11544	12883	8776	17282	2927	3807	6819	15544	14818	6344	—	7358	4029	5548	3350	4635	7552	6996	8490
New York	10988	12541	8526	9020	12747	3430	1145	12950	7980	12841	8477	5572	3936	3264	7510	11842	—	3626	4832	4280	9531	9935	6741	8951
Paris	8217	7010	11051	3210	7858	7625	6650	9630	11968	8732	4714	342	9085	9200	2486	6485	5836	—	5708	687	6671	10539	6038	11798
Rio de Janeiro	17338	13409	1953	9896	15073	4546	8547	17704	13342	7113	6035	9299	10155	7693	11562	8928	7777	9187	—	5725	9763	8389	11551	7367
Rome	8126	6175	11151	2133	7219	8363	7739	9284	12916	7743	4039	1431	10188	10243	2376	5391	6888	1105	9214	—	6229	10143	6127	11523
Singapore	4478	3914	15879	8267	2897	18359	15078	2599	10816	8660	11145	10852	14123	16610	8428	7460	15339	10737	15712	10025	—	3915	3306	5298
Sydney	8949	10160	11800	14418	9138	15343	14875	7374	8168	11040	15519	16992	12073	12969	14497	12153	15989	16962	13501	16324	6300	—	4861	1383
Tokyo	2099	6742	18362	9571	5141	14164	10137	2874	6202	13547	13480	9562	8811	11304	7485	11260	10849	9718	18589	9861	5321	7823	—	5762
Wellington	10782	12370	9981	16524	11354	13122	13451	9427	7513	11761	16050	18814	10814	11100	16549	13664	14405	18987	11855	18545	8526	2226	9273	—

MEXICO CITY
19 26°N 99 4°W

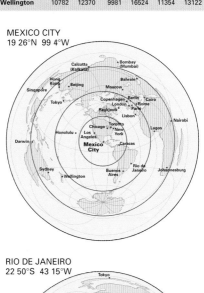

LONDON
51 28°N 0 27°W

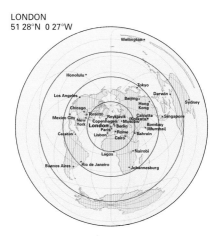

TOKYO
35 33°N 139 46°E

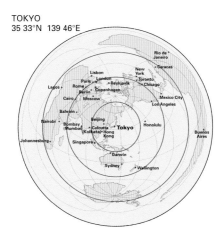

RIO DE JANEIRO
22 50°S 43 15°W

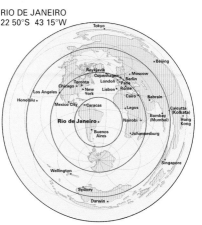

SINGAPORE
1 21°N 103 54°E

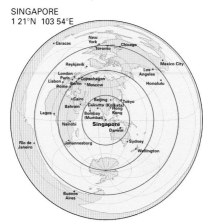

SYDNEY
33 56°S 151 10°E

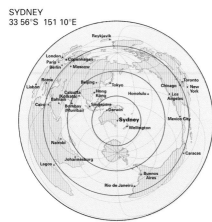

SETTLEMENTS

■ PARIS   ■ Berne   ◉ Livorno   ● Brugge   ◎ Algeciras   ○ *Frejus*   ○ *Oberammergau*   ○ *Thira*

Settlement symbols and type styles vary according to the scale of each map and indicate the importance of towns on the map rather than specific population figures

ADMINISTRATION

———— International Boundaries   – – – International Boundaries (Undefined or Disputed)   ·········· Internal Boundaries

International boundaries show the *de facto* situation where there are rival claims to territory

COMMUNICATIONS

———— Principal Roads   ⌒⌒ Principal Railways   ⊣–⊢ Railway Tunnels

⊣···⊢ Road Tunnels   – –⌒ Railways Under Construction   ⊞⊞⊞ Principal Canals

⋈ Passes   ⊕ Airfields

PHYSICAL FEATURES

⌒⌒ Perrenial Streams   ◯ Intermittent Lakes   ▲ 8848 Elevations in metres

– – – Intermittent Streams   ◌ Swamps and Marshes   ▼ 8500 Sea Depths in metres

◯ Perennial Lakes   ▨ Permanent Ice and Glaciers   *1134* Height of Lake Surface Above Sea Level in metres

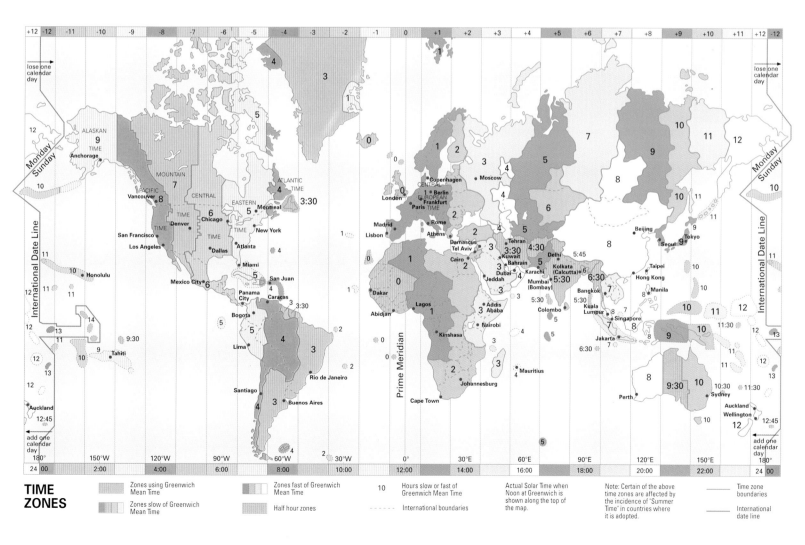

TIME ZONES

▨ Zones using Greenwich Mean Time	▨ Zones fast of Greenwich Mean Time	10 Hours slow or fast of Greenwich Mean Time	Actual Solar Time when Noon at Greenwich is shown along the top of the map.	Note: Certain of the above time zones are affected by the incidence of "Summer Time" in countries where it is adopted.
▨ Zones slow of Greenwich Mean Time	▨ Half hour zones	– – – International boundaries		

———— Time zone boundaries

———— International date line

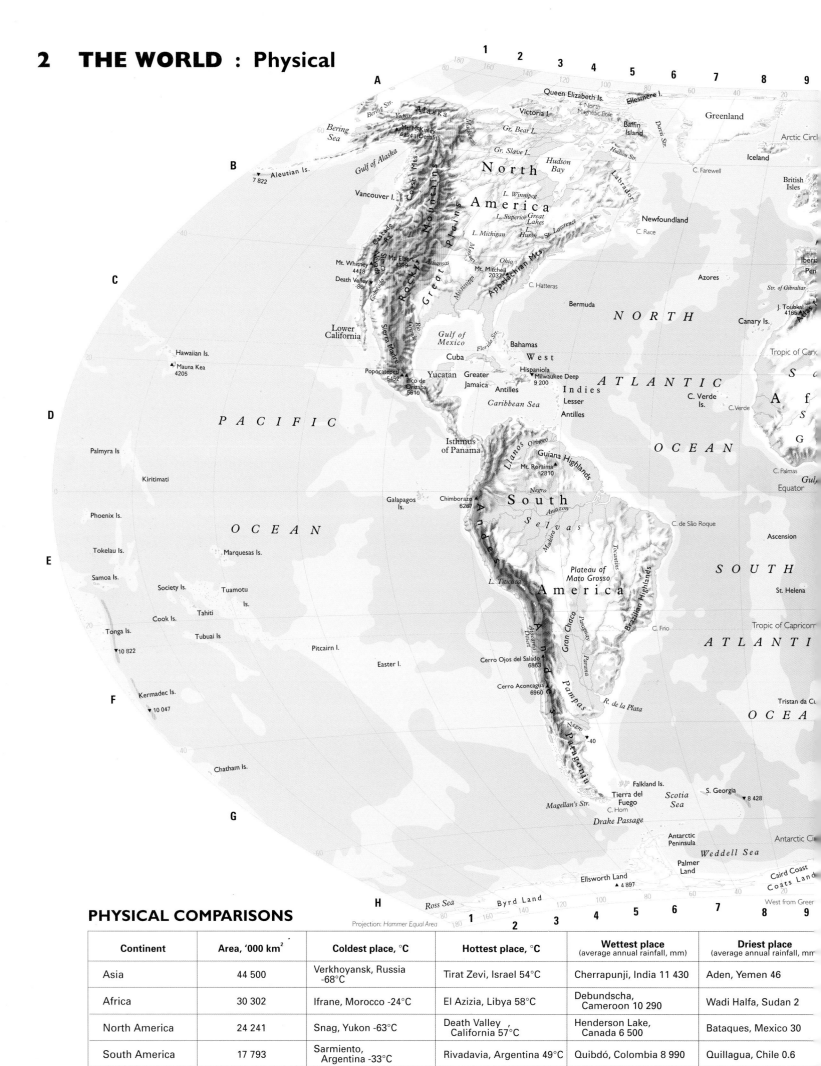

PHYSICAL COMPARISONS

Continent	Area, '000 km²	Coldest place, °C	Hottest place, °C	Wettest place (average annual rainfall, mm)	Driest place (average annual rainfall, mm)
Asia	44 500	Verkhoyansk, Russia -68°C	Tirat Zevi, Israel 54°C	Cherrapunji, India 11 430	Aden, Yemen 46
Africa	30 302	Ifrane, Morocco -24°C	El Azizia, Libya 58°C	Debundscha, Cameroon 10 290	Wadi Halfa, Sudan 2
North America	24 241	Snag, Yukon -63°C	Death Valley, California 57°C	Henderson Lake, Canada 6 500	Bataques, Mexico 30
South America	17 793	Sarmiento, Argentina -33°C	Rivadavia, Argentina 49°C	Quibdó, Colombia 8 990	Quillagua, Chile 0.6
Antarctica	14 000	Vostok -89°C	Vanda Station 15°C		
Europe	9 957	Ust'Shchugor, Russia -55°C	Seville, Spain 50°C	Crkvice, Yugoslavia 4 650	Astrakhan, Russia 160
Oceania	8 557	Charlotte Pass, Australia -22°C	Cloncurry, Australia 53°C	Tully, Australia 4 550	Mulka, Australia 100

World - largest seas, '000 km²	World - largest lakes, '000 km²	World - longest rivers, km	World - largest islands, '000 km²	World - highest peaks, m	World - deepest trenches, m
cific Ocean 165 721	Caspian Sea 424	Nile 6 690	Greenland 2 176	Himalayas: Mt. Everest 8 850	Mariana Trench 11 022
antic Ocean 81 660	Lake Superior 82	Amazon 6 280	New Guinea 777	Karakoram : K2 8 611	Tonga Trench 10 822
ian Ocean 73 442	Lake Victoria 69	Mississippi -Missouri 6 270	Borneo 725	Pamirs: Communism Pk. 7 495	Japan Trench 10 554
tic Ocean 14 351	Lake Huron 60	Yangtze-Kiang 4 990	Madagascar 590	Tian Shan: Pik Pobedy 7 444	Kuril Trench 10 542
diterranean Sea 2 966	Lake Michigan 58	Congo 4 670	Baffin Island 476	Andes: Aconcagua 6 960	Mindanao Trench 10 497
th China Sea 2 318	Aral Sea 36	Amur 4 410	Sumatra 474	Rocky Mts: Mt. McKinley 6 194	Kermadec Trench 10 047
ing Sea 2 274	Lake Tanganyika 33	Hwang-ho 4 350	Honshu 228	East Africa: Kilimanjaro 5 895	Milwaukee Deep 9 200
ibbean Sea 1 942	Lake Baikal 31	Lena 4 260	Great Britain 217	Caucasus: Elbrus 5 642	Bougainville Trench 9 140
f of Mexico 1 813	Great Bear Lake 31	Mekong 4 180	Victoria Island 212	Antarctica: Vinson Massif 4 897	South Sandwich Island Trench 8 428
of Okhotsk 1 528	Lake Malawi 31	Niger 4 180	Ellesmere Island 197	Alps: Mt. Blanc 4 807	Aleutian Trench 7 822

Projection : Hammer Equal Area

COUNTRY COMPARISONS

Country	Population in thousands 2001 estimate	Area in thous' km²	Country	Population in thousands 2001 estimate	Area in thous' km²	Country	Population in thousands 2001 estimate	Area in thous' km²	Country	Population in thousands 2001 estimate	Area in thous' km²	Country	Population in thousands 2001 estimate	Area in thous' km²
China	1 280 200	9 598	Mexico	99 600	1958	France	59 200	552	Argentina	37 500	2 767	Venezuela	24 600	
India	1 033 000	3 288	Germany	82 200	357	Italy	57 800	301	Tanzania	36 200	945	Uganda	24 000	
United States	284 500	9 373	Vietnam	78 700	332	Congo, Dem. Rep.	53 600	2 345	Sudan	31 800	2 506	Iraq	23 600	
Indonesia	206 100	1 905	Philippines	77 200	300	Ukraine	49 100	604	Algeria	31 000	2 382	Nepal	23 500	
Brazil	171 800	8 512	Egypt	69 800	1 001	Korea, South	48 800	99	Canada	31 000	9 976	Malaysia	22 700	
Pakistan	145 000	796	Turkey	66 300	779	Burma (Myanmar)	47 800	677	Kenya	29 800	580	Taiwan	22 500	
Russia	144 400	17 075	Iran	66 100	1 648	South Africa	43 600	1 220	Morocco	29 200	447	Romania	22 400	
Bangladesh	133 500	144	Ethiopia	65 400	1 128	Colombia	43 100	1 139	Afghanistan	26 800	652	Korea, North	22 000	
Japan	127 100	378	Thailand	62 400	513	Spain	39 800	505	Peru	26 100	1 285	Saudi Arabia	21 100	2
Nigeria	126 600	924	United Kingdom	60 000	243	Poland	38 600	313	Uzbekistan	25 100	447	Ghana	19 900	

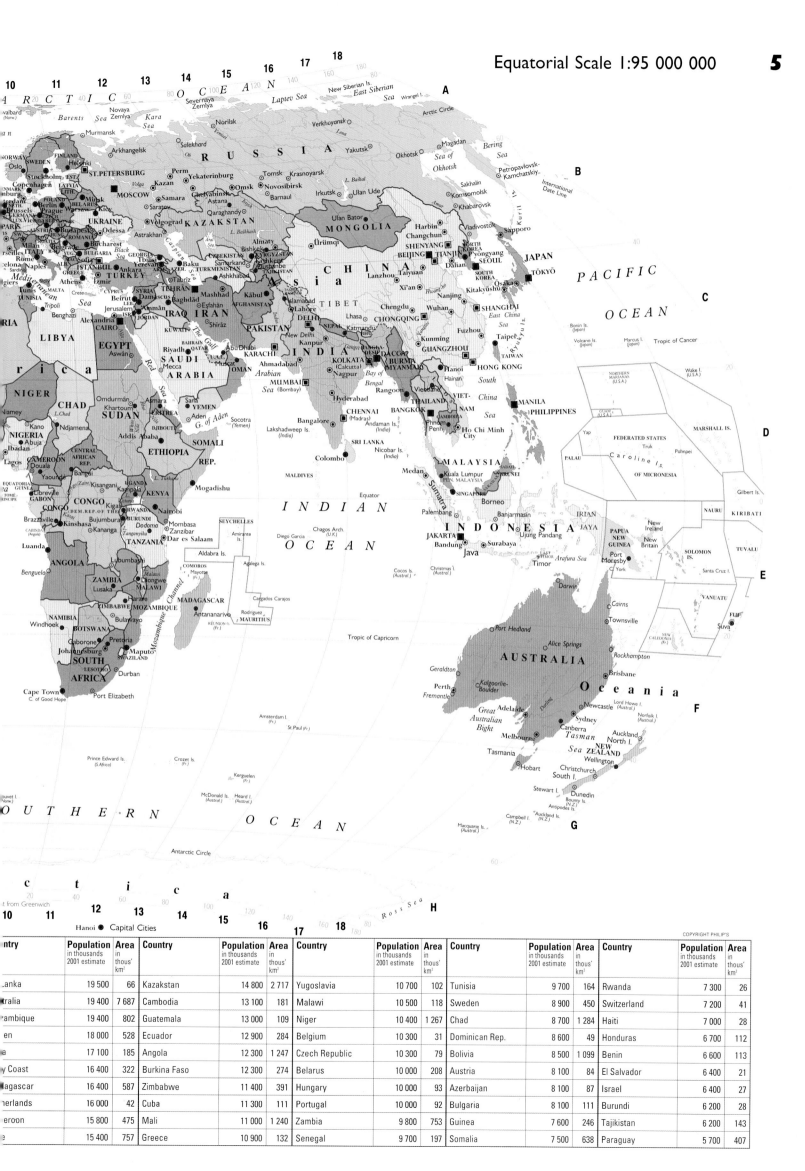

Hanoi ● Capital Cities

COPYRIGHT PHILIP'S

ntry	Population in thousands 2001 estimate	Area in thous' km²	Country	Population in thousands 2001 estimate	Area in thous' km²	Country	Population in thousands 2001 estimate	Area in thous' km²	Country	Population in thousands 2001 estimate	Area in thous' km²	Country	Population in thousands 2001 estimate	Area in thous' km²
Lanka	19 500	66	Kazakstan	14 800	2 717	Yugoslavia	10 700	102	Tunisia	9 700	164	Rwanda	7 300	26
tralia	19 400	7 687	Cambodia	13 100	181	Malawi	10 500	118	Sweden	8 900	450	Switzerland	7 200	41
rambique	19 400	802	Guatemala	13 000	109	Niger	10 400	1 267	Chad	8 700	1 284	Haiti	7 000	28
en	18 000	528	Ecuador	12 900	284	Belgium	10 300	31	Dominican Rep.	8 600	49	Honduras	6 700	112
a	17 100	185	Angola	12 300	1 247	Czech Republic	10 300	79	Bolivia	8 500	1 099	Benin	6 600	113
y Coast	16 400	322	Burkina Faso	12 300	274	Belarus	10 000	208	Austria	8 100	84	El Salvador	6 400	21
agascar	16 400	587	Zimbabwe	11 400	391	Hungary	10 000	93	Azerbaijan	8 100	87	Israel	6 400	27
herlands	16 000	42	Cuba	11 300	111	Portugal	10 000	92	Bulgaria	8 100	111	Burundi	6 200	28
eroon	15 800	475	Mali	11 000	1 240	Zambia	9 800	753	Guinea	7 600	246	Tajikistan	6 200	143
	15 400	757	Greece	10 900	132	Senegal	9 700	197	Somalia	7 500	638	Paraguay	5 700	407

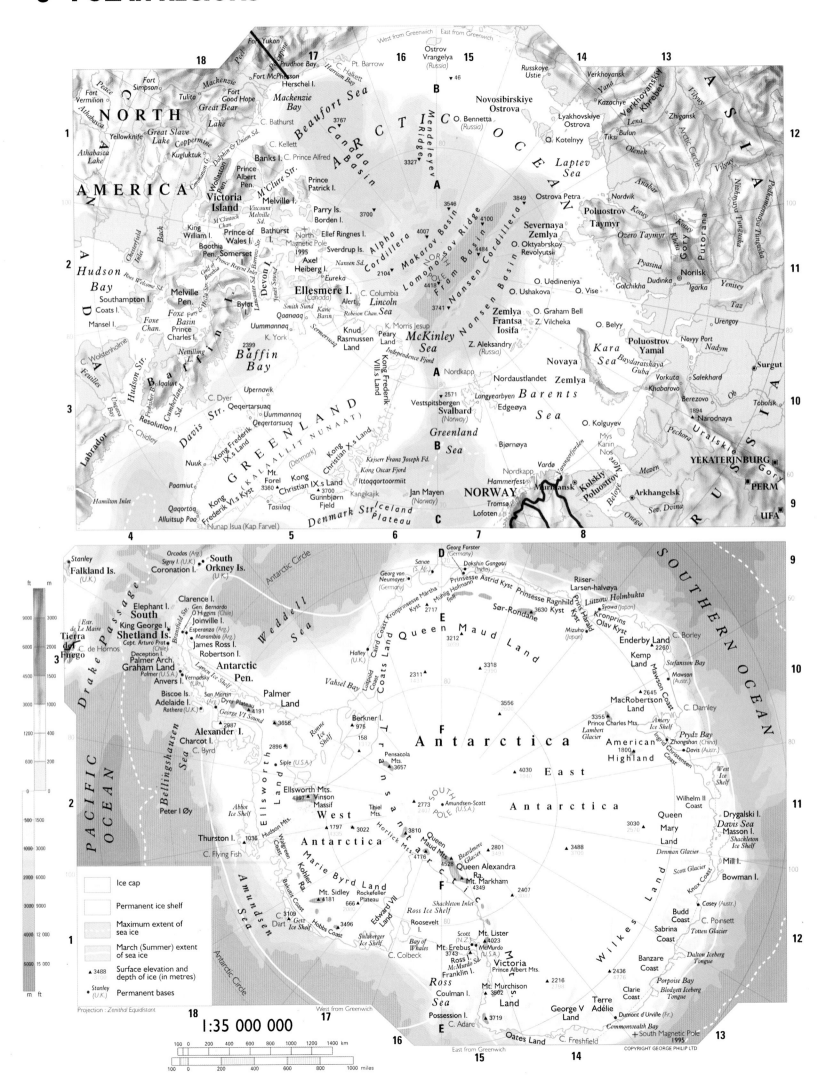

6 POLAR REGIONS

Projection : Zenithal Equidistant

1:35 000 000

Ice cap

Permanent ice shelf

Maximum extent of sea ice

March (Summer) extent of sea ice

▲3488 Surface elevation and depth of ice (in metres)

• Stanley (U.K.) Permanent bases

COPYRIGHT GEORGE PHILIP LTD

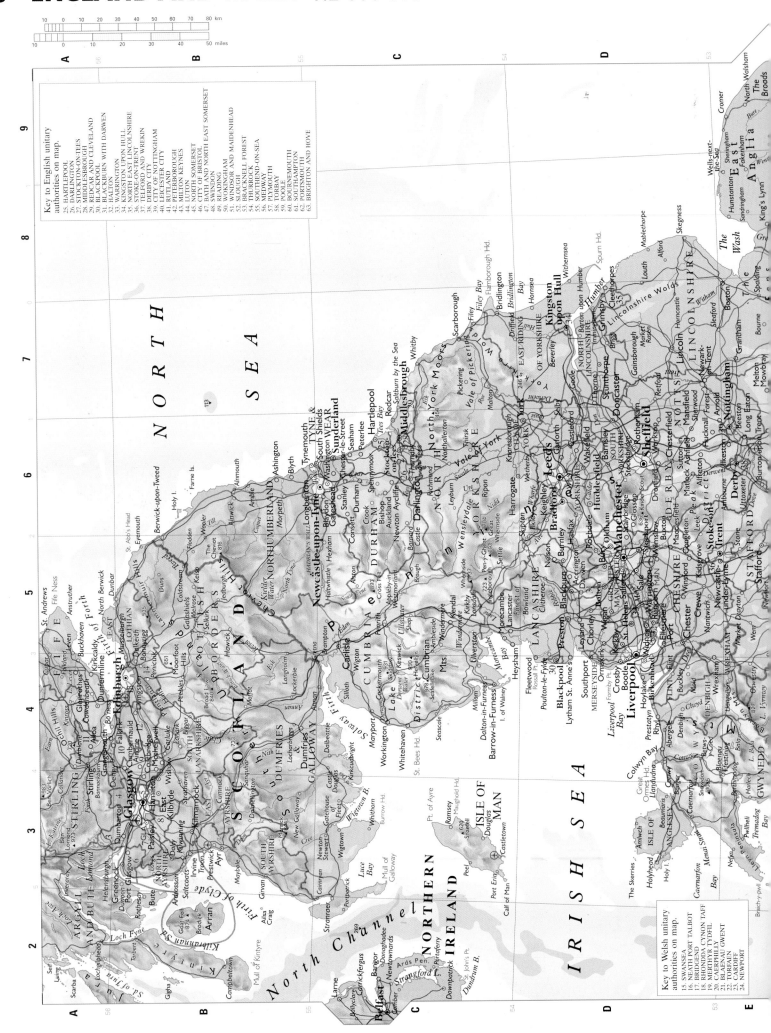

Key to English unitary
authorities on map.

25. HARTLEPOOL
26. DARLINGTON
27. STOCKTON-ON-TEES
28. MIDDLESBROUGH
29. REDCAR AND CLEVELAND
30. BLACKPOOL
31. BLACKBURN WITH DARWEN
32. HALTON
33. WARRINGTON
34. KINGSTON UPON HULL
35. NORTH EAST LINCOLNSHIRE
36. STOKE-ON-TRENT
37. TELFORD AND WREKIN
38. DERBY CITY
39. CITY OF NOTTINGHAM
40. LEICESTER CITY
41. RUTLAND
42. PETERBOROUGH
43. MILTON KEYNES
44. LUTON
45. NORTH SOMERSET
46. CITY OF BRISTOL
47. BATH AND NORTH EAST SOMERSET
48. SWINDON
49. READING
50. WOKINGHAM
51. WINDSOR AND MAIDENHEAD
52. SLOUGH
53. BRACKNELL FOREST
54. THURROCK
55. SOUTHEND-ON-SEA
56. MEDWAY
57. PLYMOUTH
58. TORBAY
59. POOLE
60. BOURNEMOUTH
61. SOUTHAMPTON
62. PORTSMOUTH
63. BRIGHTON AND HOVE

Key to Welsh unitary
authorities on map.

15. SWANSEA
16. NEATH PORT TALBOT
17. BRIDGEND
18. RHONDDA CYNON TAFF
19. MERTHYR TYDFIL
20. CAERPHILLY
21. BLAENAU GWENT
22. TORFAEN
23. CARDIFF
24. NEWPORT

ENGLAND

FRANCE

LONDON

BIRMINGHAM

WALES

POWYS · CEREDIGION · PEMBROKESHIRE · CARMARTHENSHIRE

Cardiff · **Swansea** · Newport

Bristol · **Bath** · Gloucester · Cheltenham

CORNWALL · DEVON · SOMERSET · DORSET · WILTSHIRE

Plymouth · Exeter · Torquay · Truro · Penzance · Land's End · Lizard Pt.

Bournemouth · **Southampton** · **Portsmouth** · ISLE OF WIGHT · Newport · Ryde · Cowes

HANTS · BERKSHIRE · Reading · Oxford · OXFORDSHIRE · Swindon

Brighton · Hove · Worthing · Littlehampton · Bognor Regis · Chichester

EAST SUSSEX · WEST SUSSEX · SURREY · KENT · Eastbourne · Hastings · Dover · Folkestone · Canterbury · Margate · Ramsgate · Deal

ESSEX · SUFFOLK · NORFOLK · Ipswich · Harwich · Felixstowe · Lowestoft · Colchester · Chelmsford

Cambridge · CAMBRIDGE · Peterborough · BEDFORD · Bedford · Northampton · NORTHAMPTON · Luton

Leicester · Rutland · Coventry · WARWICK · WORCESTER · HEREFORD · SHROPSHIRE · Wolverhampton · Walsall · Dudley

Strait of Dover · Calais · Boulogne-sur-Mer · Le Touquet-Paris-Plage · Berck · Dieppe · **Le Havre** · **Rouen** · NORMANDIE · HAUTE-NORMANDIE · SEINE-MARITIME · CALVADOS · MANCHE · Cherbourg · Caen · Bayeux · Lisieux · Évreux · Fécamp · Étretat

Baie de la Somme · Baie de la Seine · Cotentin

ENGLISH CHANNEL

Bristol Channel

Cardigan Bay

Lyme Bay

CHANNEL ISLANDS (U.K.) · Alderney · Guernsey · St. Peter Port · Herm · Sark · Jersey · St. Helier

Thames Estuary · Southend-on-Sea

Isles of Scilly
On same scale

Tresco · Isles of Scilly · St. Mary's · St. Ives · Camborne · Hayle · Penzance · Newlyn · Land's End

Projection: Lambert's Conformal Conic

West from Greenwich · East from Greenwich

m · ft

1000 · 500 · 200 · 100 · 0

3000 · 1500 · 600 · 300 · 0 · -50 · -150

-50 · -300 · -600

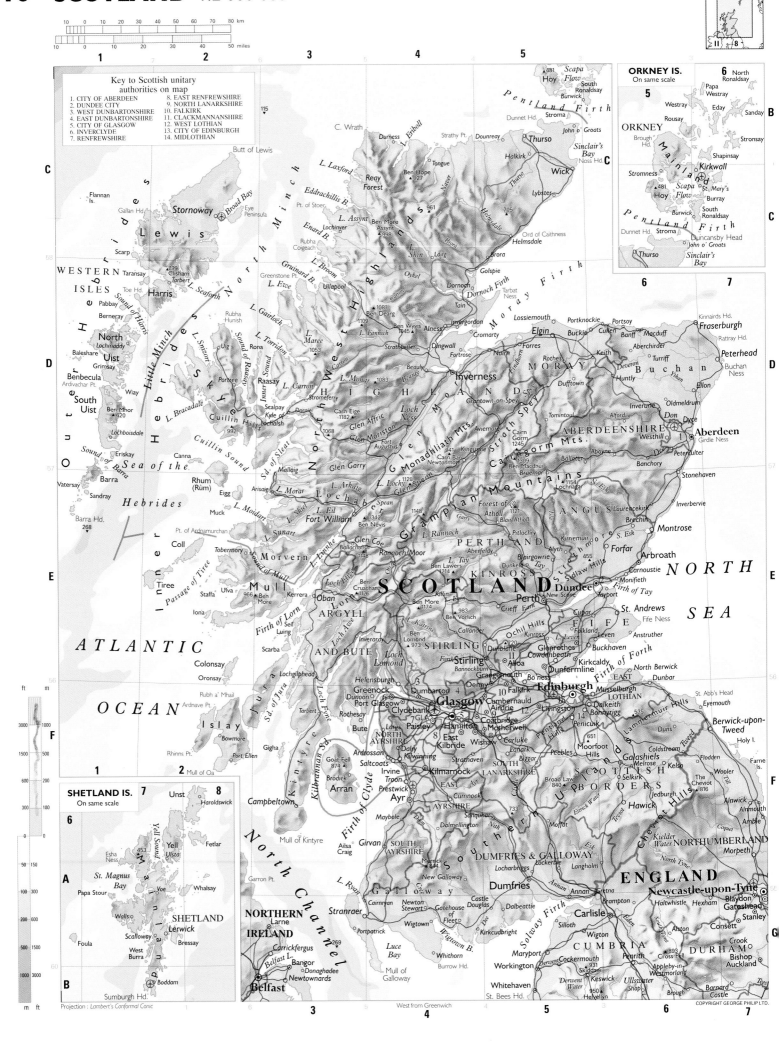

Key to Scottish unitary authorities on map
1. CITY OF ABERDEEN
2. DUNDEE CITY
3. WEST DUNBARTONSHIRE
4. EAST DUNBARTONSHIRE
5. CITY OF GLASGOW
6. INVERCLYDE
7. RENFREWSHIRE
8. EAST RENFREWSHIRE
9. NORTH LANARKSHIRE
10. FALKIRK
11. CLACKMANNANSHIRE
12. WEST LOTHIAN
13. CITY OF EDINBURGH
14. MIDLOTHIAN

ORKNEY IS.
On same scale

SHETLAND IS.
On same scale

Projection : Lambert's Conformal Conic

West from Greenwich

COPYRIGHT GEORGE PHILIP LTD.

10 10 20 30 40 50 60 70 80 km
10 10 20 30 40 50 miles

A

ATLANTIC OCEAN

Mull of Oa
Kintyre
Campbeltown
Brodick
Arran
Firth of Clyde

Malin Hd.
Tory I.
Horn Hd.
Sheep Haven
Mulroy B.
Malin Pen.
Carndonagh
Inishowen Pen.
Moville
Buncrana
Giants Causeway
Portstewart
Portrush
Ballycastle
Fair Hd.
Garron Pt.
Rathlin I.
Mts. of Antrim
Cairnryan
Stranraer
Ailsa Craig

Bloody Foreland
Inishfree B.
Aran I.
Gweedore
The Rosses
Errigal 752
683
Derryveagh Mts.
Rathmelton
L. Foyle
Coleraine
Limavady
Ballymoney
Ballymena
554 Trostan
269
Portpatrick

Crohy Hd.
Gweebarra B.
Dawros Hd.
Glenties
Lavagh More 676
Letterkenny
DONEGAL
Lifford
Strabane
LONDONDERRY
Londonderry
Sawel Mt. 683
Sperrin Mts.
Magherafelt
Randalstown
Ballyclare
NORTHERN
ANTRIM
Larne
Carrickfergus

Loughros More B.
Rossan Pt.
Killybegs
Donegal
St. John's Pt.
Donegal Bay
Ballyshannon
Bundoran
Derg
Castlederg
Sion Mills
Newtownstewart
TYRONE
Omagh
Moneymore
Cookstown
Coalisland
Dungannon
Lough Neagh
Newtownabbey
Belfast
Belfast L.
Bangor
Donaghadee
Newtownards
Comber
Ards Pen.
Portaferry

Lower L. Erne
Enniskillen
FERMANAGH
Upper L. Erne
Irvinestown
Dromore
Aughnacloy
Armagh
ARMAGH
Middletown
Keady
Blackwater
Monaghan
Craigavon
Portadown
Lurgan
Lagan
Banbridge
Tandragee
DOWN
Ballynahinch
Saintfield
Lisburn
Strangford L.
Ballyquintin Pt.
Downpatrick
Dundrum
St. John's Pt.
Dundrum B.

Sligo Bay
Sligo
Ballysadare
Colooney
L. Allen
Belturbet
Clones
MONAGHAN
Annalee
Castleblaney
Coothill
Newry
577 Slieve Gullion
Mourne Mts.
852 Slieve Donard
Warrenpoint
Greenore
Carlingford L.
Newcastle

Killala
Killala B.
Ballina
Dromore West
544
Slieve Gamph
Ballymote
L. Arrow
SLIGO
Leitrim
LEITRIM
Cavan
Carrickmacross
Kingscourt
Dundalk
LOUTH
Louth
Ardee
Dunleer
Dundalk Bay
Clogher Hd.

Erris Hd.
Broad Haven
Belmullet
Mullet Pen.
Inishkea North
Inishkea South
Blacksod Bay
Achill Hd.
Achill I.
Clare I.
Corraun Pen.
MAYO
Nephin 806
Crossmolina
Swinford
Charlestown
Ballyhaunis
ROSCOMMON
Castlerea
Ballaghaderreen
Boyle
Carrick-on-Shannon
L. Gowna
L. Sheelin
CAVAN
Oldcastle
Blackwater
Ceanannus Mor (Kells)
Drogheda

Inishturk
Killary Harbour
Inishbofin
Inishshark
Croagh Patrick 765
Mweelrea 819
Westport
Newport
Castlebar
Knock
Claremorris
Ballinrobe
Glennamaddy
Roscommon
LONGFORD
Longford
Granard
Castlepollard
MEATH
An Uaimh (Navan)
Athboy
Boyne
Balbriggan
Rush

Connemara
Clifden
Slyne Hd.
Bertraghboy B.
Kilkieran B.
Oughterard
Lough Corrib
Lough Mask
Tuam
GALWAY
Athenry
Ballinasloe
IRELAND
Connacht
Leinster
Mullingar
WESTMEATH
Moate
Inny
Trim
Royal Canal
Swords
Malahide
Lambay I.
Howth Hd.

Galway Bay
Galway
Aran Is.
Inishmore
Inishmaan
Inisheer
Black Hd.
Gort
368
Slieve Aughty
Portumna
Shannon
Loughrea
Athlone
Lough Ree
OFFALY
Tullamore
Clara
Daingean
Edenderry
Bog of Allen
Grand Canal
Maynooth
DUBLIN
Liffey
Dublin
Dun Laoghaire
Bray
Greystones

Hags Hd.
Liscannor Bay
Ennistimon
Mal Bay
Mutton I.
Milltown Malbay
Tulla
Lough Derg
Birr
Roscrea
Slieve Bloom
Arderin 528
Mountmellick
Portarlington
Portlaoise
Port Laoise
Monasterevin
Naas
Kildare
KILDARE
Droichead Nua
Athy
Poulaphouca Res.
123
WICKLOW
Wicklow
Wicklow Hd.

Loop Hd.
Kilkee
Kilrush
Shannon Airport
Sixmilebridge
CLARE
Ennis
Keeper Hill 694
Templemore
Nenagh
Killaloe
Durrow
LAOIS
Carlow
CARLOW
Muine Bheag
Tullow
Shillelagh
Gorey
Lugnaquilla 926
Avoca
Arklow
Mizen Hd.

Mouth of the Shannon
Kerry Hd.
Foynes
LIMERICK
Limerick
Rathkeale
Newcastle West
Listowel
Feale
Munster
Golden Vale
Tipperary
TIPPERARY
Thurles
Cashel
Kilkenny
KILKENNY
Callan
Mt. Leinster 796
WEXFORD
Enniscorthy
Cahore Pt.

Smerwick Harbour
Brandon Hd.
Tralee B.
Brandon Mt. 953
Dingle
Slieve Mish 853
Tralee
KERRY
Newmarket
Kanturk
Mitchelstown
Galtymore 920
Galty Mts.
Caher
Slievenamon 722
Clonmel
Comeragh Mts. 792
Carrick-on-Suir
New Ross
Wexford
Wexford Harbour
Rosslare
Greenore Pt.

Great Blasket I.
Dunmore Hd.
Dingle
Inishvickillane
Dingle Bay
Killorglin
Killarney
Laune
Maine
Newmarket
Buttevant
Fermoy
Knockmealdown Mts.
WATERFORD
Lismore
Dungarvan
Blackwater
Waterford
Tramore
Dungarvan Harbour
Tramore B.
Hook Hd.
Waterford Harbour
Saltee Is.
Carnsore Pt.

Valencia I.
Puffin I.
Great Skellig
Cahirciveen
Carrauntoohill 1041
Macgillycuddy's Reeks
Kenmare
Boggeragh Mts. 646
Macroom
Blarney
CORK
Cork
Lee
Midleton
Youghal
Youghal B.
St. David's Hd.
St. David's
St. Brides Bay

Ballinskelligs B.
Scariff I.
Kenmare River
Caha Mts. 686
Glengarriff
Dunmanway
Bandon
Bandon
Kinsale
Old Head of Kinsale
Cork Harbour
Passage West
Cobh
Crosshaven
115

Dursey I.
Crow Hd.
Castletown Bearhaven
Bear I.
Bantry Bay
Bantry
Dunmanus B.
Skull
Long I.
Mizen Hd.
Clonakilty
Clonakilty B.
Galley Hd.
Skibbereen
Baltimore
Sherkin I.
C. Clear
Clear I.

St. George's Channel
IRISH SEA
North Channel

CELTIC SEA

ft m
1500 500
600 200
300 100
0 0
50 150
100 300
200 600
500 1500
1000 3000
2000 6000
m ft

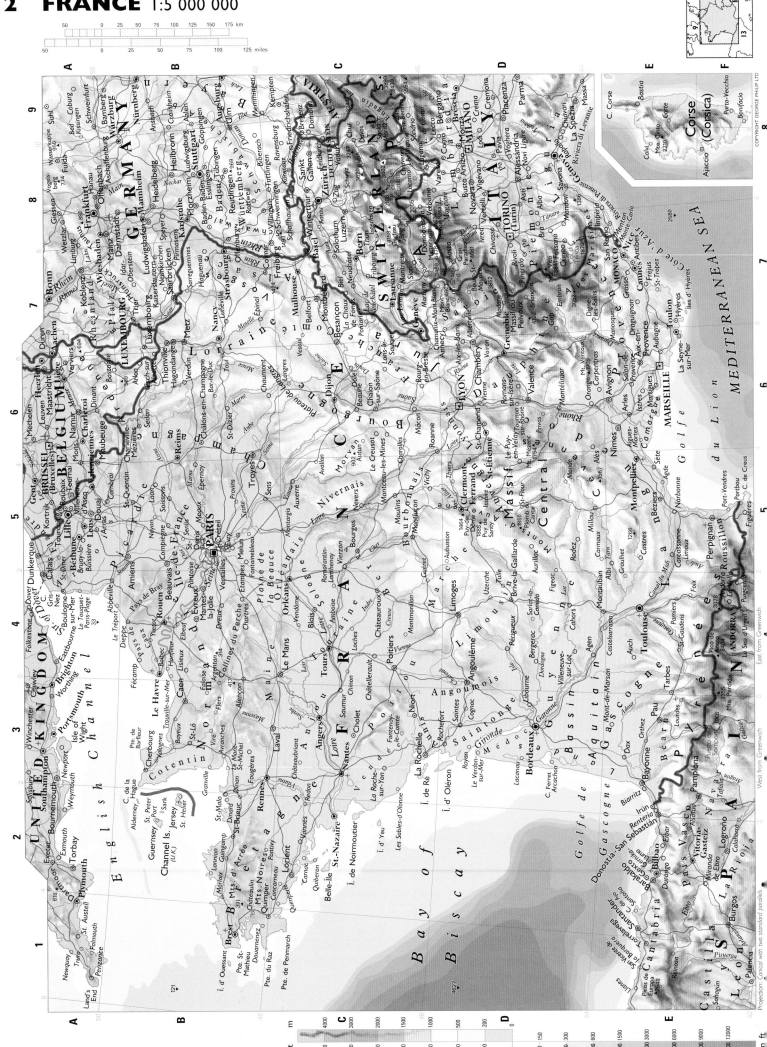

Corse (Corsica)

MEDITERRANEAN SEA

50 0 25 50 75 100 125 150 175 km

50 0 25 50 75 100 125 miles

FRANCE

SPAIN

PORTUGAL

MADRID

LISBOA

BARCELONA

Valencia

Sevilla

Málaga

Zaragoza

Porto

MOROCCO

ALGERIA

ANDORRA

Mallorca

Menorca

Pyrenees

MEDITERRANEAN SEA

Balearic Sea

Bay of Biscay

ATLANTIC OCEAN

Golfe du Lion

Golfo de Valencia

G. de Cádiz

Str. of Gibraltar

Costa Brava

Costa Dorada

Costa Blanca

Costa del Sol

Castilla y León

Castilla-La Mancha

Navarra

País Vasco

Algarve

Projection: Conical with two standard parallels

West from Greenwich   East from Greenwich

COPYRIGHT GEORGE PHILIP LTD

m   ft
6000 2000
4500 1500
3000 1000
1500 500
600   200
0   0
50   -100–300
-200 600
-500 1500
-1000 3000
-2000 6000
-3000 9000
-4500 12000
ft   m

50 0 25 50 75 100 125 150 175 km
50 0 25 50 75 100 125 miles

3 4 5 6 7

SWITZERLAND **AUSTRIA**
Rhine Chur Wildspitze Grossglockner Badgastein Steiermark Graz
Davos Lienz Villach Klagenfurt Wolfsberg
Domodossola Bolzano Merano Bressanone Karnische Alpen Maribor Nagykani
Matterhorn Mont Blanc Ortles Trento Belluno Vittório Veneto Udine Karawanken Kranj Celje
Aosta Gran Paradiso Como Lecco Garda Schio Bassano del Grappa Pordenone Gorízia Triglav Kobarid **LJUBLJANA** Zagreb **SLOVENIA** Varaždin Koprivnica Bjelovar

A L P S

Lyonnais **LYON** Annecy Verbánia Lago di Garda Riva Rovereto Vicenza Treviso Mira Gorízia Trieste Koper Postojna Rijeka Karlovac **CROAT**
Chamonix Maggiore Bérgamo Brescia Verona Pádova Venézia (Venice) Golfo di Venézia Istra Krk Pula Senj Sisak

B Grenoble Biella Novara **MILANO** Monza Crema Mantova Legnago Rovigo Chióggia Rovinj Cres Velika Kapela Bosanska Gradiška
Massif du Pelvoux **TORINO** (Turin) Vigévano Lodi Pavia Cremona Po Adige Pula Rt. Kamenjak Lošinj Pag Banja Luka
Montélimar Chivasso Piacenza Parma Modena Ferrara Comácchio Gospić Gračač
Pinerolo Piemonte Alessándria Novi Ligure Réggio nell'Emília Bologna Lugo Ravenna Cres Kварner Krk Zadar **HE**

FRANCE Cuneo Savona Génova Carpi Sassuolo Imola Faenza Forlì Rimini Pešaro Fano Ugljan Pašman Šibenik
Mondovì Alba Rapallo Chiávari La Spézia Massa Carrara Mte. Cimone Cesena Senigállia Falconara Marittima Ancona Solta Brač
Impéria San Remo Riviera di Ponente Viaréggio Pistóia Lucca Prato Firenze (Florence) **SAN MARINO** Fabriano Civitanova Marche Macerata Fermo Vis Pelješac

MONACO Nice Monte-Carlo Riviera di Levante Pisa Livorno Cáscina Arno Scandicci Arezzo Città di Castello Perúgia Macerata San Benedetto del Tronto Korčul Lastovo
Cannes Antibes Menton Rosignano Marittimo Volterra Siena L. Trasimeno Assisi Mte. Vettore Ascoli Piceno Teramo Montesilvano Marina

C **MARSEILLE** Toulon Hyères Iles d' Hyères Côte d'Azur **LIGURIAN** Capraia Piombino Portoferráio Elba Grosseto L. di Bolsena Orvieto Spoleto Terni Gran Sasso d'Italia Pescara Chieti

SEA Pianosa Giglio Orbetello Mte. Argentario Viterbo Rieti L'Aquila Lanciano
Montecristo Civitavécchia L. di Bracciano Guidónia Montecélio Tívoli Avezzano Mte. Amaro Vasto Térmoli

D Corse (France) Ajaccio Porto-Vecchio Bonifacio **VATICAN CITY** **ROMA** Velletri Frosinone Isérnia Campobasso Sannicandro Gargánico Mte. Calvo Manfredónia
Bouches de Bonifacio Maddalena Pomézia Aprilia Latina Fondi Fórmia Cassino Benevento Cerignola Foggia
Asinara C. del Falcone Golfo dell' Asinara Ólbia Golfo Aranci Terracina Ánzio Gaeta Caserta Barletta Trani Molfetta
Porto Tórres Sássari Ísole Ponziane Ventotene Aversa Avellino Altamura Bari
Alghero Bosa Nuoro C. Comino Ísole Ponziane Pozzuoli **NÁPOLI** Nocera Inferiore Putignano Monópoli

E Bosa Mti. del Gennargentu G. di Monte Santu Íschia Torre del Greco Battipáglia Potenza Matera Martina
Sorgono C. di Monte Santu **Sardegna** (Italy) Capri Castellammare di Stabia Salerno Sala Consilina
G. di Oristano Oristano Árbatax Lanusei Laúria Agri Tára
Terralba Iglésias Portoscuso Carbónia Corigliano Cálabro Rossano

San Pietro Sant' Antíoco **Cágliari** Quartu Sant' Élena **TYRRHENIAN** Cetraro Cosenza Crotone
G. di Pálmas G. di Cágliari C. Carbonara **SEA** Nicastro Catanzaro
C. Spartivento Strómboli Ísole Eólie Sambiase Vibo Valéntia

C. Bougaroun Ustica (Italy) Salina Palmi Scilla **Messina**
Collo Skikda C. de Fer Lípari Vulcano Taurianova Réggio di Calábria
El-Milia Annaba C. Rosa Ísole Égadi Érice Trápani Palermo Bagheria Milazzo Barcellona Pozza di Gotto **Messina** C. Spartivento

F **ALGERIA** Azzaba El Kala Bizerte Favignana Partinico Alcamo Termini Imerese Cefalù Giarre Str. di Messina
Mila Constantine Tabarka Menzel-Bourguiba Mateur Marsala Castelvetrano Caltanissetta Enna Adrano Etna Acireale
Aïn M'lila Guelma Golfe de Tunis Mazara del Vallo Sciacca Platáni Canicattì Paternò **Catánia**
Sedrata Souk-Ahras Manouba Ariana La Marsa Ra's aṭ Ṭib (C. Bon) Porto Empédocle Licata Caltagirone Lentini Augusta

G **TUNISIA** **Tunis** Nabeul Hammamet Pantelleria (Italy) Favara Agrigento Gela Ragusa Siracusa
Oum el Bouaghi Ain Beida Béja Zaghouan Golfe de Hammamet Ra's Muṣṭafá Vittória Módica Avola
Khenchela Makthar Hamman Sousse Ísole Pelagie (Italy) Gozo Valletta Íspica C. Passero
Tébessa Kalaa-Kebira Sousse Linosa Rabat **MALTA**
Kasserine Sbeïtla Kairouan M'saken Monastir Mahdia Lampione Ísole Pelagie (Italy) **MEDITER**
Lampedusa

ADRIATIC SEA

Golfo di Génova

Corse

Golfo di Oristano

ft m
12000 4000
9000 3000
6000 2000
4500 1500
3000 1000
1500 500
600 200
0 0
m ft
50 150
100 300
200 600
500 1500
1000 3000
2000 6000
3000 9000
4000 12000

Projection: Conical with two standard parallels

1 2 3 4 5 6 7

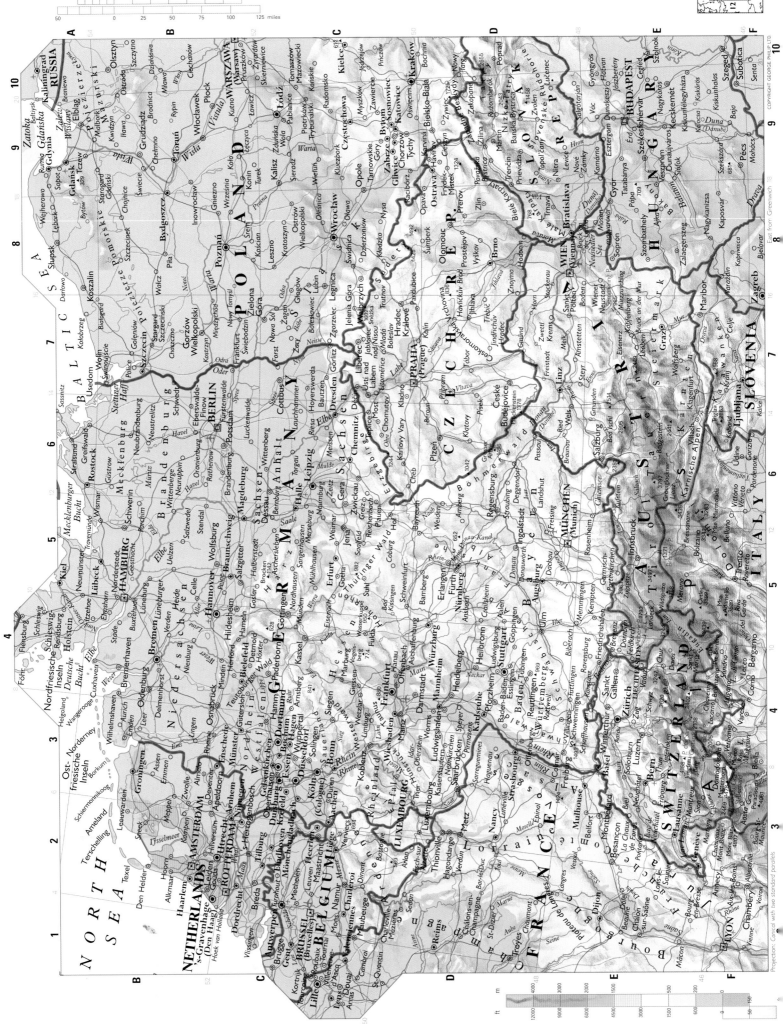

50 0 100 200 300 400 km
50 0 50 100 150 200 250 miles

East from Greenwich

Projection: Conic with two standard parallels

C A S P I A N   S E A

R U S S I A
KALMYKIA
Astrakhan
Volga
Fort Shevchenko
Makhachkala
Derbent
DAGESTAN
CHECHENIA
Grozny
NORTH OSSETIA
KABARDINO-BALKARIA
Nalchik
Pyatigorsk
Kislovodsk
Stavropol
Nevinnomyssk
Cherkessk
KARACHEY-CHERKESSIA
Maykop
ADYGEA
Krasnodar
Novorossiysk
Tuapse
Sochi
Rostov
Novocherkassk
Shakhty
Taganrog
Azov
Yeysk
Salsk
Volgodonsk
Tikhoretsk
Armavir
Labinsk
Kropotkin
Budennovsk
Elista

CAUCASUS MOUNTAINS
Elbrus 5642

GEORGIA
TBILISI
Batumi
Poti
Sokhumi
ABKHAZIA
AJARIA
Gagra
Rustavi
Telavi
Tskhinvali

AZERBAIJAN
BAKI (Baku)
Sumqayt
Naftalan
Gäncä
NAGORNO-KARABAKH
Naxçivan
Länkäran

ARMENIA
YEREVAN
Gyumri
Vanadzor

I R A N
TABRIZ
Orumiyeh
Maragheh
Marand
Khvoy
Ardabil
Zanjan
Bakhtaran

K U R D I S T A N
Kirkuk
Arbil
Al Mawsil (Mosul)
Al Amarah
BAGHDAD
Ba'qubah
NINAWA

M A J Q
Mesopotamia
Tash Sham
Ar Ramadi
As Sulaymaniyah
Sananandaj
Saqqez

S A U D I   A R A B I A

S Y R I A
HALAB (Aleppo)
Hims
DIMASHQ (Damascus)
Ar Raqqah
Dayr az Zawr
Al Hasakah
Al Qamishli
Nusaybin
Gaziantep

T U R K E Y
Erzurum
Van
Diyarbakir
Elaziğ
Malatya
Sivas
Kayseri
ANKARA
Konya
Adana
Mersin
Iskenderun
Antakya
Kahramanmaras
Osmaniye
Trabzon
Rize
Giresun
Ordu
Samsun
Amasya
Tokat
Çorum
Kastamonu
Zonguldak
Sakarya
Kocaeli (İzmit)
ISTANBUL
BURSA
Eskişehir
Kütahya
Afyon
Uşak
Denizli
İZMIR (Smyrna)
Manisa
Balıkesir
Çanakkale
Aydın
Muğla
Antalya
Isparta
Burdur
Toros Daglari

L E B A N O N
BAYRUT (Beirut)
Tarabulus
Saydā

ISRAEL
TEL AVIV-YAFO
Jerusalem
Gaza
Hefa (Haifa)

J O R D A N
AMMAN
Dead Sea
Al 'Aqabah
Elat

C Y P R U S
Nicosia
Limassol
Larnaca

E G Y P T
EL QÄHIRA (Cairo)
EL GÎZA
EL ISKANDARÎYA (Alexandria)
Dumyät
Tanta
Zagazig
Ismä'ilîya
El Suweis (Suez)
Bür Sa'id (Port Said)
Marsä Matrüh
El 'Alamein

L I B Y A
Tubruq
Darnah
Bardiyah

M E D I T E R R A N E A N   S E A

B L A C K   S E A

U K R A I N E
DNIPROPETROVSK
DONETSK
Zaporizhzhya
Mariupol
Kryvyy Rih
Mykolaiv
Kherson
Melitopol
ODESA
CRIMEA
Simferopol
Sevastopol
Yalta
Kerch
Feodosiya
Yevpatoriya

MOLDOVA
Chişinău
Tiraspol
Balţi

R O M A N I A
BUCUREŞTI (Bucharest)
Iaşi
Galaţi
Brăila
Constanţa
Ploieşti
Braşov
Cluj-Napoca
Sibiu
Timişoara
Craiova
Arad
Oradea
Baia Mare

HUNGARY
Szeged

YUGOSLAVIA
BEOGRAD
SERBIA
Niš
Kragujevac
Novi Sad
Priština
KOSOVO
MONTENEGRO
Podgorica

B U L G A R I A
SOFIA
Plovdiv
Varna
Burgas
Ruse
Pleven
Stara Planina
Rhodopi Planina

MACEDONIA
Skopje
Bitola

A L B A N I A
Tirana
Durrës
Vlorë

G R E E C E
ATHINAI (Athens)
Thessaloniki
Patrai
Larisa
Volos
Pindos Oros
Peloponnisos
Kriti (Crete)
Iráklion
Khaniá
Rhodos
Lésvos
Khios
Kikládhes
Dhodhekánisos

Æ G E A N   S E A

Sea of Azov

RUSSIA	
1	Adygea
2	Karachey-Cherkessia
3	Kabardino-Balkaria
4	North Ossetia
5	Ingushetia
6	Chechenia
7	Dagestan
8	Mordvinia
9	Chuvashia
10	Mari El
11	Tatarstan
12	Udmurtia
13	Khakassia
AZERBAIJAN	
14	Naxçivan
GEORGIA	UKRAINE
15 Ajaria	17 Crimea
16 Abkhazia	

Projection: Conical Orthomorphic with two standard parallels

East from Greenwich

OCEAN

Laptev Sea

East Siberian Sea

Severnaya Zemlya

Poluostrov Taymyr
Gory Byrranga

R U S S I A

S A K H A

Khrebet Cherskogo

Verkhoyanskiy Khrebet

Sredinnyy Khrebet

Koryakskoye Nagorye

Poluostrov Kamchatka

Sea of Okhotsk

Kolymskoye Nagorye

Yakutsk

Bering Sea

Krasnoyarsk

Bratsk

Irkutsk

Ulan Ude

Stanovoy Khrebet

Yablonovyy Khrebet

Khrebet Dzhugdzur

Sakhalin

Kurilskiye Ostrova

Khabarovsk

Komsomolsk

Sikhote Alin

Vladivostok

Hokkaidō

SAPPORO

MONGOLIA

Ulaanbaatar

Hangayn Nuruu

Hentiyn Nuruu

Da Hinggan Ling

Dongbei

HARBIN

QIQIHAR

CHANGCHUN

JILIN

Mudanjiang

Honshū

JAPAN

OSAKA

C H I N A

Gobi

BEIJING

SHENYANG

ANSHAN

FUSHUN

NORTH KOREA

PYONGYANG

SOUTH KOREA

SŎUL

INCH'ŎN

TAEJŎN

TAEGU

PUSAN

Sea of Japan (East Sea)

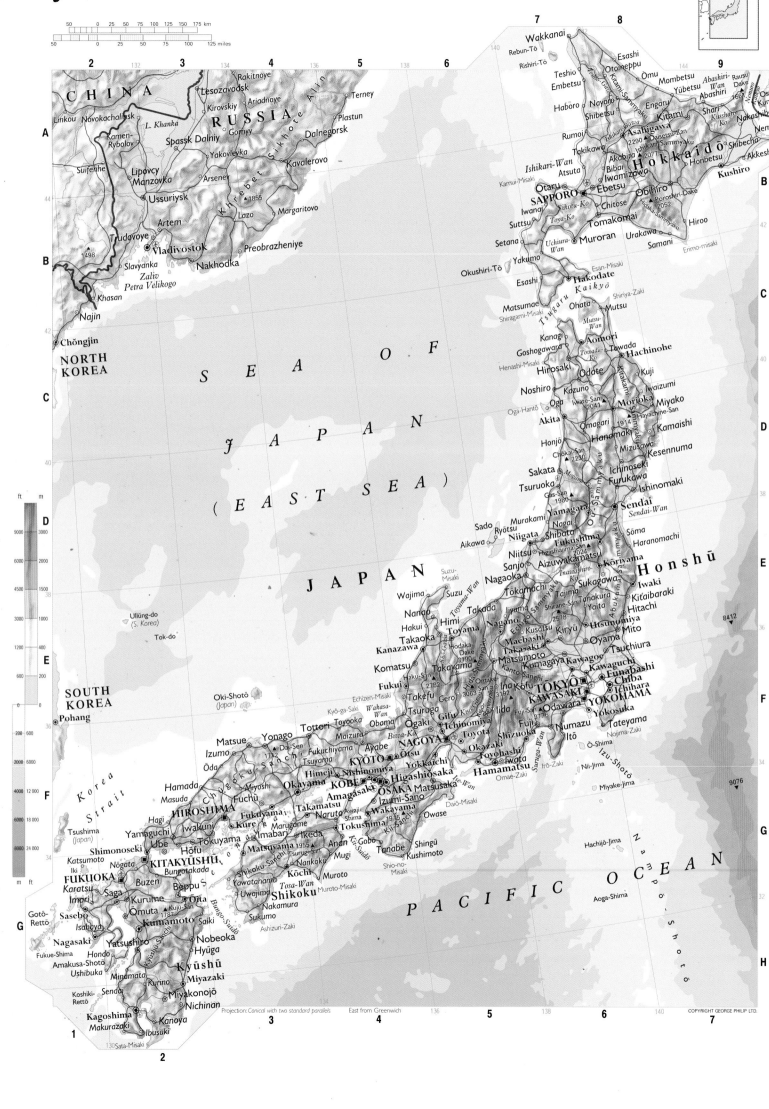

50   0   25   50   75   100   125   150   175 km
50   0   25   50   75   100   125 miles

7   **8**   **9**

Wakkanai
Rebun-Tō
Rishiri-Tō   Esashi
Teshio   Ōmu   Mombetsu
Embetsu   Nayoro   Yūbetsu   Abashiri-Wan
Haboro   Shibetsu   Engaru   Abashiri
Rumoi   Kitami   Shari   Rausu-Dake
Asahigawa   2290   Daisetsu-Zan   Nakashibetsu
Akabira   2077   Kunashiri
Takikawa   Ishikari Sammyaku   Ostrov
Bibai   Honbetsu   Shibecha   Kushiro
Ebetsu   Obihiro   Akkeshi

HOKKAIDŌ

CHINA

RUSSIA

Linkou
Novokachalinsk   Iesozavodsk
Kamen-   Kirovskiy   Ariadnoye   Terney
Rybolov   Spassk Dalniy   Plastun
Manzovka   Yakovleyka
Suifenhe   Arseney   Kavalerovo
Ussuriysk   Lazo   Margaritovo
Artem   Dalnegorsk

Trudovoye
Vladivostok   Preobrazheniye
Slavyanka
Nakhodka
Khasan
Najin
Chŏngjin

**NORTH
KOREA**

SEA   OF

JAPAN

(EAST   SEA)

JAPAN

**SOUTH
KOREA**

Pohang

Honshū

PACIFIC   OCEAN

Kyūshū

Shikoku

Projection: Conical with two standard parallels   East from Greenwich   COPYRIGHT GEORGE PHILIP LTD.

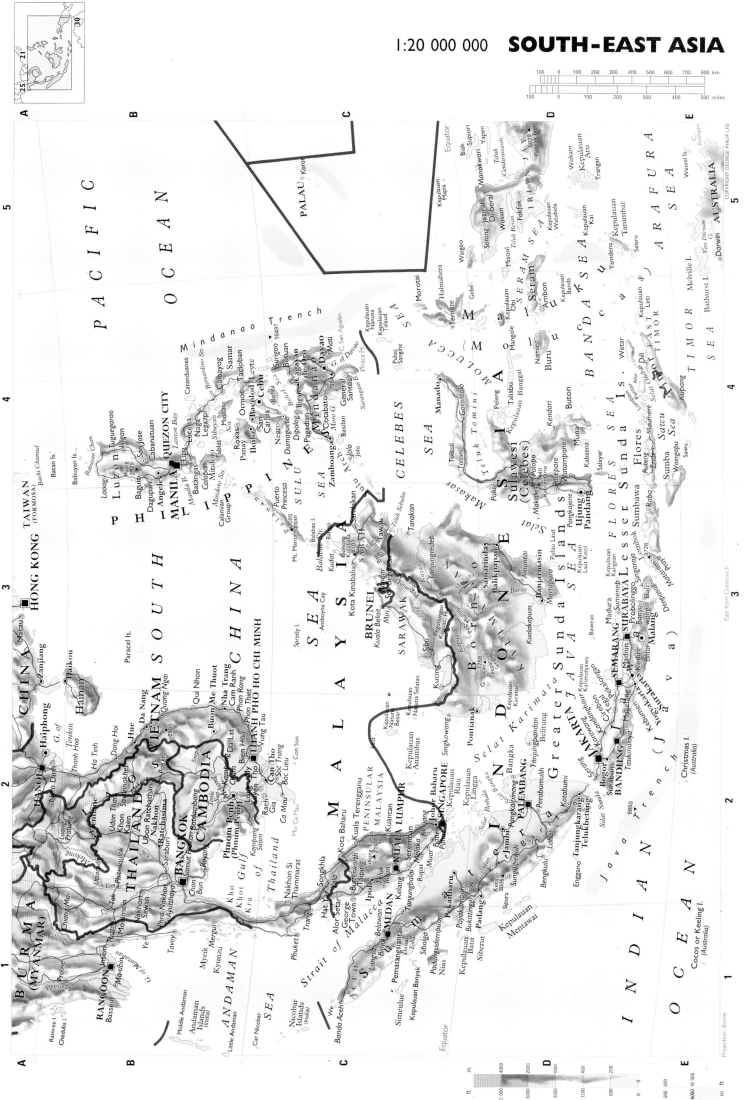

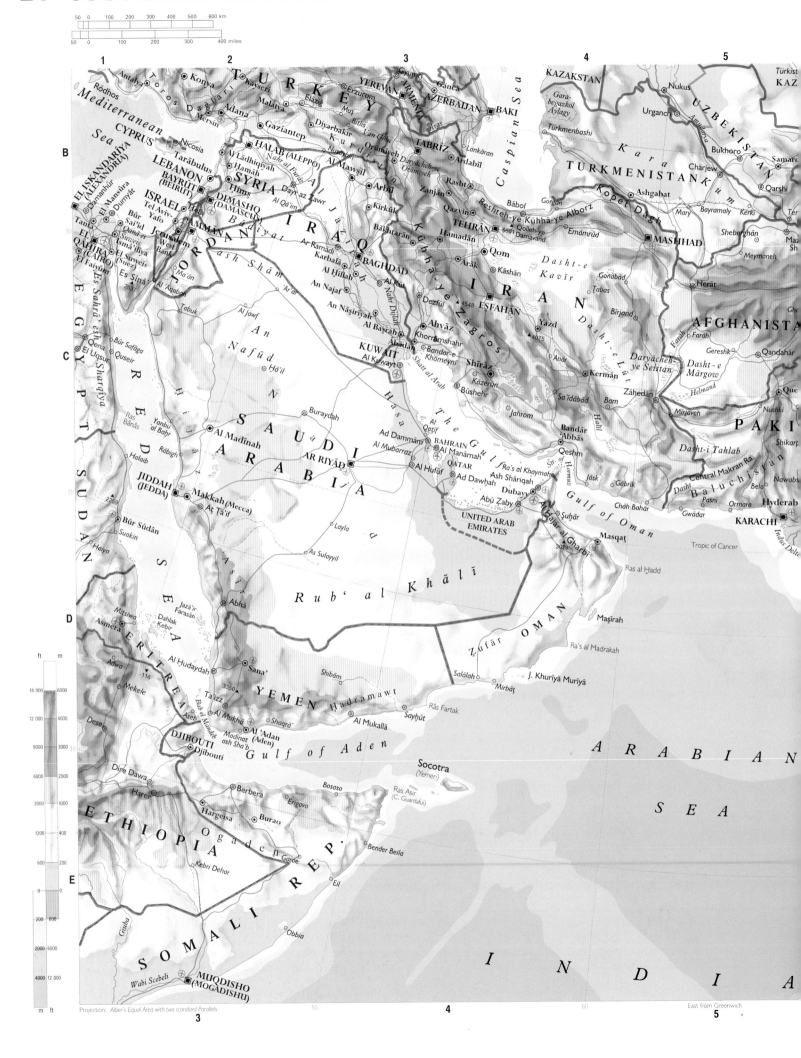

1 2 3 4 5

Ródhos
Antalya
Toros Dağları
Konya
Kayseri
TURKEY
Gyumri
YEREVAN
ARMENIA
Ganca
KAZAKSTAN
Nukus
Türkist
KAZ
Mediterranean
Sea
CYPRUS
Nicosia
Adana
Mersin
Gaziantep
Malatya
Elazığ
Muş
Erzurum
Van Gölü
Diyarbakır
Bitlis
AZERBAIJAN
BAKI
Aras
Garabogazköl
Aylagy
Turkmenbashi
Urganch
UZBEKISTAN
Bukhoro
Samarc
B
ELISKANDARIYA
(ALEXANDRIA)
Tarābulus
LEBANON
HALAB (ALEPPO)
Al Lādhiqīyah
Al Mawsil
Kurdistan
Oroumiyeh
Daryācheh-ye
Oroumiyeh
Ardabil
Lānkāran
Rasht
Caspian Sea
TURKMENISTAN
Kara
Kum
Chärjew
Kerki
Ter
Damanhûr
BAYRUT
(BEIRUT)
Ḥimş
SYRIA
Ḥamāh
Dayr az Zawr
Al Furāt
Arbīl
Zanjān
TABRĪZ
Qazvīn
Gorgan
Bābol
Reshteh-ye Kūhhā-ye Alborz
Ashgabat
Mary
Bayramaly
Sheberghān
Maz
El Manstira
ISRAEL
Tel Aviv
DIMASHQ
(DAMASCUS)
Al Qā'im
Kirkūk
Bākhtarān
TEHRĀN
Qolleh-ye
Damavand
Emāmrūd
MASHHAD
Meymaneh
Bûr Sa'îd
Tanta
Suweis
(Suez)
Damietta
Jerusalem
West Bank
AMMĀN
JORDAN
Ba'qūbah
Ar Ramādī
BAGHDĀD
Karbalā'
Al Ḥillah
An Najaf
An Nāṣirīyah
Hamadān
Qom
Ārāk
Kāshān
Qolleh-ye
Dasht-e
Kavīr
Gonābād
Tabas
Birjand
AFGHANISTA
Herāt
Farāh
Gereshk
QANDAHĀR
Ghc
EGYPT
El QĀHIRA (CAIRO)
El Faiyûm
Isma'iliya
Ma'ān
Al 'Aqabah
Tabuk
Al Jawf
'Ar'ar
An Nafūd
Ḥā'il
Al Kūt
An Nāṣirīyah
Al Baṣrah
KUWAIT
Al Kuwayt
Shatt al Arab
Dezfūl
ESFAHĀN
Ahvāz
Khorramshahr
Abadan
Bandar-e Khomeyni
Būshehr
Shīrāz
Kāzerūn
Yazd
Anār
IRAN
Dasht-e Lūt
Zāhedān
Kermān
Sa'īdābād
Jahrom
Dasht-e
Seistan
Daryācheh-ye
Seistan
Dasht-e
Mārgow
Helmand
Mirjaveh
Nushki
PAKI
Que
Es Sahrâ' esh Sharqîya
El Uqsur
Qena
Quseir
Ras Bânâs
RED
Tabuk
SAUDI
ARABIA
Buraydah
Al Madīnah
Rābigh
Ad Dammām
Al Mubarraz
BAHRAIN
Al Manāmah
Al Hufūf
QATAR
Ad Dawhah
Qatīf
Ḥasa
The Gulf
Ra's al Khaymah
Ash Shāriqah
Dubayy
Abū Ẓaby
UNITED ARAB
EMIRATES
Bandar 'Abbās
Qeshm
Str. of Hormuz
Jāsk
Chāh Bahār
Gābrīk
Dasht
Central Makran Ra.
Dasht-i Tahlab
Pasni
Gwādar
Ormara
Bela
Nawabs
Shikar
Hyderab
KARACHI
Indus Delte
SUDAN
Yanbu' al Bahr
Ḥalaib
JIDDAH
(JEDDA)
Makkah (Mecca)
Aṭ Ṭā'if
AR RIYĀḌ
Layla
As Sulayyil
Rub' al Khālī
OMAN
Suḥār
Al Hajar al Gharbī
Masqat
Ras al Ḥadd
Tropic of Cancer
SEA
Bûr Sûdân
Suakin
Haiya
Mitsiwa
Asmera
Dahlak Kebir
Jazā'ir Farasān
ERITREA
Abhā
Zufār
Ra's al Madrakah
Maṣīrah
D
Adwa
Mekele
Al Hudaydah
Sana'
Shibām
Ḥaḍramawt
Salālah
J. Khurīyā Murīyā
Mirbāṭ
Ras Fartak
Giba
Dese
Ta'izz
Al Mukhā
Shaqrā'
YEMEN
Al Mukallā
Sayḥūt
A R A B I A N
ETHIOPIA
Dire Dawa
Harer
Bāb al Mandab
Madīnat ash Sha'b
Al 'Adan
(Aden)
DJIBOUTI
Djibouti
Gulf of Aden
Socotra
(Yemen)
Bosaso
Ras Asir
(C. Guardafui)
SEA
Hargeisa
Berbera
Burao
Erigavo
Garoe
Bender Beila
Ogaden
Kebri Dehar
Eil
E
SOMALI REP.
Obbia
Giuba
Wabi Scebeli
MUQDISHO
(MOGADISHU)
I N D I A

ft m
18 000 6000
12 000 4000
9000 3000
6000 2000
3000 1000
1200 400
600 200
0
200 600
2000 6000
4000 12 000
m ft

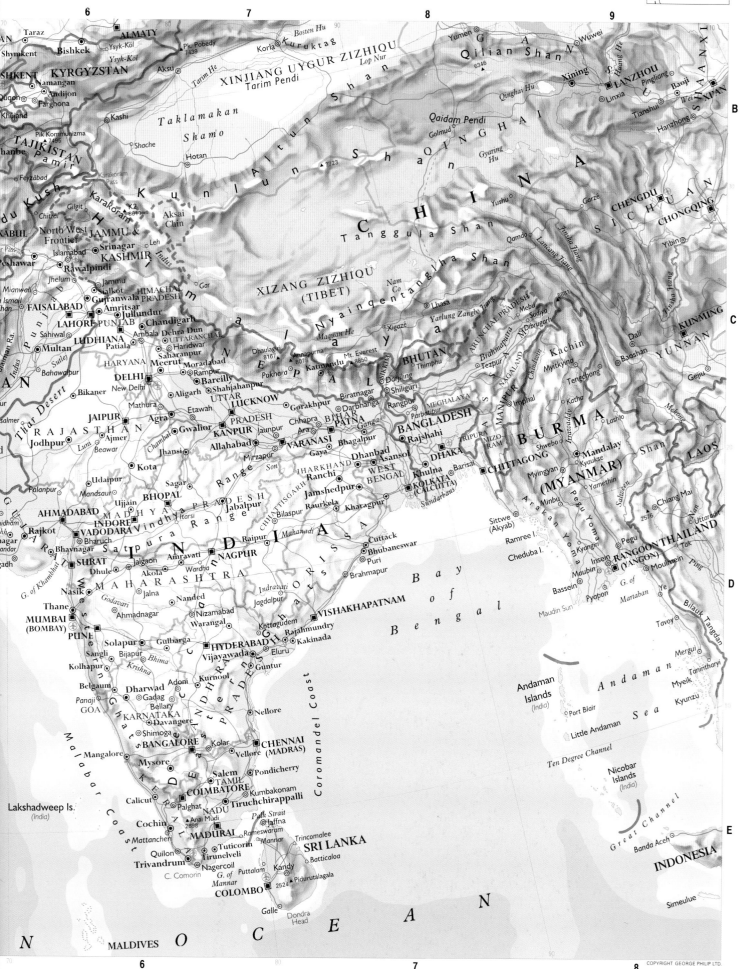

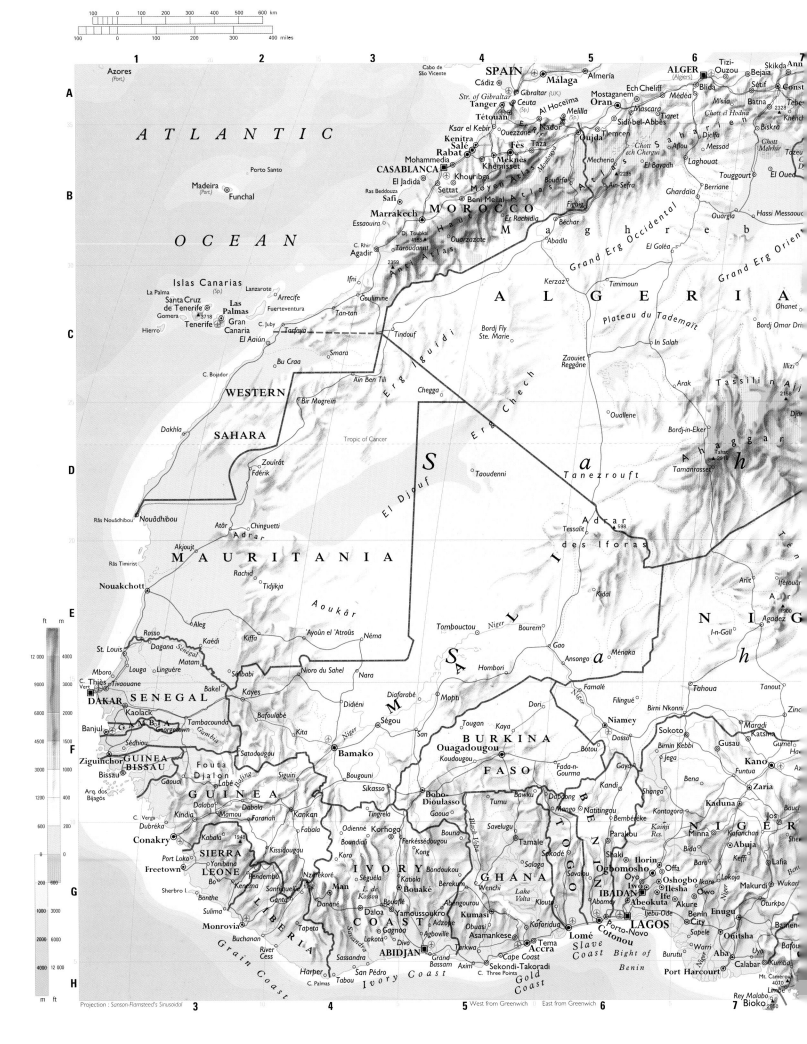

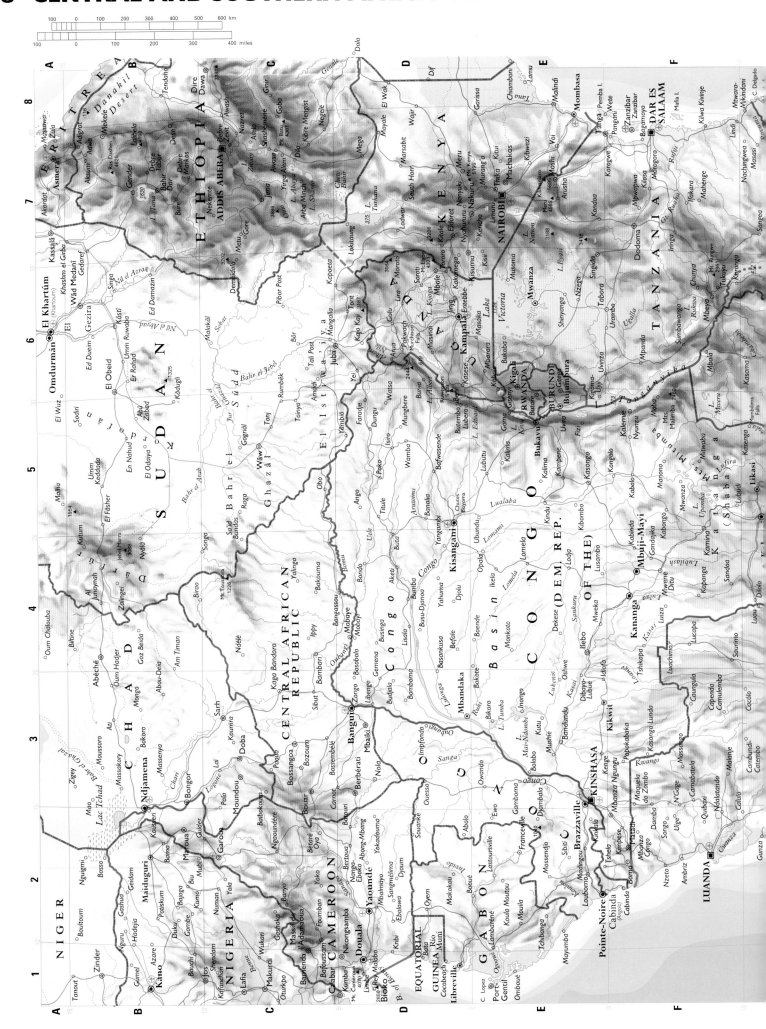

MADAGASCAR
On same scale as General Map

COPYRIGHT GEORGE PHILIP LTD.

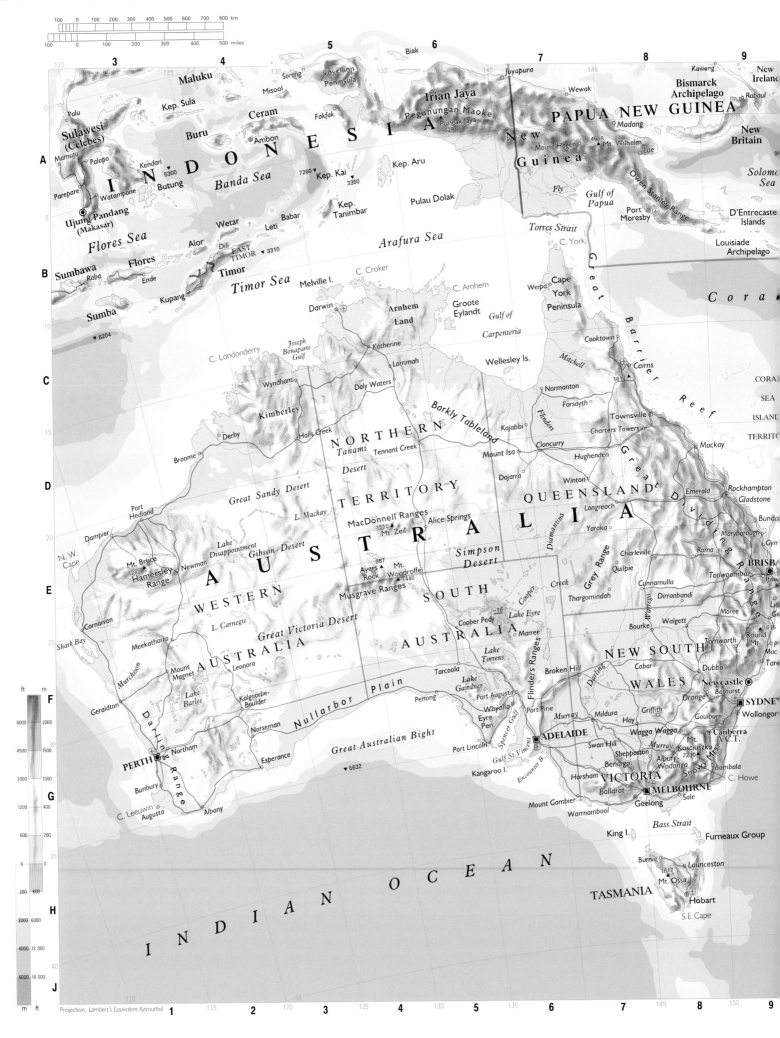

100 0 100 200 300 400 500 600 700 800 km
100 0 100 200 300 400 500 miles

INDONESIA

Maluku
Palu
Kep. Sula
Misool
Sorong
Ceram
Fakfak
Vogelkop Peninsula
Biak
Irian Jaya
Pegunungan Maoke
Puncak Jaya 5029
Jayapura
Wewak
Kavieng
New Ireland
Bismarck Archipelago
Rabaul
PAPUA NEW GUINEA
Madang
Mount Hagen
Mt. Wilhelm 4508
Lae
New Britain
Solomon Sea

Sulawesi (Celebes)
Mamuju
Palopo
Buru
Kendari
Butung
Watampone
Ambon
Banda Sea
5300
Kep. Kai 7260
Kep. Aru
3350
New Guinea
Fly
Owen Stanley Range
Gulf of Papua
Port Moresby
D'Entrecasteaux Islands

Parepare
Ujung Pandang (Makasar)
Wetar
Leti
Babar
Kep. Tanimbar
Pulau Dolak
Arafura Sea
Torres Strait
C. York
Louisiade Archipelago

Flores Sea
Alor
Dili
EAST TIMOR 3310
Flores
Ende
Kupang
Timor
Timor Sea
Melville I.
C. Croker
C. Arnhem
Weipa
Cape York Peninsula
Great Barrier Reef
Coral

Sumbawa
Raba
6204
Sumba
Darwin
Arnhem Land
Groote Eylandt
Gulf of Carpentaria
Wellesley Is.
Cooktown
Cairns 1611
CORAL SEA

C. Londonderry
Joseph Bonaparte Gulf
Katherine
Larrimah
Normanton
Forsayth
Mitchell
Townsville
ISLAND TERRITO

Wyndham
Daly Waters
Barkly Tableland
Kajabbi
Flinders
Charters Towers
Mackay

Kimberley
Halls Creek
NORTHERN
Tanami Desert
Tennant Creek
Cloncurry
Mount Isa
Hughenden
Derby
Broome
Dajarra
Winton
QUEENSLAND
Great
Emerald
Rockhampton
Gladstone

Port Hedland
Great Sandy Desert
L. Mackay
TERRITORY
MacDonnell Ranges 1510
Mt. Zeil
Alice Springs
Longreach
Yaraka
Diamantina
Dividing
Maryborough

Dampier
N.W. Cape
Lake Disappointment
Gibson Desert
AUSTRALIA
867
Ayers Rock
Mt. Woodroffe 1440
Simpson Desert
Cooper
Grey Range
Charleville
Quilpie
Roma
BRISB

Mt. Bruce 1235
Hamersley Range
Newman
WESTERN
Musgrave Ranges
SOUTH
Creek
Thargomindah
Cunnamulla
Dirranbandi
Toowoomba
Ipsw

Carnarvon
Meekatharra
L. Carnegie
AUSTRALIA
Great Victoria Desert
16
Lake Eyre
AUSTRALIA
Warrego
Bourke
Walgett
Moree
Lis

Shark Bay
Mount Magnet
Leonora
Coober Pedy
Marree
Flinders Ranges
NEW SOUTH
Cobar
Dubbo
Tamworth
Round Mt 1615
Tare

Geraldton
Murchison
Lake Barlee
Kalgoorlie-Boulder
Tarcoola
Lake Torrens
Broken Hill
Darling
WALES
Orange
Bathurst
Newcastle

Penong
Port Augusta
Port Pirie
Lake Gairdner
WALES
Griffith
Mildura
Bendigo
SYDNEY
Wollongong

Norseman
Nullarbor Plain
Eyre Pen.
Whyalla
Murray
Hay
Wagga Wagga
Goulburn
Canberra A.C.T.

PERTH
Northam
Esperance
Great Australian Bight
Port Lincoln
Spencer Gulf
Gulf St. Vincent
ADELAIDE
Swan Hill
Shepparton
Albury
Kosciuszko 2230
Snowy Mts.
Bombala
C. Howe

Bunbury
Darling Range
Kangaroo I.
Encounter B.
Horsham
VICTORIA
Murray
Wodonga
Sale

C. Leeuwin
Augusta
Albany
5632
Mount Gambier
Ballarat
MELBOURNE
Geelong
Warrnambool

King I.
Bass Strait
Furneaux Group

INDIAN OCEAN

Burnie
Launceston
TASMANIA
Mt. Ossa 1617
Hobart
S.E. Cape

ft m
6000 2000
4500 1500
3000 1000
1200 400
600 200
0 0
200 600
2000 6000
4000 12 000
6000 18 000
m ft

Projection: Lambert's Equivalent Azimuthal

M e l a n e s i a

Bougainville
t. Balbi

Choiseul

Santa Isabel

New
Georgia

**SOLOMON
ISLANDS**

Malaita

Honiara ▲2439
Guadalcanal

San
Cristóbal ▼7223

Rennell

Sea

Santa Cruz
Is.

Fataka

Banks Is.

Espíritu Santo ▲1879

Malakula

VANUATU
(New Hebrides)

Îles D'Entrecasteaux

Port-Vila ○ Efate

Îles Bélep

Erromango

Îles Loyauté ▲1628

Tanna

New
Caledonia
(Fr.)

Noumea

Aneityum

▼7569

Matthew I.

Ceve-i-Ra

K I R I B A T I

Tamana

Baker
(U.S.A.) Equator

▼6195

Namumea

Abariringa

Phoenix Is.

Carondelet

TUVALU
(Ellice Is.) Funafuti ○ Fongafale

Nukulaelae

Tokelau Is.
(N.Z.)

Rotuma

Mata-Utu⊕○ Uvea
Wallis & Futuna
Horn *(Fr.)*

Niuafo'ou

SAMOA
Savai'i ○ ⊕Apia
'Upolu

Tutuila

American
Samoa

Vanua Levu

Viti Levu

▲1323 Suva **FIJI**

Kandavu

Lau Group

Vava'u Group

Ha'apai Group

TONGA

Nuku'alofa ⊕
Tongatapu Group

⊕Niue
(N.Z.)

P A C I F I C

▼5303

O C E A N

10 882 ▼ ▲

Tonga Trench

Tropic of Capricorn

Norfolk I.
(Austral.)

Lord Howe I.
(Austral.) ▼734

Raoul

Kermadec Is.
(N.Z.)

Lord Howe Ridge

10 047 ▼

Kermadec Trench

asman Sea

North C.

Kaitaia

Whangarei

Auckland ⊙

Hamilton

North Island
Bay of
Plenty
Tauranga

NEW

New Plymouth

Rotorua ○ Gisborne

Raupehu
▲2797

ZEALAND

Wanganui

Napier

Palmerston
North

Nelson

Masterton

▼5267

Greymouth

Blenheim

Cook Strait

Wellington

South Island

Aoraki Mt. Cook
3753 ● **Christchurch**

Southern Alps

Queenstown

Timaru

Invercargill ○ Dunedin
Stewart I.

International Date Line

Chatham Is.
(N.Z.)

A

B

C

D

E

F

G

H

J

10   11   12   13   East from Greenwich   14   15   West from Greenwich   16   17   18

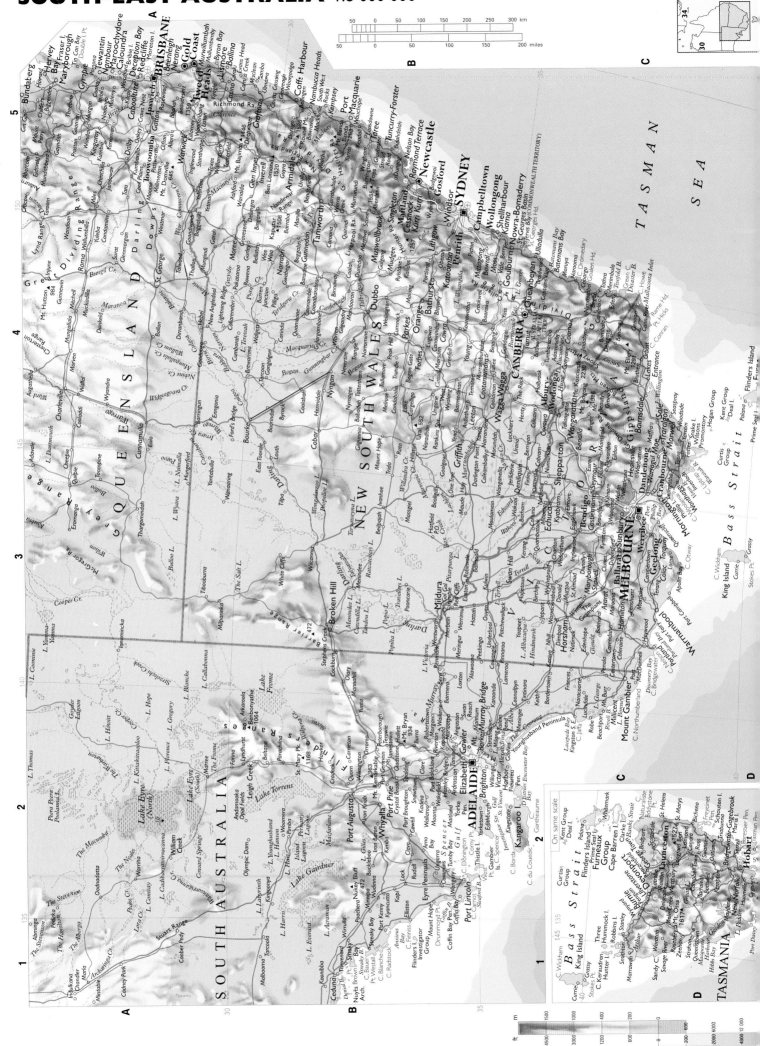

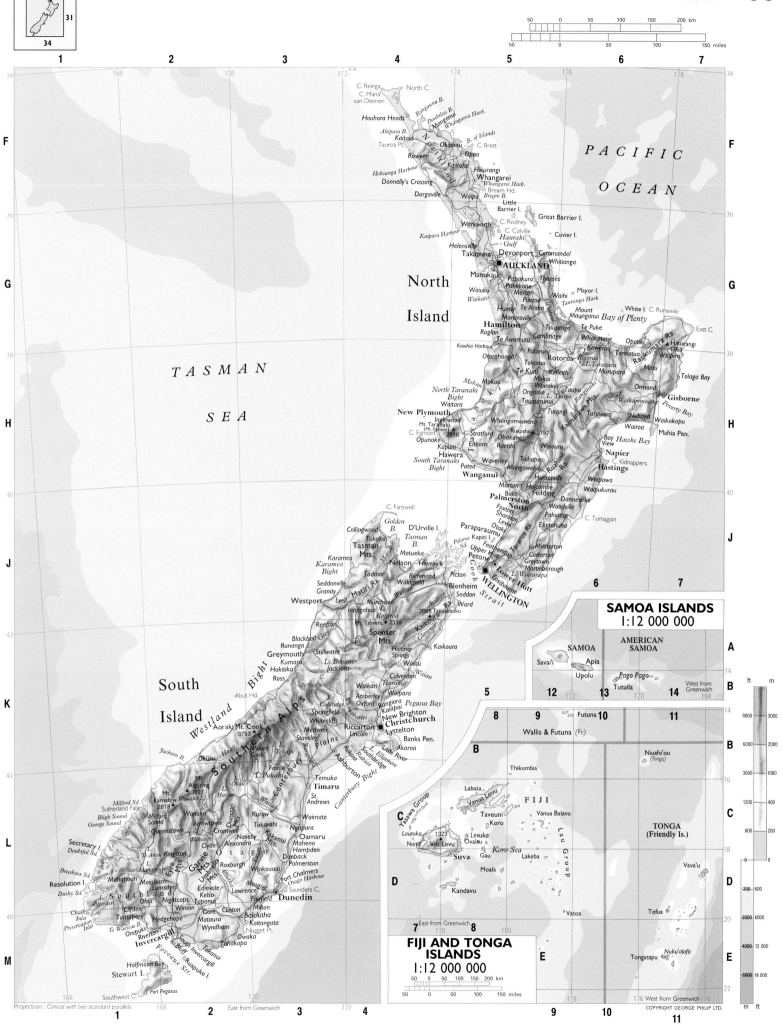

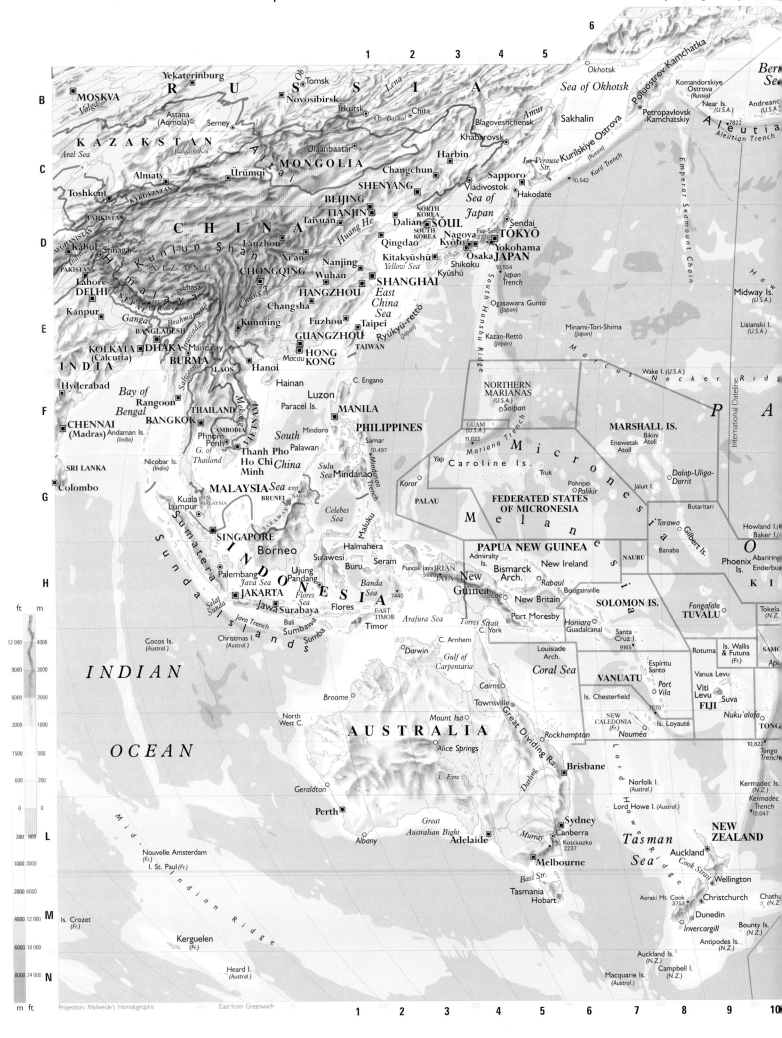

Arctic Circle

ALASKA
(U.S.A.)
Anchorage

Bristol Bay

Gulf of Alaska

Juneau

15

ROCKY

C A N A D A

16   17   18   19   20

Prince of Wales I.
(U.S.A.) Prince Rupert
Queen Charlotte Is.
(Canada)

Edmonton

L. Winnipeg

Newfoundland

N O R T H

B

Vancouver
Vancouver I.   Victoria
Seattle

Calgary   Regina   Winnipeg

St. Lawrence

Québec

St. John's

Portland

Snake

Boise

Missouri

L. Superior

Minneapolis

L. Michigan   L. Huron
Toronto   Ottawa
Detroit   L. Ontario
L. Erie   Boston

Montréal

C

C. Mendocino

Salt Lake
City

Denver

CHICAGO
Pittsburgh

Buffalo

NEW YORK CITY
PHILADELPHIA
Baltimore
Washington D.C.

A T L A N T I C

6741

Sacramento

SAN FRANCISCO

4418

Kansas City

St. Louis
Memphis

Cincinnati

Appalachian Mts.

Atlanta

D

UNITED STATES

LOS ANGELES
San Diego

Phoenix

Dallas

C. Hatteras

Bermuda
(U.K.)

Sargasso Sea

Mississippi

Houston

Jacksonville

Guadalupe
(Mex.)

Ciudad
Juárez

San Antonio

New
Orleans

Gulf of Mexico

Miami

BAHAMAS

O C E A N

E

Ridge

Tropic of Cancer

Baja California

Golfo de California

M E X I C O

Monterrey

La Habana

CUBA

West Indies

Honolulu
Oahu   HAWAIIAN IS.
4205   (U.S.A.)
Hawaii

C. San Lucas

C I F I C

C. San Lucas

Guadalajara

Is. Revilla Gigedo
(Mex.)

Acapulco

MEXICO
Puebla
5700

Mérida

Canal de Yucatán

Florida St.

HAITI
9200
DOMINICAN REP.
7680
JAMAICA   Kingston   PUERTO
RICO
(U.S.A.)

Leeward
Is.

F

nston I.
(U.S.A.)

Palmyra Is.
(U.S.A.)

North West Christmas Ridge

Teraina

Tabuaeran
Kiritimati

BELIZE

GUATEMALA
Guatemala   HONDURAS

Caribbean Sea

BARBADOS

Windward Is.

San Salvador
EL SALVADOR   NICARAGUA
Managua

Barranquilla

Maracaibo

I. Clipperton
(Fr.)

COSTA
RICA   Colón   Panamá
PANAMA

San José

Caracas

Orinoco

VENEZUELA

G

L I N E   I S.

Equator

Jarvis I.
(U.S.A.)

Galápagos
(Ecuador)

I. del Coco
(Costa Rica)

Medellín

Bogotá

E A N

B A T I

Malden I.

Starbuck I.

I. de Malpelo
(Colombia)

Cali

COLOMBIA

Quito
ECUADOR

Amazonas

H

Tongareva

Pukapuka   Manihiki

Is. Marquises

Guayaquil

Iquitos

BRAZIL

Vostok I.

Caroline I.
(Millennium I.)
Flint I.

C. Paliñas

Suwarrow Is.

Is. de la
Société

Is. Tuamotu

Trujillo

6369

PERU

J

Australseamount Chain

Papeete
Tahiti

Cuzco

L. Titicaca   Nevada Ancohuma
6550

Cook Is.
(N.Z.)

FRENCH POLYNESIA

Mururoa

Arequipa
6866
Peru-
Chile   Arica

La Paz

BOLIVIA

Rarotonga

Is. Tubuai

Iquique

Tropic of Capricorn

Antofagasta

PARAGUAY

Asunción

K

Ducie I.

Pitcairn I.
(U.K.)

Rapa

Sala-y-Gómez

San Felix
(Chile)

I. de Pascua
(Chile)

8050
Trench

San Ambrosio
(Chile)

San Miguel
de Tucumán

Pôrto
Alegre

Arch. de
Juan Fernández
(Chile)

Valparaíso

Córdoba

Aconcagua
6960   Rosario

URUGUAY

SANTIAGO
Concepción

BUENOS
AIRES

Montevideo

Río de la Plata

L

East Pacific Ridge

Chile Rise

ARGENTINA

SOUTH

M

Pacific-Antarctic Ridge

Patagonia

6212

ATLANTIC

OCEAN

Punta Arenas

Falkland Is.
(U.K.)

South Georgia
(U.K.)

N

Est. de Magallanes
Tierra del Fuego

C. de Hornos

West from Greenwich

COPYRIGHT GEORGE PHILIP LTD.

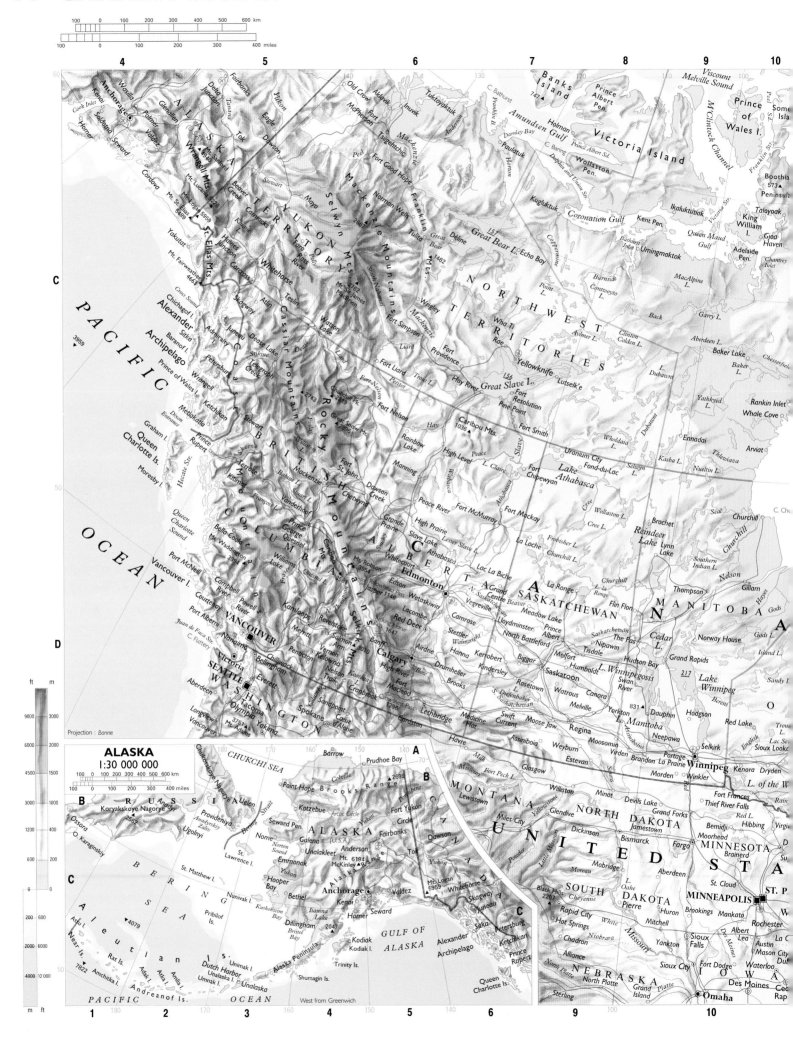

100 0 100 200 300 400 500 600 km
100 0 100 200 300 400 miles

4   **5**   **6**   **7**   **8**   **9**   **10**

C

PACIFIC OCEAN

Projection : Bonne

ft   m
9000   3000
6000   2000
4500   1500
3000   1000
1200   400
600   200
0   0
200   600
2000   6000
4000   12 000
m   ft

D

ALASKA
1:30 000 000

100 0 100 200 300 400 500 600 km
100 0 100 200 300 400 miles

CHUKCHI SEA

RUSSIA

BERING SEA

B

C

Aleutian Is.

PACIFIC OCEAN

West from Greenwich

1   **2**   **3**   **4**   **5**   **6**   **9**   **10**

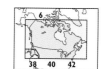

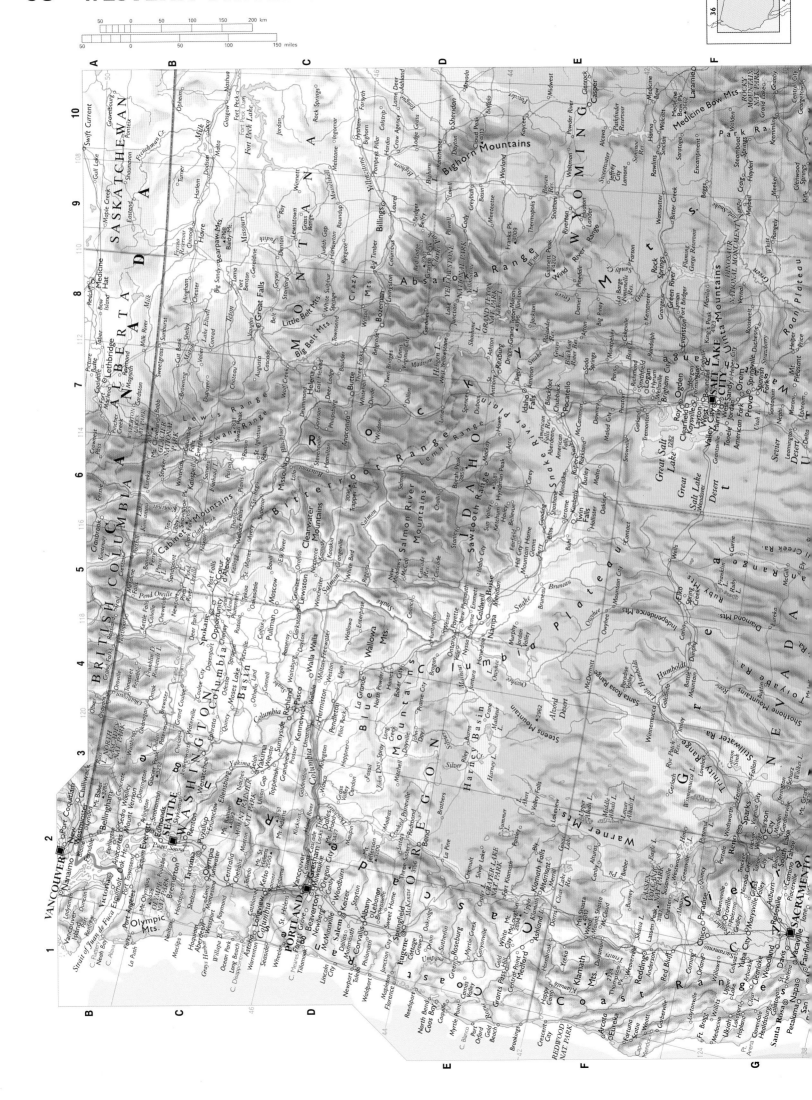

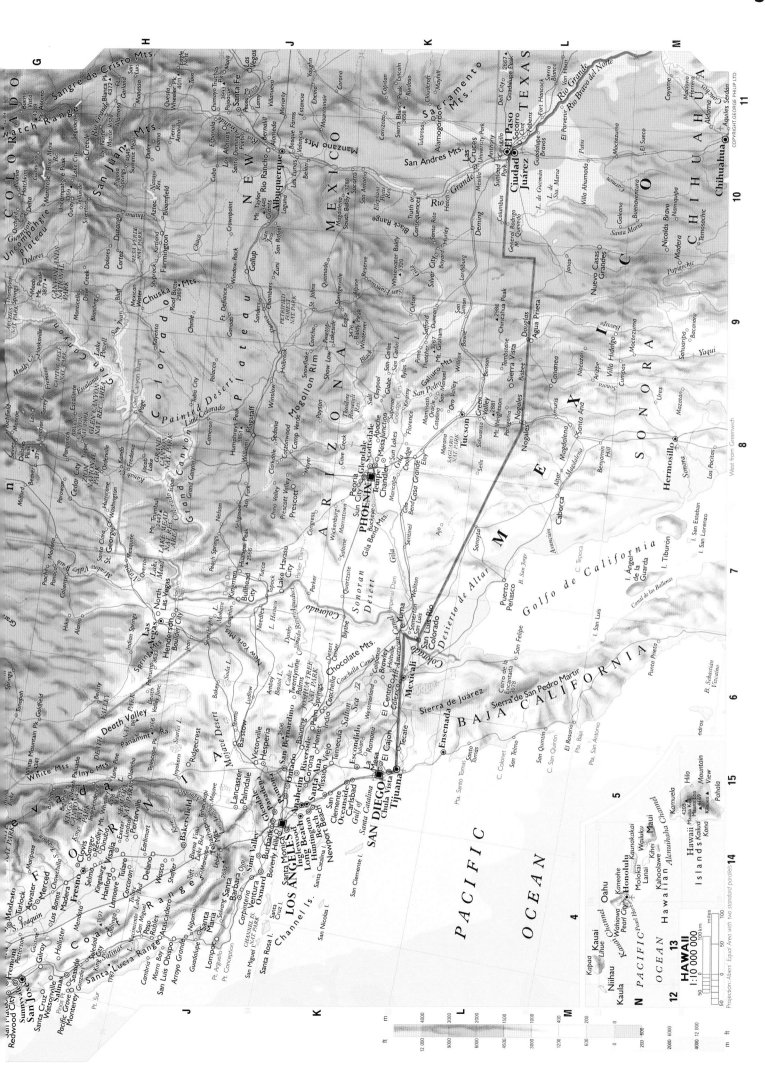

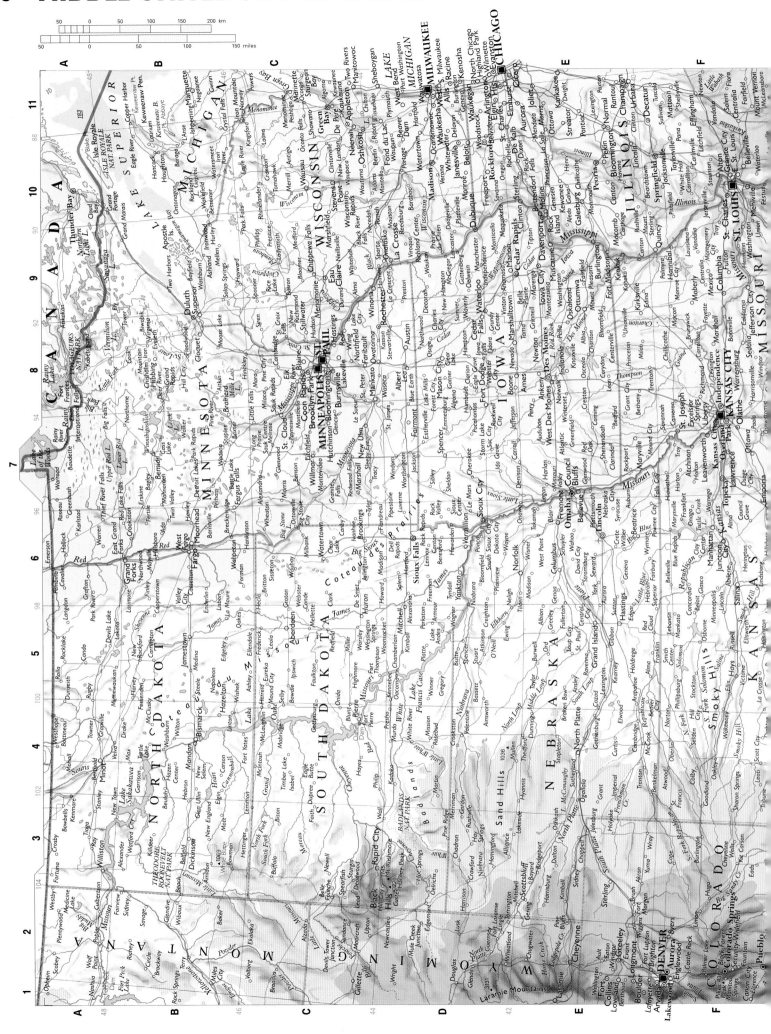

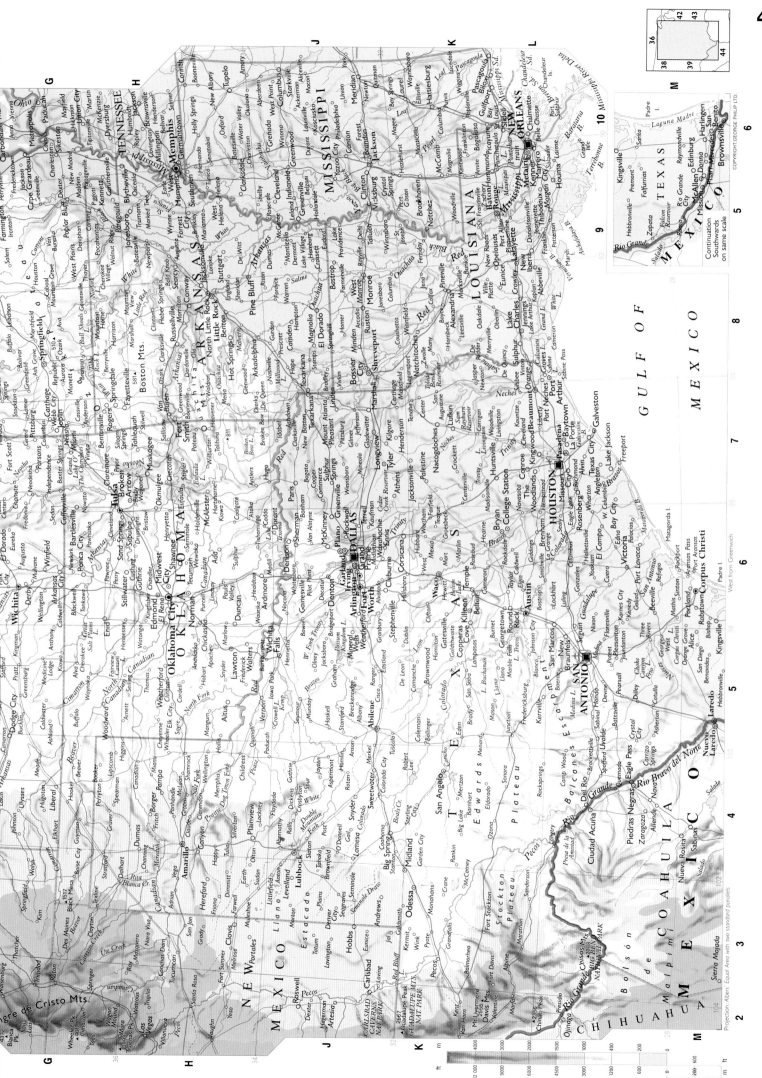

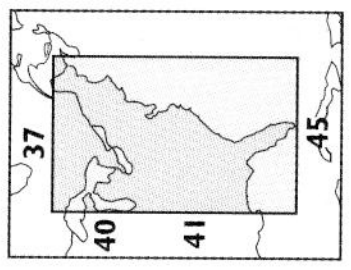
37
40
41
45

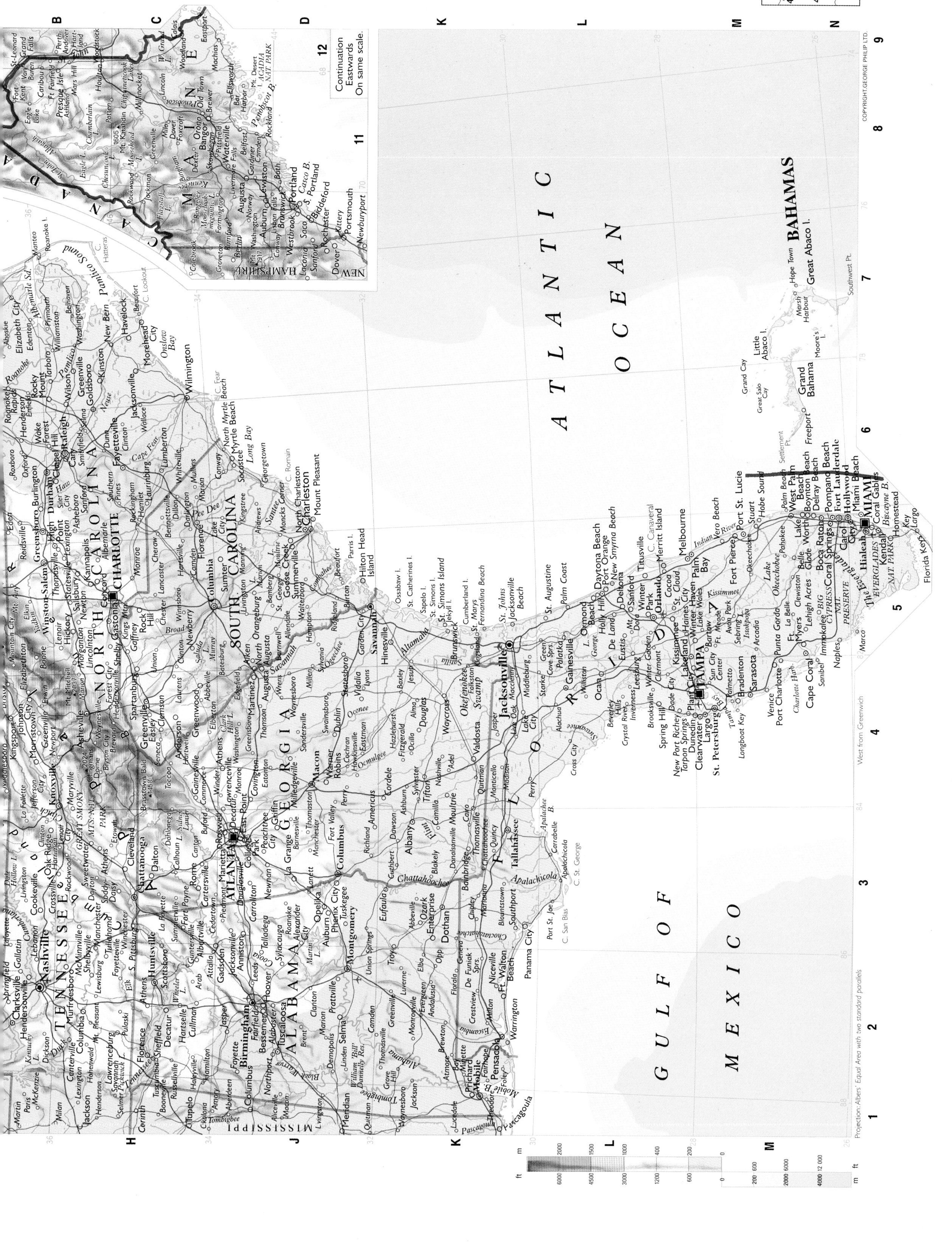
ATLANTIC
OCEAN
GULF OF
MEXICO
BAHAMAS
TENNESSEE
NORTH CAROLINA
SOUTH CAROLINA
GEORGIA
ALABAMA
FLORIDA
MISSISSIPPI
MAINE
NEW HAMPSHIRE
CANADA
ATLANTA
CHARLOTTE
TAMPA
MIAMI
Nashville
Jacksonville
Tallahassee
Savannah
Charleston
Orlando
Birmingham
Montgomery
Mobile
Continuation Eastwards On same scale.
West from Greenwich
Projection: Albers' Equal Area with two standard parallels
COPYRIGHT, GEORGE PHILIP LTD.

ATLANTIC OCEAN

PUERTO RICO d
1:3 000 000

PUERTO RICO
(U.S.A.)

Pta. Agujereada
Isabela
Aguadilla
Arecibo
Manati
Barceloneta
Vega Baja
Bayamón
SAN JUAN
Rio Grande
Carolina
Fajardo
Dewey
Culebra
Mayagüez
San Sebastián
Adjuntas
Utuado
Cordillera Central
▲C de Punta 1338
Caguas
Cayey
Humacao
Naguabo
Vieques
Esperanza
San German
Yauco
Urayon Mts.
Coamo
Yabucoa
Pta. Aguila
Guanica
Ponce
Guayama
I. Caja de Muertos

ST. LUCIA f
1:1 000 000

Cap Point
Pte. Hardy
Gros Islet
Esperance Bay
Castries
Marquis
Babonneau
L'Anse la Raye
Canaries
Dennery
Millet
Soufrière ▲750
Soufrière Bay ▲960 Mt. Gimie
Petit Piton ▲750
Gros Piton Pt. ▲796
Gros Piton
Micoud
Vierge Pt.
Choiseul
ST. LUCIA
Laborie
Vieux Fort
C. Moule à Chique

VIRGIN IS. e
1:2 000 000

Rufling Pt.
The Settlement
Anegada
East Pt.
Virgin Islands
(U.K.)
Great Camanoe
Jost Van Dyke I.
Guana I. 521
Virgin Is.
(U.S.A.)
Hans Lollik I.
Tortola
Beef I.
Virgin Gorda
Road Town
Spanish Town
Cruz Bay
Charlotte Amalie
St. Thomas I.
St. John I.
Peter I.

ATLANTIC OCEAN
Crabhill
North Point
Spring Hall
Fustic
Boscobelle
▲245 Belleplaine
Speightstown
BARBADOS
Westmoreland
Bathsheba
Hillcrest
Alleynes Bay
▲340 Mt. Hillaby
Martin's Bay
Holetown
Massiah Street
Jackson
Bridgefield
Black Rock
Ellerton
Six Cross Roads
Bridgetown
Oistins
The Crane
St. Martins
Carlisle Bay
Worthing
Oistins
Chancery Lane
Bay
South Point

BARBADOS g
1:1 000 000

Columbia
Wilmington
ATLANTA
Augusta
Long Bay
C. Fear
Macon
Charleston
bus
Savannah
Altamaha
any
Jacksonville
lahassee
Daytona Beach
Orlando
C. Canaveral
AMPA
Melbourne
etersburg
West Palm Beach
Sarasota
L. Okeechobee
Grand Bahama I.
MIAMI
Fort Lauderdale
Freeport
Great Abaco I.
Bimini Is.
New Providence I.
Key West
Eleuthera I.
Nassau
BAHAMAS
Andros I.
Cat I.
San Salvador I.
HABANA
Matanzas
Cárdenas
Sagua la Grande
Santa Clara
del Rio
Güines
Great Exuma I.
Long I.
ane Batabanó
G. de Batabanó
Placetas
Morón
C U B A
Cienfuegos
Trinidad
Sancti-Spíritus
Ciego de Avila
Camagüey
Crooked I.
Acklins I.
I. de la Juventud
Victoria de Las Tunas
Nuevitas
Holguín
Banes
Mayaguana I. (U.K.)
Turks & Caicos Is. (U.K.)
2005
Manzanillo
Bayamo
Santiago de Cuba
Guantánamo
Baracoa
Great Inagua
7680
Cayman Is.
Grand Cayman (U.K.)
Montego Bay
Gonaïves
St-Marc
Jérémie
Cap-Haïtien
Port-de-Paix
Puerto Plata
Monte Christi
3175
Santiago de los Cabelleros
San Francisco de Macorís
9200
PUERTO RICO
(U.S.A.)
La Vega
La Romana
Arecibo
SAN JUAN
Virgin Is.
(U.K. - U.S.A.)
Anguilla (U.K.)
St-Martin (Fr. - Neth.)
St-Barthelemy (Fr.)
ST. KITTS & NEVIS
Mandeville
Spanish Town
JAMAICA
Kingston
Les Cayes
Jacmel
HAITI
PORT-AU-PRINCE
DOMINICAN REP.
San Juan
Bani
Barahona
San Pedro de Macorís
SANTO DOMINGO
Canal de la Mona
(Mona Passage)
Mayagüez
Ponce
Caguas
St. Croix (U.S.A.)
Basseterre
ANTIGUA & BARBUDA
St. John's
Montserrat (U.K.)
GUADELOUPE (Fr.)
Pointe-à-Pitre
Basse-Terre
DOMINICA
Roseau
Paso de los Vientos
(Windward Passage)
Hispaniola
Anti
l les
Lesser
Leeward
Is.
Fort-de-France
MARTINIQUE (Fr.)
Castries
ST. LUCIA
Kingstown
BARBADOS
Bridgetown
Is. Santanilla
(Honduras)
ST. VINCENT & THE GRENADINES
Windward
Is.
GRENADA
St. George's
Tobago
L. de Caratasca
C. Gracias a Dios
Puerto Cabezas
La Blanquilla (Ven.)
Port of Spain
TRINIDAD & TOBAGO
San Fernando
Río Grande
I. de Providencia (Colombia)
Bluefields
I. de San Andrés (Colombia)
Pta. Gallinas
Aruba (Neth.)
Curaçao
Willemstad
Bonaire
NETH. ANTILLES
Punta Fijo
I. de Margarita
Porlamar
Carúpano
Güiria
Pen. de la Guajira
Ríohacha
Coro
San Felipe
Puerto Cabello
Maiquetía
La Tortuga
Cumaná
G. de Paria
Santa Marta
Sierra Nevada de Santa Marta
5800
BARRANQUILLA
MARACAIBO
Maracay
Barquisimeto
CARACAS
Barcelona
2596
Maturín
Cartagena
Soledad
Calamar
L. de Cabimas
VALENCIA
Puerto La Cruz
El Tigre
Tucupita
Valledupar
L. Maracaibo
Valera
Acarigua
Ciudad Guayana
COSTA RICA
Limón
3432
Irazú
Cartago
Colón
Sincelejo
Mompós
Valera
Barinas
Apure
San Fernando de Apure
Orinoco
Ciudad Bolívar
Georgetown
Sur
Volcán Barú 3475
David
Puerto Armuelles
PANAMÁ
Panamá
Panama Canal
G. del Darién
Montería
Magdalena
Mérida
5007
Caicara
Embalse de Guri
Tumeremo
Bartica
New Amsterdam
Linden
Wismar
Santiago
Chitré
La Palma
El Real
Puerto Wilches
Barrancabermeja
Cúcuta
San Cristóbal
Pamplona
Bucaramanga
Arauca
V E N E Z U E L A
Caura
Caroní
Mt. Roraima 2810
G U Y A N A
Pen. de Azuero
I. de Coiba
Arch. de las Perlas
G. de Panamá
Riosucio
3960
Yarumal
Angel Falls
Cuyuni
Esequibo
SURINAM
C. Corrientes
Antioquia
Bello
MEDELLÍN
Quibdó
Sogamoso
Tunja
Puerto Carreño
Sierra Pacaraima
Boa Vista
COLOMBIA
Manizales
Pereira
Tolima 5215
Ibagué
BOGOTÁ
Villavicencio
Meta
Puerto Ayacucho
Ventuari
Sierra Parima
Armenia
Girardot
Puerto Inírida
Buenaventura
Palmira
Huila 5750
CALI
Neiva
Guaviare
Orinoco
Casiquiare
Popayán
Volcán Puracé 4646
B R A Z I L
Equator

C A R I B B E A N   S E A

Straits of Florida

C. Romain
C. Sable

A
B
C
D
E
F
G

West from Greenwich

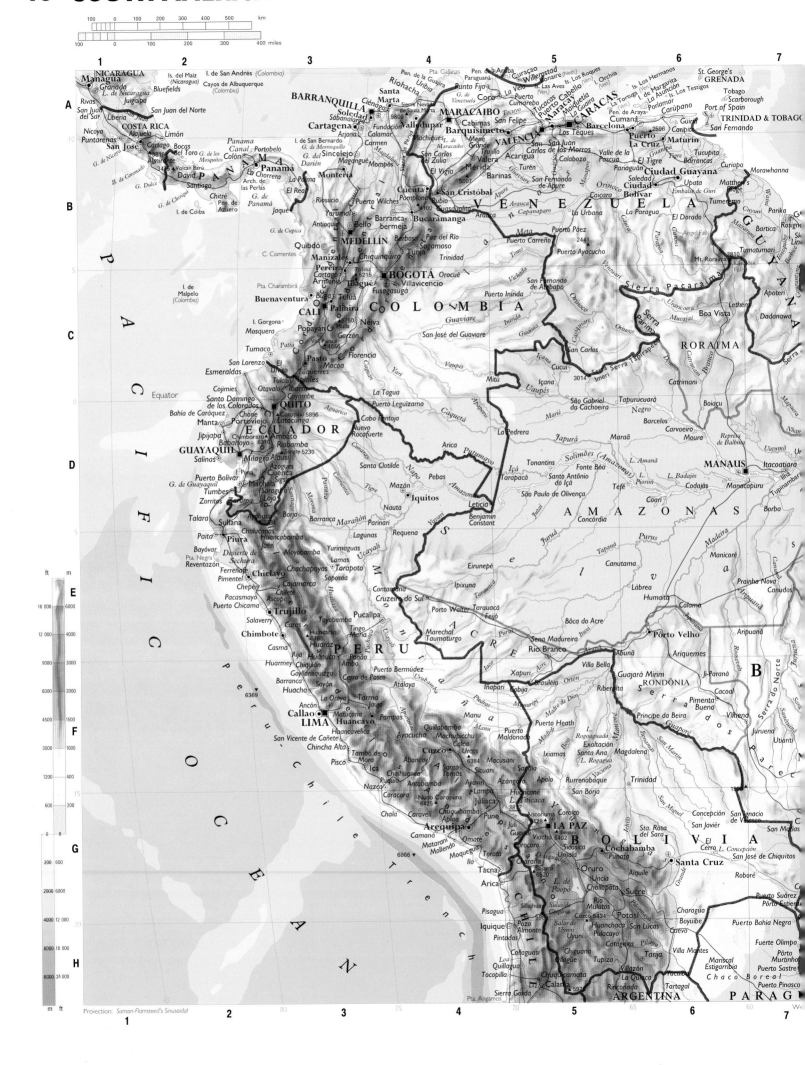

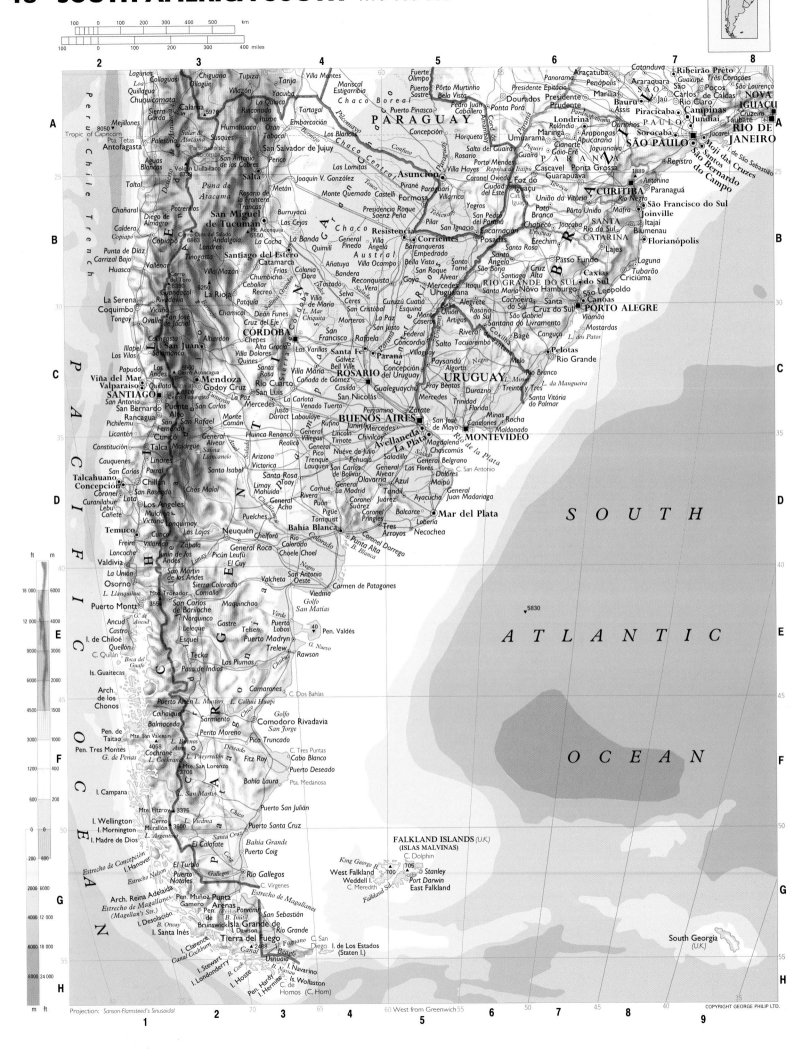

Projection: Sanson-Flamsteed's Sinusoidal

INDEX

The index contains the names of all the principal places and features shown on the maps. The alphabetical order of names composed of two or more words is governed primarily by the first word and then by the second. This is an example of the rule:

New South Wales □   **30** **G8**
New York □   **42** **D8**
New Zealand ■   **34** **M9**
Newark, Del., U.S.A.   **42** **F8**
Newark, N.J., U.S.A.   **42** **E8**

Physical features composed of a proper name (Erie) and a description (Lake) are positioned alphabetically by the proper name. The description is positioned after the proper name and is usually abbreviated:

Erie, L.   **42** **D5**
Everest, Mt.   **25** **C7**

Where a description forms part of a settlement name or administrative name, however, it is always written in full and put in its true alphabetical position:

Lake Charles   **41** **K8**
Mount Isa   **30** **E6**

The number in bold type which follows each name in the index refers to the number of the map page where that place or feature will be found. This is usually the largest scale at which the place or feature appears.

The letter and figure which are immediately after the page number give the grid square on the map page, within which the feature is situated. The letter represents the latitude and the figure the longitude. In some cases the feature itself may fall within the specified square, while the name is outside.

Rivers are indexed to their mouths or confluences and carry the symbol → after their names. A solid square ■ follows the name of a country, while an open square □ refers to a first order administrative area.

A

A Coruña 13 A1
Aachen 16 C3
Aarau 12 C8
Aare → 12 C8
Aba 26 G7
Ābādān 24 B3
Abakan 19 D10
Abaringa 34 H10
Abbaye, Pt. 42 B1
Abbeville, France 12 A4
Abbeville, Ala., U.S.A. 43 K3
Abbeville, La., U.S.A. 41 L8
Abbeville, S.C., U.S.A. 43 H4
Abeokuta 26 G6
Aberaeron 9 E3
Aberchirder 10 D6
Abercorn 32 A5
Aberdare 9 F4
Aberdeen, Australia 32 B5
Aberdeen, China 21 G11
Aberdeen, U.K. 10 D6
Aberdeen, Ala., U.S.A. 43 J1
Aberdeen, Idaho, U.S.A. 38 E7
Aberdeen, Md., U.S.A. 42 F7
Aberdeen, S. Dak., U.S.A. 40 C5
Aberdeen, Wash., U.S.A. 38 C2
Aberdeenshire □ 10 D6
Aberdyfi 9 E3
Aberfeldy 10 E5
Abergavenny 9 F4
Abergele 9 D4
Abernathy 41 J4
Abert, L. 38 E3
Aberystwyth 9 E3
Abhā 24 D3
Abidjan 26 G5
Abilene, Kans., U.S.A. 40 F6
Abilene, Tex., U.S.A. 41 J5
Abingdon, U.K. 9 F6
Abingdon, U.S.A. 43 G5
Abitibi, L. 37 D12
Abminga 32 A1
Aboyne 10 D6
Absaroka Range 38 D9
Abu Dhabi = Abū Ẓaby 24 C4
Abū Kamāl 24 C4
Abuja 26 G7
Abut Hd. 33 K3
Acadia Nat. Park 43 C11
Acaponeta 44 C3
Acapulco 44 D5
Acarigua 46 B5
Accomac 42 G8
Accra 26 G5
Accrington 8 D5
Aceh □ 23 C1
Achill Hd. 11 C1
Achill I. 11 C1
Achinsk 19 D10
Ackerman 41 J10
Acklins I. 45 C10
Aconcagua, Cerro 48 C3
Açores, Is. do 26 A1
Acraman, L. 32 B2
Acre = 'Akko 24 C2
Acre □ 46 E4
Acre → 46 E5
Ad Dammām 24 C4
Ad Dawḥah 24 C4
Ada, Minn., U.S.A. 40 B6
Ada, Okla., U.S.A. 41 H6
Adair, C. 37 A12
Adak I. 36 C2
Adamaoua, Massif de l' 26 G7
Adaminaby 32 C4
Adams, N.Y., U.S.A. 42 D7
Adams, Wis., U.S.A. 40 D10
Adams Mt. 38 D5
Adana 17 C6
Adapazarı = Sakarya 17 B4
Adare, C. 5 E15
Adavale 32 A3
Addis Ababa 28 C7
Adel 43 K4
Adelaide 32 B2
Adelaide I. 5 C3
Adelaide Pen. 36 B10
Adélie, Terre 5 C10
Aden = Al 'Adan 24 D3
Aden, G. of 24 D3
Adirondack Mts. 42 D8
Adjuntas 45 d
Admiralty Is. 34 H6
Adoni 25 M10
Adour → 12 E3
Adra 13 D4
Adrano 14 F6
Adrar des Iforas 26 C5
Adrian, Mich., U.S.A. 42 E3
Adrian, Tex., U.S.A. 41 H3
Adwa 24 D2
Adriatic Sea 6 G9
Ægean Sea 15 E11
Aerht'ai Shan 20 B4
Afghanistan ■ 24 B5
Afton 38 E8
Agadez 26 E7
Agadir 26 B4
Agartala 25 C9
Agde 12 E5
Agen 12 D4
Ağrı Dağı 17 C4
Agra 25 F10
Agrigento 14 F5
Agua Prieta 44 A3
Aguadilla 45 d
Aguascalientes 44 C4
Aguila, Punta 45 d
Aguijereada, Pta. 45 d
Agulhas, C. 29 E3
Ahipara B. 33 H4
Ahmadabad 25 H8
Ahmadnagar 25 K9
Ahoskie 43 G7
Ahvāz 24 B3
Ahvenanmaa = Åland 7 F11
Aihui 21 A7
Aiken 43 J5
Ailsa Craig 10 F3
Ainsworth 40 D5
Air 26 E7
Air Force I. 37 B12
Airdrie, Canada 38 C6
Airdrie, U.K. 10 F5
Aire → 8 D7
Aisne → 12 B5
Aitkin 40 B7
Aix-en-Provence 12 E6
Aix-la-Chapelle = Aachen 16 C3
Aix-les-Bains 12 D6
Aizawl 25 H9
Ajaccio 12 F8
Ajanta Ra. 25 J9
Ajmer 25 F9
Ajo 39 K7
Akaroa 33 K4
Akimiski I. 37 C11

Akita 22 D7
'Akko 24 C2
Aklavik 36 B6
Akmolinsk = Astana 18 D8
Akola 25 C6
Akpatok I. 37 B13
Akron, Colo., U.S.A. 40 E3
Akron, Ohio, U.S.A. 42 E5
Aksai Chin 25 B6
Aksu 20 B3
Aktyubinsk = Aqtöbe 18 D6
Akure 26 G7
Akyab = Sittwe 25 C8
Al 'Adan 24 D3
Al 'Aqabah 24 D2
Al Başrah 24 B3
Al Ḥajar al Gharbī 24 C4
Al Ḥillah 24 B3
Al Ḥudaydah 24 D3
Al Ḥufūf 24 C3
Al Jazirah 24 C3
Al Jawf 24 C2
Al Kūt 24 B3
Al Kuwayt 24 C3
Al Lādhiqīyah 24 B2
Al Madīnah 24 C2
Al Manāmah 24 C4
Al Mawṣil 24 B3
Al Mubarraz 24 C3
Al Mukallā 24 D3
Al Mukhā 24 D3
Al Qā'im 24 C3
Al Quds = Jerusalem 17 D5
Alabama □ 43 K2
Alabaster 43 J2
Alachua 43 L4
Alameda 39 H6
Alamogordo 39 K11
Alamosa 39 H11
Åland 7 F11
Alaska □ 36 B5
Alaska, G. of 36 C5
Alaska Peninsula 36 C4
Alaska Range 36 B4
Alava, C. 38 B1
Alba-Iulia 15 A10
Albacete 13 C5
Albacutya, L. 32 C3
Albanel, L. 37 C12
Albania ■ 15 D9
Albany, Australia 33 G2
Albany, Ga., U.S.A. 43 K3
Albany, N.Y., U.S.A. 42 D9
Albany, Oreg., U.S.A. 38 D2
Albany, Tex., U.S.A. 41 J5
Albany → 37 C11
Albemarle 43 H5
Albemarle Sd. 43 H7
Albert, L., Africa 28 D6
Albert, L., Australia 32 C2
Albert Lea 40 D8
Albertville, France 12 D7
Albertville, U.S.A. 43 H2
Albi 12 E5
Albion, Mich., U.S.A. 42 D3
Albion, Nebr., U.S.A. 40 E6
Ålborg 7 F5
Alborz, Reshteh-ye Kūhhā-ye 24 B4
Albuquerque 39 J10
Albury-Wodonga 30 H8
Alcalá de Henares 13 B4
Alchevsk 18 E5
Alcova 38 E10
Aldabra Is. 27 G8
Aldan 19 D13
Aldan → 19 C13
Aldeburgh 9 E9
Alderney 9 H5
Aldershot 9 F7
Aleksandrovsk-Sakhalinskiy 19 D15
Alençon 12 B4
Aleppo = Ḥalab 24 B2
Alès 12 D6
Alessándria 12 D8
Ålesund 7 E9
Aleutian Is. 36 C2
Aleutian Trench 34 C10
Alexander 40 B3
Alexander Arch. 36 C6
Alexander City 43 J3
Alexander I. 5 C3
Alexandra, Australia 32 C4
Alexandra, N.Z. 33 L2
Alexandria = Iskandarīya 27 B11
Alexandria, La., U.S.A. 41 K8
Alexandria, Minn., U.S.A. 40 C7
Alexandria, S. Dak., U.S.A. 40 D6
Alexandria, Va., U.S.A. 42 F7
Alexandria Bay 42 C8
Alexandrina, L. 32 C2
Alford, Aberds., U.K. 10 D6
Alford, Lincs., U.K. 8 D8
Alfreton 8 D6
Algarve 13 D1
Algeciras 13 D3
Algemesí 13 C5
Alger 26 A6
Algeria ■ 26 C6
Algiers = Alger 26 A6
Algoa B. 29 E4
Algoma 42 C2
Alhambra 39 J4
Ali Sabieh 24 D3
Aliağa 15 E12
Alicante 13 C5
Alice 41 M5
Alice Springs 30 E5
Aliceville 43 J1
Aligarh 25 F11
Aliwal North 29 E4
Alkmaar 16 B3
Allagash → 43 B11
Allahabad 25 G12
Allanridge 29 D4
Allegan 42 D3
Allegheny → 42 E6
Allegheny Mts. 42 G6
Allen, Bog of 11 C5
Allen, L. 11 B3
Allendale 43 J5
Allentown 42 E8
Alleppey 25 Q10
Alliance, Nebr., U.S.A. 40 D3
Alliance, Ohio, U.S.A. 42 E5
Allier → 12 C5
Alloa 10 E5
Alma, Ga., U.S.A. 43 K4
Alma, Mich., U.S.A. 42 D3

Alma, Nebr., U.S.A. 40 E5
Alma Ata = Almaty 18 E8
Almansa 13 C5
Almanzor, Pico 13 B3
Almaty 18 E8
Almelo 16 B3
Almería 13 D4
Almora 25 E11
Alness 10 D4
Alnmouth 8 B6
Alnwick 8 B6
Alor 23 D4
Alor Setar 23 C2
Alpena 42 C4
Alpine, Ariz., U.S.A. 39 K9
Alpine, Tex., U.S.A. 41 K3
Alps 12 C8
Alsace 12 B7
Alsask 36 C9
Alston 8 C5
Altai = Aerht'ai Shan 20 B4
Altamaha → 43 K5
Altamura 14 D7
Altanbulag 20 A5
Altay 20 B3
Alton, U.K. 9 F7
Alton, U.S.A. 40 F9
Altoona 42 E6
Alturas 38 F3
Altun Shan 20 C3
Alva 41 G5
Alvarado 44 D5
Alvin 41 L7
Alvord Desert 38 E4
Alwar 25 F10
Alxa Zuoqi 20 C5
Alyth 10 E5
Alzada 38 F3
Amadeus, L. 30 E5
Amadjuak L. 37 B12
Amagasaki 22 F4
Amarillo 41 H4
Amazon = Amazonas → 47 D9
Amazonas □ 46 E6
Amazonas → 47 D9
Ambala 25 D10
Ambato 46 D3
Ambergris Cay 44 D7
Amberley 33 K4
Amble 8 B6
Ambleside 8 C5
Ambon 23 D4
Amboy 39 J6
Amboyna Cay 23 C3
Amchitka I. 36 C1
Ameca 44 C4
American Falls 38 E7
American Falls Reservoir 38 E7
American Fork 38 F8
American Highland 5 D6
American Samoa ■ 35 J10
Americus 43 J3
Amersfoort 16 B3
Amery Ice Shelf 5 D6
Ames 40 E8
Amherst 43 H7
Amiata, Mte. 12 C9
Amidon 40 B3
Amiens 12 B5
Amirante Is. 4 E9
Amistad, Presa de la 44 B4
Amite 41 K9
Amlia I. 36 C2
'Ammān 24 B2
Ammanford 9 F4
Ammon 38 E8
Amory 43 J1
Amos 37 D12
Amoy = Xiamen 21 D6
Amravati 25 J10
Amreli 25 J7
Amritsar 25 D9
Amroha 25 E11
Amsterdam, Neths. 16 B3
Amsterdam, U.S.A. 42 D8
Amudarya → 18 E6
Amundsen Gulf 36 A7
Amundsen Sea 5 D15
Amuntai 23 D3
Amur → 19 D15
An Nafūd 24 C3
An Najaf 24 B3
An Nāṣirīyah 24 B3
An Uaimh 11 C5
Anaconda 38 C7
Anacortes 38 B2
Anadarko 41 H5
Anadolu 17 C4
Anadyr 19 C18
Anadyrskiy Zaliv 19 C19
Anaheim 39 K5
Anambas, Kepulauan 23 C2
Anamosa 40 E9
Anápolis 47 G9
Anār 24 B4
Anatolia = Anadolu 17 C4
Anchorage 36 B5
Ancohuma, Nevada 46 G5
Ancona 14 C5
Ancud 48 E2
Anda 21 B7
Andalucía □ 13 D3
Andalusia 43 K2
Andaman Is. 25 D8
Andaman Sea 25 D9
Andamooka Opal Fields 32 B2
Anderson, Alaska, U.S.A. 36 B5
Anderson, Calif., U.S.A. 38 F2
Anderson, Ind., U.S.A. 42 E3
Anderson, Mo., U.S.A. 41 G7
Anderson, S.C., U.S.A. 43 H4
Anderson → 36 B7
Andes, Cord. de los 46 H5
Andhra Pradesh □ 25 L11
Andijon 18 E8
Andkhvoy 24 B5
Andorra ■ 13 A6
Andover 9 F6
Andreanof Is. 36 C2
Ándria 14 D7
Andros 15 F11
Andros I. 45 C9
Androscoggin → 43 D10
Anegada 45 e
Aneityum 34 E12
Angara → 19 D10
Angarsk 19 D11
Angaston 32 B2
Ånge 7 E10
Ángel de la Guarda, I. 44 B2
Angel Falls 46 B6
Ángeles 23 B4
Angermanälven → 7 E11
Angers 12 C3
Angesön 32 B2
Anglesey, Isle of □ 8 D3
Angmering 9 G7
Angol 48 D2
Angola ■ 28 G3
Angoulême 12 D4
Angoumois 12 D4
Angra do Heroísmo 26 A1
Angren 18 E8

Ankaboa, Tanjona 29 J8
Ankang 21 C5
Ankara 17 C5
Ankeny 40 E8
Ann, C. 42 D10
Ann Arbor 42 D4
Annaba 26 A7
Annalee → 11 B4
Annam 23 B3
Annan 10 G5
Annan → 10 G5
Annapolis 42 F7
Annapurna 25 C7
Annecy 12 D7
Anning 20 D5
Anniston 43 J3
Annobón 26 H6
Annotto Bay 44 a
Anqing 21 C6
Anshan 21 B7
Anshun 20 D5
Ansley 40 E5
Anson 41 J5
Anson B. 30 C5
Ansonia 42 E9
Anstruther 10 E6
Antabamba 46 F4
Antakya 17 C6
Antalya 17 C4
Antananarivo 29 H9
Antarctic Pen. 5 C4
Antarctica 5 E7
Antero, Mt. 39 G10
Anthony, Kans., U.S.A. 41 G5
Anthony, N. Mex., U.S.A. 39 K10
Antibes 12 E7
Anticosti, Î. d' 37 D13
Antigo 40 C10
Antigonish 37 D13
Antigua & Barbuda ■ 45 D12
Antilles = West Indies 45 E12
Antipodes Is. 34 M9
Antlers 41 H7
Antofagasta 48 A2
Anton 41 J3
Antrim 11 B5
Antrim, Mts. of 11 A5
Antsiranana 29 G9
Antwerp = Antwerpen 16 C3
Antwerpen 16 C3
Anvers = Antwerpen 16 C3
Anxi 20 B4
Anxious B. 32 B1
Anyang 21 C6

Arklow 11 D5
Arles 12 E6
Arlington, Oreg., U.S.A. 38 D3
Arlington, S. Dak., U.S.A. 40 C6
Arlington, Tex., U.S.A. 41 J6
Arlington, Va., U.S.A. 42 F7
Arlington, Wash., U.S.A. 38 B2
Arlington Heights 42 D2
Arlon 16 D3
Armagh 11 B5
Armagh □ 11 B5
Armavir 17 A6
Armenia 46 C3
Armenia ■ 17 B6
Armidale 32 B5
Armour 40 D5
Arnaud → 37 B12
Arnett 41 G5
Arnhem 16 C3
Arnhem, C. 30 C6
Arnhem Land 30 C5
Arno Bay 32 B2
Arnold 40 E4
Arnprior 42 C7
Arno → 12 C4
Arran 10 F3
Arras 12 A5
Arrecife 26 C3
Arrow, L. 11 B3
Arrowtown 33 L2
Arroyo Grande 39 J3
Artesia 41 J2
Arthur → 32 G3
Arthur's Pass 33 K3
Artigas 48 C5
Artois 12 A5
Aru, Kepulauan 23 D5
Arua 28 D6
Aruanã 47 F8
Aruba ■ 45 E11
Arunachal Pradesh □ 25 C9
Arusha 28 E7
Arvada, Colo., U.S.A. 40 F2
Arvada, Wyo., U.S.A. 38 D10
Arxan 21 B6
As Sulaymānīyah 24 B3
Asahigawa 22 B8
Asansol 25 C7
Asbury Park 42 E9
Ascension I. 4 E9
Aseb 24 D3
Ash Fork 39 J7
Ash Grove 41 G8
Ash Shāriqah 24 C4
Ashbourne 8 D6
Ashburton 33 K3
Ashburton → 30 D2
Ashby de la Zouch 8 E6
Ashdown 41 J8
Asheboro 43 H6
Asheville 43 H4
Ashford, Australia 32 A5
Ashford, U.K. 9 F8
Ashgabat 18 F6
Ashibetsu 22 B8
Ashington 8 B6
Ashizuri-Zaki 22 C3
Ashkhabad = Ashgabat 18 F6
Ashland, Kans., U.S.A. 41 G5
Ashland, Ky., U.S.A. 42 F4
Ashland, Ohio, U.S.A. 42 E4
Ashland, Oreg., U.S.A. 38 E2
Ashland, Va., U.S.A. 42 G7
Ashley 40 B5
Ashtabula 42 E5
Ashton 38 D8
Ashuanipi, L. 37 C13
'Āṣī → 24 B2
Asir, Ras 24 D4
Askersund 7 G11
Asmera 24 D2
Aspen 39 G10
Aspermont 41 J4
Aspiring, Mt. 33 L2
Assam □ 25 C9
Assen 16 B4
Assiniboia 36 D9
Assisi 14 C5
Asti 12 D8
Astoria 38 C2
Astrakhan 17 A7
Asturias □ 13 A3
Asunción 48 B5
Aswân 27 D12
Atacama, Desierto de 48 A3
Atacama Gulf = Gulf, The 24 C4
Atbara 27 E12
'Atbara, Nahr → 27 E12
Atchafalaya → 41 L9
Atchison 40 F7
Ath 16 C3
Athabasca 36 C8
Athabasca → 36 B8
Athabasca, L. 36 C9
Athenry 11 C3
Athens = Athínai 15 F10
Athens, Ala., U.S.A. 43 H2
Athens, Ga., U.S.A. 43 J4
Athens, Ohio, U.S.A. 42 F4
Athens, Tenn., U.S.A. 43 H3
Athens, Tex., U.S.A. 41 J7
Athínai 15 F10
Athlone 11 C4
Atholl, Forest of 10 E5
Athy 11 C5
Atka I. 36 C2
Atkinson 40 D5
Atlanta, Ga., U.S.A. 43 J3
Atlanta, Tex., U.S.A. 41 J7
Atlantic 40 E7
Atlantic City 42 F8
Atlas Mts. = Haut Atlas 26 B4

B

Bab el Mandeb 24 D3
Babahoyo 46 D3
Babine L. 36 C7
Bābol 24 B4
Babruysk 18 D4
Babuyan Chan. 23 B4
Babuyan Is. 23 B4
Bac Lieu 23 C2
Bacabal 47 D10
Bacău 15 A12
Back → 36 B10
Bacolod 23 B4
Bad → 40 C4
Bad Axe 42 D4
Bad Lands 40 D3
Badajoz 13 C2
Badalona 13 B7
Baden-Württemberg □ 16 D4
Badin 25 G6
Badlands Nat. Park 40 D3
Baffin B. 37 A13
Baffin I. 37 B12
Baggs 38 F10
Bagley 40 B7
Bago = Pegu 25 D8
Bagshot 9 F7
Baguio 23 A4
Bahamas ■ 45 C10
Bahawalpur 25 E7
Bahía = Salvador 47 F11
Bahía □ 47 F10
Bahía Blanca 48 D4
Bahrain ■ 24 C4
Baia Mare 17 E10
Baião 47 D9
Baie Comeau 37 D13
Baie Verte 37 D14
Baikal, L. = Baykal, Oz. 19 D11
Baile Atha Cliath = Dublin 11 C5
Bainbridge 43 K3
Bairnsdale 32 C4
Bayin 20 C5
Baja, Pta. 44 B1
Baja California 44 A1
Bajimba, Mt. 32 A5
Baker, Calif., U.S.A. 39 H6
Baker, Mont., U.S.A. 40 B2
Baker, Oreg., U.S.A. 38 D5
Baker City 38 D5
Baker I. 34 G10
Baker L. 36 B10
Baker Lake 36 B10
Baker Mt. 38 B3
Bakersfield 39 J4
Baki 17 B7
Baky = Baki 17 B7
Bakony 16 E8
Bakony Forest 16 E8
Bala, L. = Tegid, Llyn 8 E4
Balabac I. 23 C3
Balabac Str. 23 C3
Balaghat 25 B6
Balaklava 32 B2
Balakovo 18 D5
Balashov 18 D5
Balaton 16 E8
Balbina, Reprêsa de 46 D7
Balboa 44 H14
Balbriggan 11 C5
Balcarce 48 D5
Balclutha 33 M2
Bald Knob 41 H9
Baldwin 42 D3
Baldy Peak 39 K9
Baleares, Is. 13 C7
Balearic Is. = Baleares, Is. 13 C7

Baudette 40 A7
Bauer, C. 32 B1
Bauru 47 H9
Bavaria = Bayern □ 16 D5
Bawean 23 D3
Baxley 43 K4
Baxter Springs 41 G7
Bay City, Mich., U.S.A. 42 D4
Bay City, Tex., U.S.A. 41 L7
Bay Minette 43 K2
Bay Roberts 37 D14
Bay St. Louis 41 K10
Bay Springs 41 K10
Bayamo 45 C9
Bayamón 45 d
Bayan Har Shan 20 C4
Bayanhongor 20 B5
Bayard, Nebr., U.S.A. 40 E3
Bayard, N. Mex., U.S.A. 39 K9
Bayern □ 16 D5
Bayeux 12 B3
Baykal, Oz. 19 D11
Bayombong 23 A4
Bayonne 12 E3
Bayreuth 16 D5
Bayrūt 17 C5
Baytown 41 L7
Beachport 32 C3
Beachy Hd. 9 G8
Beacon 32 B2
Beaconsfield 9 F7
Beagle, Canal 48 H3
Bear I. 11 E2
Bear L. 38 E8
Beardmore Glacier 5 E11
Beardstown 40 F9
Béarn 12 E3
Beatrice 40 E6
Beatton → 36 C7
Beatty 38 H5
Beauce, Plaine de la 12 B4
Beaudesert 32 A5
Beaufort, Malaysia 23 C3
Beaufort, N.C., U.S.A. 43 H7
Beaufort, S.C., U.S.A. 43 J5
Beaufort Sea 4 B18
Beaufort West 29 E3
Beauly → 10 D4
Beaumaris 8 D3
Beaumont 41 K7
Beaune 12 C6
Beaver, Okla., U.S.A. 41 G4
Beaver, Utah, U.S.A. 39 G7
Beaver → 36 C9
Beaver City 40 E5
Beaver Dam 40 D10
Beaver Falls 42 E5

Beeville 41 L6
Bega 32 C4
Bei Jiang → 21 D6
Bei'an 21 B7
Beijing 21 C6
Beira 29 H6
Beirut = Bayrūt 17 C5
Beja 13 C2
Béja 14 A1
Bejaïa 26 A7
Békéscsaba 16 E11
Bela 25 F5
Belarus ■ 18 D4
Belau = Palau ■ 23 C4
Belawan 23 C1
Belcher Is. 37 C12
Belém 47 D9
Belep, Is. 34 N11
Belfast, U.K. 11 B6
Belfast, U.S.A. 43 C11
Belfast L. 11 B6
Belfield 40 B3
Belfort 12 C7
Belfry 38 D9
Belgaum 25 M9
Belgium ■ 16 C3
Belgorod 18 D5
Belgrade = Beograd 15 B9
Belitung 23 D2
Belize ■ 44 D7
Belize City 44 D7
Bell I. 37 C14
Bell Ville 48 C4
Bella Coola 36 C7
Bellaire 42 E5
Bellary 25 M10
Bellata 32 A4
Belle-Chasse 41 L10
Belle Fourche 40 C3
Belle Fourche → 40 C3
Belle Glade 43 M5
Belle-Ile 12 C2
Belle Isle 37 C14
Belle Isle, Str. of 37 C14
Belle Plaine 40 E8
Belledonne 12 D7
Bellefontaine 42 E4
Bellefonte 42 E6
Belleplaine 42 E8
Belleville, Canada 37 D12
Belleville, Ill., U.S.A. 40 F10
Belleville, Kans., U.S.A. 40 F6
Bellevue, Idaho, U.S.A. 38 E6
Bellevue, Nebr., U.S.A. 40 E7
Bellevue, Ohio, U.S.A. 42 E4
Bellingham 38 B2
Bellingshausen Sea 5 C17
Bellinzona 12 C8
Belmont 32 B5
Belmopan 44 D7
Belogorsk 19 D14
Belonia 25 C9
Beloit, Kans., U.S.A. 40 F5
Beloit, Wis., U.S.A. 40 D10
Belorussia = Belarus ■ 18 D4
Belovo 18 D9
Belpre 42 F5
Belton 41 K6
Belturbet 11 B4

Berkner I. 5 D18
Berkshire Downs 9 F6
Berlin, Germany 16 B6
Berlin, Md., U.S.A. 42 F8
Berlin, N.H., U.S.A. 42 C10
Berlin, Wis., U.S.A. 42 D1
Bermejo → 48 B5
Bermuda ■ 4 C6
Bernalillo 39 J10
Berne = Bern 12 C7
Berneray 10 D1
Berry, Australia 32 B5
Berry, France 12 C5
Bertraghboy B. 11 C2
Berwick 42 E7
Berwick-upon-Tweed 8 B6
Berwyn Mts. 8 E4
Besançon 12 C7
Bessemer, Ala., U.S.A. 43 J2
Bessemer, Mich., U.S.A. 40 B9
Bethany 40 E7
Bethel 36 B3
Bethlehem, S. Africa 29 K5
Bethlehem, U.S.A. 42 E8
Béthune 12 A5
Bettendorf 40 E9
Betws-y-Coed 8 D4
Beulah, N. Dak., U.S.A. 40 B4
Beverley 8 D7
Beverly Hills 39 J4
Beverly 42 D10
Bexhill 9 G8
Beziers 12 E5
Bhagalpur 25 C7
Bharuch 25 C6
Bhavnagar 25 J8
Bhilwara 25 C6
Bhima → 25 L10
Bhopal 25 H10
Bhubaneshwar 25 C7
Bhuj 25 H6
Bhusawal 25 J9
Bhutan ■ 25 C8
Biafra, B. of = Bonny, Bight of 28 D1
Biak 23 D5
Białystok 17 B11
Biarritz 12 E3
Bicester 9 F6
Bicheno 32 G4
Biddeford 43 D10
Bideford 9 F3
Bideford Bay 9 F3
Bié, Planalto de 29 G3
Biel 12 C7
Bielefeld 16 B4
Bielsko-Biała 17 D9
Bien Hoa 23 B2
Bienne = Biel 12 C7
Bienville, L. 37 C12
Big Belt Mts. 38 C8
Big Bend Nat. Park 41 L3
Big Black → 41 J9
Big Blue → 40 F6
Big Cypress Nat. Preserve 43 M5
Big Cypress Swamp 43 M5
Big Falls 40 A8
Big Fork → 40 A8
Big Horn Mts. 38 D10
Big Muddy Cr. → 40 A2
Big Pine 39 H4
Big Piney 38 E8
Big Rapids 42 D3
Big Sandy 38 B8
Big Sioux → 40 D6
Big Spring 41 J4
Big Stone City 40 C6
Big Stone Gap 43 G4
Big Stone L. 40 C6
Big Timber 38 D9
Big Trout L. 37 C11
Biggar, Canada 36 C9
Biggar, U.K. 10 F5
Biggenden 32 A5
Biggleswade 9 E7
Bighorn → 38 C10
Bighorn L. 38 D9
Bighorn Mts. 38 D10
Bihar □ 25 C7
Bijapur 25 C6
Bijar 24 B3
Bikaner 25 C8
Bikini Atoll 34 F8
Bilaspur 25 C7
Bilbao 13 A4
Billabong Cr. → 32 C4
Billings 38 D9
Bilma 26 E8
Biloxi 41 K10
Bina-Etawah 25 C10
Binalong 32 B4
Binatang = Bintangor 23 C3
Bingara 32 A5
Binghamton 42 D8
Bioko 28 D1
Birch Hills 36 C9
Bird I. 32 A5
Birdsville 30 F6
Birjand 24 B4
Birkenhead 8 D4
Birmingham, U.K. 9 E6
Birmingham, U.S.A. 43 J2
Birr 11 C4
Biscay, B. of 12 D2
Biscayne B. 43 N5
Bishop, Calif., U.S.A. 39 H4
Bishop, Tex., U.S.A. 41 M6
Bishop Auckland 8 C6
Bishop's Stortford 9 F8
Biskra 26 B7
Bismarck 40 B4
Bismarck Arch. 34 H6
Bissau 26 F2
Bitter Creek 38 F9
Bitterfontein 29 E2
Bitterroot Range 38 C6
Biwa-Ko 22 B5
Biwabik 40 B8
Bixby 41 H7
Blysk 18 D9
Black → Ariz., U.S.A. 39 K8
Black → Ark., U.S.A. 41 H9
Black → Wis., U.S.A. 40 D9

49

Black Forest = Schwarzwald 16 D4
Black Forest 40 F2
Black Hd. 11 C2
Black Hills 40 D3
Black L. 42 C3
Black Mesa 41 G3
Black Mts. 9 F4
Black Range 39 K10
Black River 44 a
Black River Falls 40 C9
Black Rock 45 g
Black Sea 17 B5
Black Volta → 26 G5
Black Warrior → 43 J2
Blackball 33 K3
Blackburn 8 D5
Blackfoot 38 E7
Blackfoot → 38 C7
Blackfoot River Reservoir 38 E8
Blackpool 8 D4
Blacksburg 42 G7
Blacksod B. 11 B1
Blackstone 42 G7
Blackwater →, Meath, Ireland 11 C4
Blackwater →, Waterford, Ireland 11 D4
Blackwater →, U.K. 11 B5
Blackwell 41 G6
Blaenau Ffestiniog 8 E4
Blaenau Gwent □ 9 F4
Blagoveshchensk 19 D13
Blaine, Minn., U.S.A. 40 C8
Blaine, Wash., U.S.A. 38 B2
Blair 40 E6
Blair Athol 32 C4
Blairgowrie 10 E5
Blake Pt. 40 A10
Blakely 43 K3
Blanc, Mont 12 D7
Blanca Peak 39 H11
Blanche, C. 32 B1
Blanche, L. 32 A2
Blanco 41 K5
Blanco, C. 38 E1
Blandford Forum 9 G5
Blanding 39 H9
Blanquilla, I. 45 E12
Blantyre 29 H6
Blarney 11 E3
Blaydon 8 C6
Blayney 32 B4
Blenheim 31 J13
Bletchley 9 F7
Blida 26 A6
Bligh Sound 33 L1
Bliss 38 E6
Blitar 23 D3
Block I. 42 E10
Bloemfontein 29 K5
Bloemhof 29 K5
Blois 12 C4
Bloody Foreland 11 A3
Bloomer 40 C9
Bloomfield, Iowa, U.S.A. 40 E8
Bloomfield, N. Mex., U.S.A. 39 H10
Bloomfield, Nebr., U.S.A.
Bloomington, Ill., U.S.A. 40 E10
Bloomington, Ind., U.S.A. 42 F2
Bloomington, Minn., U.S.A. 40 C8
Bloomsburg 42 E7
Blountstown 43 K3
Blue Earth 40 D8
Blue Mesa Reservoir 39 G10
Blue Mountain Pk. 44 a
Blue Mountains, The 44 a
Blue Mts. 38 D4
Blue Nile = Nîl el Azraq → 27 E12
Blue Rapids 40 F6
Blue Ridge Mts. 43 G5
Bluefield 42 G5
Bluefields 45 E8
Bluff, N.Z. 33 M2
Bluff, U.S.A. 39 H9
Bluffton 42 F2
Blumenau 48 B7
Blunt 40 C5
Bly 38 E3
Blyth 8 C6
Blythe 39 K6
Blytheville 41 H10
Bo Hai 21 C6
Bo 26 G3
Bobadah 32 B4
Bobo-Dioulasso 26 F5
Boca Raton 43 M5
Bochum 16 C3
Boddam 10 D7
Bodensee 16 E5
Bodmin 9 G3
Bodmin Moor 9 G3
Boerne 41 L5
Bogan → 32 A4
Bogan Gate 32 B4
Boggabilla 32 A5
Boggabri 32 B5
Boggeragh Mts. 11 D3
Bognor Regis 9 G7
Bogong, Mt. 32 C4
Bogotá 46 C4
Bohemian Forest = Böhmerwald 16 D6
Böhmerwald 16 D6
Bohol □ 23 C4
Bohol Sea 23 C4
Boise 38 E5
Boise City 41 G3
Bokhara → 32 A4
Bole 26 G5
Bolivar, Mo., U.S.A. 41 G8
Bolivar, Tenn., U.S.A. 41 H10
Bolivia ■ 46 G6
Bollon 32 A4
Bologna 14 B4
Bolshevik, Ostrov 19 B11
Bolshoi Kavkaz = Caucasus Mountains 18 E5
Bolt Head 9 G4
Bolton 8 D5
Bolzano 14 A4
Boma 28 F2
Bombala 32 C4
Bombay = Mumbai 25 K8
Bonaire 45 E11
Bonang 32 C4
Bo'ness 10 E5
Bonifacio 12 F8
Bonifacio, Bouches de 12 F8
Bonin Is. = Ogasawara Gunto 34 G14
Bonn 16 C3
Bonne Terre 41 G9
Bonners Ferry 38 B5
Bonney, L. 32 C3
Bonnyrigg 10 F5
Booker 41 G4
Boolaboolka L. 32 B3
Booligal 32 B3
Boone, Iowa, U.S.A. 40 D8
Boone, N.C., U.S.A. 43 G5
Booneville, Ark., U.S.A. 41 H8
Booneville, Miss., U.S.A. 41 H10
Boonville, Ind., U.S.A. 42 F2
Boonville, Mo., U.S.A. 40 F8
Boonville, N.Y., U.S.A. 42 D8
Boorindal 32 B4
Boorowa 32 B4
Boothia, Gulf of 37 A11

Boothia Pen. 36 A10
Bootle 8 D4
Borah Peak 38 D7
Borås 7 F6
Borba 32 C2
Bordeaux 12 D3
Borden Pen. 37 A11
Borders = Scottish Borders □ 10 F6
Bordertown 32 C3
Borehamwood 9 F7
Borger 41 H4
Borgholm 7 F7
Borisov = Barysaw 17 A9
Borkum 16 B3
Borneo 23 C3
Bornholm 7 F7
Borth 9 E3
Bosaso 24 D3
Boscastle 9 G3
Boscobelle 44 b
Bosnia-Herzegovina ■ 14 B7
Bosporus = İstanbul Boğazı 15 D13
Bosque Farms 39 J10
Bossier City 41 J8
Bosten Hu 20 B3
Boston, U.K. 8 E7
Boston, U.S.A. 42 D10
Boston Mts. 41 H8
Bothnia, G. of 7 E8
Bothwell 32 D4
Botletle → 29 J4
Botoșani 17 A3
Botswana ■ 29 J4
Bottineau 40 A4
Bouaké 26 G4
Bouar 28 C3
Bougainville I. 34 H7
Bougie = Bejaia 26 A7
Bouillante 44 b
Boulder, Colo., U.S.A. 40 E2
Boulder, Mont., U.S.A. 38 C7
Boulder City 39 J6
Boulogne-sur-Mer 12 A4
Bountiful 38 F8
Bounty Is. 34 M9
Bourbonnais 42 E2
Bourg-en-Bresse 12 C6
Bourgogne 12 C6
Bourke 32 B4
Bourne 8 E7
Bournemouth 9 G6
Bouvetøya 5 G10
Bovill 38 C5
Bow → 36 C8
Bowbells 40 A3
Bowdle 40 C5
Bowen Mts. 32 C4
Bowie, Ariz., U.S.A. 39 K9
Bowie, Tex., U.S.A. 41 J6
Bowland, Forest of 8 D5
Bowling Green, Ky., U.S.A. 42 G2
Bowling Green, Ohio, U.S.A. 42 E4
Bowman 40 B3
Bowral 32 B5
Bowraville 32 B5
Box Cr. → 32 B3
Boyce 41 K8
Boyne → 11 C5
Boyne City 42 C3
Boynton Beach 43 M5
Boysen Reservoir 38 E9
Bozeman 38 D8
Bozen = Bolzano 14 A4
Bräcke 7 E7
Bracadale, L. 10 D2
Brackettville 41 L4
Bracknell 9 F7
Bracknell Forest □ 9 F7
Bradenton 43 M4
Bradford, U.K. 8 D6
Bradford, U.S.A. 42 E6
Bradley 41 J8
Brady 41 K5
Braga 13 B1
Brahmapur 25 D7
Braich-y-pwll 8 E3
Braidwood 32 C4
Braintree 9 F8
Brak → 28 C3
Brampton 8 C5
Brandon → 42 B6
Branco → 46 C6
Brandenburg, Germany 16 B6
Brandenburg □ 16 B6
Brandon, Canada 36 D10
Brandon B. 11 D1
Brandon Mt. 11 D1
Branson 41 G8
Brantford 42 D6
Bras d'Or L. 43 C11
Brasília 47 G9
Braşov 15 B11
Brassey, Banjaran 23 C3
Brasstown Bald 43 H4
Bratislava 16 D8
Bratsk 19 D11
Brattleboro 42 D9
Braunau 16 D6
Braunschweig 16 B5
Braunton 9 F3
Bravo del Norte, Rio → = Grande, Rio → 41 N6
Brawley 39 K6
Bray 11 C5
Brazil ■ 47 F2
Brazos → 41 L7
Brazzaville 28 E3
Breaksea Sd. 33 L1
Bream B. 33 F5
Bream Hd. 33 F5
Brechin 10 E6
Breckenridge, Colo., U.S.A. 38 G10
Breckenridge, Minn., U.S.A. 40 B6
Breckenridge, Tex., U.S.A. 41 J5
Breckland 9 E8
Brecon 9 F4
Brecon Beacons 9 F4
Breda 16 C2
Bredasdorp 29 L4
Bregenz 16 E4
Bremen 16 B4
Bremerhaven 16 B4
Bremerton 38 C2
Brenham 41 K6
Brennerpass 16 E5
Brent 9 F7
Brentwood 9 F8
Bréscia 14 B4
Breslau = Wrocław 16 C8
Bressay 10 A7
Brest, Belarus 17 B6
Brest, France 12 B1
Brest-Litovsk = Brest 17 B6
Bretagne 12 B2
Brett, C. 33 F5
Brevard 43 H4
Brewarrina 32 A4
Brewer 43 C11
Brewster 42 E9
Brewton 43 K2
Brezhnev = Naberezhnyye Chelny 18 D6
Bribie I. 32 A5
Bridgefield 44 b
Bridgend 9 F4
Bridgeport, Calif., U.S.A. 39 G4
Bridgeport, Conn., U.S.A. 42 E9
Bridgeport, Nebr., U.S.A. 40 E3
Bridgeport, Tex., U.S.A. 41 J6
Bridger 38 D9
Bridgeton 42 F8
Bridgetown, Australia 30 G2
Bridgetown, Barbados 44 b
Bridgwater 9 F4

Bridgewater, C. 32 C3
Bridgewater-Gagebrook 32 A4
Bridgnorth 9 E5
Bridgwater 9 F5
Bridgwater B. 9 F4
Bridlington 8 C7
Bridlington B. 8 C7
Bridport, Australia 32 D4
Bridport, U.K. 9 G5
Brig 12 C7
Brigg 8 D7
Brigham City 38 F7
Bright 32 C4
Brighton, Australia 32 A1
Brighton, U.K. 9 G7
Brighton, U.S.A. 40 F2
Brindisi 15 D7
Brinkley 41 H9
Brisbane 32 A5
Bristol, U.K. 9 F5
Bristol, Conn., U.S.A. 42 E9
Bristol, Tenn., U.S.A. 43 G4
Bristol B. 36 C4
Bristol Channel 9 F3
Bristow 41 H6
British Columbia □ 36 C7
British Indian Ocean Terr. = Chagos Arch. 5 E13
British Isles 7 B9
Brittany = Bretagne 12 B2
Brixham 9 G4
Brixton 44 a
Brno 16 D8
Broad → 43 J5
Broad B. 10 C2
Broad Haven 11 B2
Broad Law 10 F5
Broads, The 8 E9
Broadus 40 C2
Brochet 36 C9
Brock 37 A11
Brocken 16 C5
Brockport 42 D7
Brockton 42 D10
Brockville 42 D8
Brockway 40 B2
Brodeur Pen. 37 A11
Brodick 10 F3
Brogan 38 D5
Broken Arrow 41 G7
Broken Bow, Nebr., U.S.A. 40 E5
Broken Bow, Okla., U.S.A. 41 H7
Broken Bow Lake 41 H7
Broken Hill 32 B3
Bromley 9 F8
Bromsgrove 9 E5
Brookhaven 41 K9
Brookings, Oreg., U.S.A. 38 E1
Brookings, S. Dak., U.S.A. 40 C6
Brooklyn Park 40 C8
Brooks 36 C8
Brooks Range 36 B5
Brooksville 43 L4
Brookville 42 E6
Broom, L. 10 D3
Broome 30 D3
Brora 10 C5
Brora → 10 C5
Brosna → 11 C4
Brothers 38 E3
Brough 8 C5
Brough Hd. 10 B5
Brown, Pt. 32 B1
Brown Willy 9 G3
Brownfield 41 J3
Browning 38 B7
Brownsville, Oreg., U.S.A. 38 D2
Brownsville, Tenn., U.S.A. 41 H10
Brownsville, Tex., U.S.A. 41 N6
Brownwood 41 K5
Bruay-la-Buissière 12 A5
Bruce, Mt. 30 E2
Bruce Rock 30 G2
Bruck 16 E8
Bruges = Brugge 16 C1
Brugge 16 C1
Bruneau 38 E6
Bruneau → 38 E6
Brunei = Bandar Seri Begawan 23 C3
Brunei ■ 23 C3
Brunner, L. 33 K3
Brunswick = Braunschweig 16 B5
Brunswick, Ga., U.S.A. 43 K5
Brunswick, Maine, U.S.A. 43 D11
Brunswick, Md., U.S.A.
Brunswick, Mo., U.S.A. 40 F8
Brunswick, Pen. de 48 G2
Bruny I. 32 D4
Brush 40 E2
Brussel 16 C2
Brussels = Brussel 16 C2
Bruthen 32 C4
Bruxelles = Brussel 16 C2
Bryan, Ohio, U.S.A. 42 E3
Bryan, Mt. 32 B2
Bryansk 18 D4
Bryce Canyon Nat. Park 39 H7
Brynmawr 9 F4
Bryson City 43 H4
Bucaramanga 46 B4
Buchan 10 D6
Buchan Ness 10 D7
Buchanan 26 G3
Buckeye 39 K7
Buckhannon 42 F5
Buckhaven 10 E5
Buckie 10 D6
Buckingham 9 E7
Buckinghamshire □ 9 F7
Buckley → 32 C2
Bucklin 41 G5
Bucureşti 15 B12
Bucyrus 42 E4
Budapest 16 E10
Bude 9 G3
Budgewoi 32 B5
Buena Vista, Colo., U.S.A. 39 G10
Buena Vista, Va., U.S.A. 42 G6
Buena Vista Lake Bed 39 J4
Buenaventura 46 C3
Buenos Aires 48 C5
Buffalo, N.Y., U.S.A. 42 D6
Buffalo, Okla., U.S.A. 41 G5
Buffalo, Wyo., U.S.A. 38 D10
Buford 38 D9
Bug → 17 B9
Bug → 17 D9
Bugun Shara 20 B5
Bujumbura 28 E5
Bukavu 28 E5
Bukhoro 18 F7
Bukittinggi 23 D2
Bulahdelah 32 B5
Bulawayo 29 J5
Bulgaria ■ 15 C11
Bulgan 20 B5
Bull Shoals L. 41 G8
Bullhead City 39 J6
Bulloo → 32 A3
Bulls 33 J5
Bunbury 30 G2
Buncrana 11 A4
Bundaberg 32 A5
Bundi 25 G9
Bungay 9 E9
Bunji 25 B9
Bunkie 41 K8
Bunnell 43 L5
Buon Ma Thuot 23 B2

Bûr Sa'îd 27 B12
Bûr Sûdân 27 E13
Burao 24 D4
Buraydah 24 C3
Burbank 39 J4
Bure → 8 E9
Burgas 15 C12
Burgos 13 A4
Burgundy = Bourgogne 12 C6
Burkburnett 41 H5
Burkina Faso ■ 26 F5
Burley 38 E7
Burlington, Colo., U.S.A. 40 F3
Burlington, Iowa, U.S.A. 40 E9
Burlington, Kans., U.S.A. 40 F7
Burlington, N.C., U.S.A. 43 G6
Burlington, Vt., U.S.A. 42 C9
Burlington, Wash., U.S.A. 38 B2
Burlington, Wis., U.S.A.
Burlyu-Tyube 18 E8
Burma ■ 25 D10
Burnet 41 K5
Burnham-on-Sea 9 F5
Burnie 30 J8
Burnley 8 D5
Burns 38 E4
Burnside → 36 B9
Burnsville 40 C8
Burra 32 B2
Burray 10 C6
Burren Junction 32 B4
Burrenjuck Res. 32 B4
Burrow Hd. 10 G4
Burry Port 9 F3
Bursa 15 D13
Burton 43 J5
Burton upon Trent 8 E6
Buru 23 D4
Burundi ■ 28 E5
Burwell 40 E5
Burwick 10 C6
Bury 8 D5
Bury St. Edmunds 9 E8
Buryatia □ 19 D11
Büshehr 24 C4
Bushmills 11 A5
Businga 28 D4
Butaritari 34 G9
Bute 10 F3
Butha Qi 21 B7
Butler, Mo., U.S.A. 40 F7
Butler, Pa., U.S.A. 42 E6
Buton 23 D4
Butte, Mont., U.S.A. 38 C7
Butterworth 23 C2
Buttevant 11 D3
Butuan 23 C4
Butung = Buton 23 D4
Buxtehude 16 B5
Buxton 8 D6
Buzău 15 B12
Byelorussia = Belarus ■ 18 D3
Byers 40 F2
Bylas 39 K8
Bylot I. 37 A12
Byrock 32 B4
Byron Bay 32 A5
Byrranga, Gory 19 B11
Bytom 16 C9

C

Ca Mau 23 C2
Ca Mau, Mui 23 C2
Cabanatuan 23 B4
Cabimas 46 A4
Cabinda 28 F2
Cabinda □ 28 F2
Cabinet Mts. 38 C6
Cabonga, Réservoir 37 D12
Cabool 41 G8
Caboolture 32 A5
Cabot Str. 37 D14
Čačak 15 C9
Cáceres, Brazil 46 G7
Cáceres, Spain 13 C2
Cachoeira do Sul 48 C6
Cachoeiro de Itapemirim 47 H10
Caddo 41 H6
Cader Idris 8 E4
Cadibarrawirracanna, L. 32 A2
Cadillac 42 C3
Cádiz 13 D2
Cadiz 42 F4
Cadney Park 32 A1
Caen 12 B3
Caernarfon 8 D3
Caernarfon B. 8 D3
Caerphilly 9 F4
Cagayan de Oro 23 C4
Cágliari 14 E3
Caguas 45 d
Caha Mts. 11 E2
Caher 11 D4
Caherciveen 11 E1
Cahore Pt. 11 D5
Cahors 12 D4
Cairn Gorm 10 D5
Cairn Toul 10 D5
Cairngorm Mts. 10 D5
Cairnryan 10 G3
Cairns 32 A4
Cairo = El Qâhira 27 B12
Cairo, Ga., U.S.A. 43 K3
Cairo, Ill., U.S.A. 41 G10
Caithness, Ord of 10 C5
Caja de Muertos, I. 45 d
Cajamarca 46 E3
Calabar 26 H7
Calábria □ 14 E7
Calais, France 12 A4
Calais, U.S.A. 43 C12
Calamian Group 23 B3
Calapan 23 B4
Calbayog 23 B4
Calcutta = Kolkata 25 D7
Caldwell, Idaho, U.S.A. 38 E5
Caldwell, Kans., U.S.A. 41 G6
Caldwell, Tex., U.S.A. 41 K6
Caledon 29 L3
Caledon → 29 L5
Calexico 39 K6
Calf of Man 8 C3
Calgary 36 C8
Cali 46 C3
Caliente 39 H6
California □ 39 H4
California, G. de 44 B2
Callabonna, L. 32 A3
Callan 11 D4
Callander 10 E4
Callao 46 F3
Calne 9 F6
Caltanissetta 14 F6
Calvi 12 E8
Calvinia 29 L3
Cam → 9 E8
Camabatela 28 F3
Camacupa 28 G3
Camagüey 45 C9
Camargue 12 E6
Camas 38 D2
Camas Valley 38 E2
Cambay, G. of = Khambhat, G. of 25 J8
Cambodia ■ 23 B2
Camborne 9 G2
Cambrai 12 A5
Cambria 39 J3

Cambrian Mts. 9 E4
Cambridge, Jamaica 44 a
Cambridge, N.Z. 33 G5
Cambridge, U.K. 9 E8
Cambridge, Mass., U.S.A. 42 D10
Cambridge, Minn., U.S.A. 40 C8
Cambridge, Nebr., U.S.A. 40 E5
Cambridge, Ohio, U.S.A. 42 E5
Cambridge Bay 36 B9
Cambridgeshire □ 9 E7
Camden, Ala., U.S.A. 43 J2
Camden, Ark., U.S.A. 41 J8
Camden, Maine, U.S.A. 43 C11
Camden, N.J., U.S.A. 42 F8
Camden, S.C., U.S.A. 43 H5
Cameron, Ariz., U.S.A. 39 J8
Cameron, La., U.S.A. 41 L8
Cameron, Mo., U.S.A. 40 F7
Cameron, Tex., U.S.A. 41 K6
Cameroon ■ 28 C2
Cameroun, Mt. 28 D1
Camira Creek 32 A5
Camp Hill 42 E7
Camp Verde 39 J8
Camp Wood 41 L4
Campánia □ 14 D6
Campbell I. 34 N8
Campbell Town 32 D4
Campbellsville 42 G3
Campbellton 37 D13
Campbelltown 32 B5
Campeche 44 D6
Campeche, Golfo de 44 D6
Camperdown 32 C3
Campina Grande 47 E11
Campinas 47 H9
Campo Grande 47 H8
Campos 47 H10
Camrose 36 C8
Can Tho 23 B2
Canada ■ 36 C10
Canadian 41 H4
Canadian → 41 H7
Çanakkale 15 D12
Çanakkale Boğazı 15 D12
Canandaigua 42 D7
Cananea 44 A2
Canarias, Is. 26 C2
Canaries 44 c
Canary Is. = Canarias, Is. 26 C2
Canaveral, C. 43 L5
Canberra 32 C4
Canby, Calif., U.S.A. 38 F3
Canby, Minn., U.S.A. 40 C6
Canby, Oreg., U.S.A. 38 D2
Cancún 44 C7
Candela 44 B4
Candia = Iráklion 15 G11
Canea = Khaniá 15 G11
Canna 10 D2
Cannes 12 E7
Canno... Cannock 8 E5
Cannon Ball → 40 B4
Cañon City 40 F2
Canora 36 C9
Canowindra 32 B4
Cantabria □ 13 A4
Cantábrica, Cordillera 13 A3
Canterbury 9 F9
Canterbury Bight 33 L3
Canterbury Plains 33 K3
Canton = Guangzhou 21 D6
Canton, Ga., U.S.A. 43 H3
Canton, Ill., U.S.A. 40 E9
Canton, Miss., U.S.A. 41 J9
Canton, Ohio, U.S.A. 42 E5
Canton, N.Y., U.S.A. 42 C8
Canton, S. Dak., U.S.A. 40 D6
Canton L. 41 G5
Canyon 41 H4
Canyonlands Nat. Park 39 G9
Canyonville 38 E2
Cap-Chat 37 D13
Cap-Haïtien 45 D10
Cap Pt. 44 b
Cape Barren I. 32 D4
Cape Breton I. 37 D13
Cape Charles 42 G8
Cape Coast 26 G5
Cape Coral 43 M5
Cape Dorset 37 B12
Cape Fear → 43 H6
Cape Girardeau 41 G10
Cape May 42 F8
Cape May Point 42 G8
Cape Town 29 L3
Cape Verde Is. ■ 2 D8
Cape York Peninsula 30 C7
Capela 47 F11
Capella 32 C4
Capesterre-Belle-Eau 44 b
Capitan 39 K11
Capitol Reef Nat. Park 39 G8
Capri 14 D6
Captain's Flat 32 C4
Caquetá → 46 D5
Caracal 15 B11
Caracas 46 A5
Caratasca, L. 45 D8
Caratinga 47 G10
Caravaca de la Cruz 13 C5
Caravelas 47 G11
Caravelle, Presqu'île de la 44 c
Carballo 13 A1
Carberry 36 D10
Carbó 44 B2
Carbondale, Colo., U.S.A. 38 G10
Carbondale, Ill., U.S.A. 41 G10
Carbondale, Pa., U.S.A. 42 E8
Carbonear 37 D14
Carbónia 14 E3
Carcassonne 12 E5
Carcross 36 B6
Cárdenas 45 C8
Cardiff 9 F4
Cardigan 9 E3
Cardigan B. 9 E3
Cardston 36 D8
Cardwell 32 A4
Carei 16 E12
Cariacica 47 H10
Caribbean Sea 45 E10
Cariboo Mts. 36 C7
Caribou 43 B12
Caribou → 36 B10
Carinda 32 B4
Carinthia = Kärnten □ 16 E8
Carlin 38 F5
Carlingford L. 11 B5
Carlinville 40 F10
Carlisle, U.K. 8 C5
Carlisle, U.S.A. 42 E7
Carlow 11 D5
Carlow □ 11 D5
Carlsbad, Calif., U.S.A. 39 K5
Carlsbad, N. Mex., U.S.A. 41 J2
Carlsbad Caverns Nat. Park 41 J2
Carluke 10 F5
Carmacks 36 B6
Carmarthen 9 F3
Carmarthen B. 9 F3
Carmarthenshire □ 9 F4
Carmaux 12 D5
Carmen 44 D6
Carmi 42 F1
Carmichael 39 G3
Carn Ban 10 D4
Carn Eige 10 D3
Carnac 12 C2
Carnarvon, Australia 30 E1
Carnarvon, S. Africa 29 L4
Carnegie, L. 30 F3
Carnic Alps = Karnische Alpen 16 E7
Carnot 28 C3
Carnoustie 10 E6
Carnsore Pt. 11 D5

Carnsore Pt. 11 D5
Caro 42 D4
Carol City 43 N5
Carolina, Brazil 47 E9
Carolina, Puerto Rico 45 d
Caroline I. 35 H12
Caroní → 46 B6
Carpathians 17 A2
Carpații Meridionali 15 B11
Carpentaria, G. of 30 C6
Carpentras 12 D6
Carpi 14 B4
Carrabelle 43 L3
Carrara 14 B4
Carrick-on-Shannon 11 C3
Carrick-on-Suir 11 D4
Carrickfergus 11 B6
Carrickmacross 11 C5
Carrieton 32 B2
Carrington 40 B5
Carrizo Cr. → 41 G3
Carrizo Springs 41 L5
Carrizozo 39 K11
Carroll 40 D7
Carrollton, Ga., U.S.A. 43 J3
Carrollton, Ill., U.S.A. 40 F9
Carrollton, Ky., U.S.A. 42 F3
Carrollton, Mo., U.S.A. 40 F8
Carron → 10 D4
Carron, L. 10 D3
Carson 38 G4
Carson City 38 G4
Carson Sink 38 G4
Cartagena, Colombia 46 A3
Cartagena, Spain 13 D5
Cartago 46 C3
Carterton 33 J5
Carthage, Mo., U.S.A. 41 G7
Carthage, N.Y., U.S.A. 42 D8
Carthage, Tex., U.S.A. 41 J7
Cartwright 37 C14
Caruaru 47 E11
Carúpano 46 A6
Caruthersville 41 G10
Cary 43 H6
Casa Grande 39 K8
Casablanca 26 B4
Cascade, Idaho, U.S.A. 38 D5
Cascade, Mont., U.S.A. 38 C8
Cascade Locks 38 D3
Cascade Ra. 38 D3
Cascade Reservoir 38 D5
Cascavel 47 H8
Casco B. 43 D11
Casiguran 23 B4
Casino 32 A5
Casiquiare → 46 C5
Casper 38 E10
Caspian Sea 18 E6
Cass Lake 40 B7
Cassiar Mts. 36 C6
Castellammare di Stábia 14 D6
Castellón de la Plana 13 C5
Castelo Branco 13 C2
Castelsarrasin 12 E4
Castilla-La Mancha □ 13 C4
Castilla y León □ 13 B3
Castle Dale 38 G8
Castle Douglas 10 G5
Castle Rock 40 F2
Castlebar 11 C2
Castleblayney 11 B5
Castlederg 11 B4
Castleford 8 D6
Castlegar 36 D8
Castleisland 11 D2
Castlemaine 32 C3
Castlepollard 11 C4
Castlereagh □ 11 B6
Castlereagh → 32 B4
Castletown 8 C3
Castletown Bearhaven 11 E2
Castres 12 E5
Castries 44 b
Castro 48 E2
Castuera 13 C3
Cat I. 45 C9
Catalão 47 G9
Catalonia = Cataluña □ 13 B6
Cataluña □ 13 B6
Catandaunes □ 23 B4
Catánia 14 F6
Catanzaro 14 E7
Caterham 9 F7
Cathcart 29 L5
Catoche, C. 44 C7
Catskill 42 D9
Catskill Mts. 42 D8
Cauca → 46 B4
Caucasus Mountains 18 E5
Caungula 28 F3
Cavalier 40 A6
Cavan 11 C4
Cavan □ 11 C4
Cave Creek 39 K7
Cavendish 32 C3
Cawndilla L. 32 B3
Cawnpore = Kanpur 25 F12
Caxias 47 D10
Caxias do Sul 48 B6
Cayenne 47 B8
Cayman Is. ■ 45 D8
Cayuga L. 42 D7
Ceanannus Mor 11 C5
Ceará = Fortaleza 47 D11
Cebu 23 B4
Cecil Plains 32 A5
Cedar → 40 E9
Cedar City 39 H7
Cedar Creek Reservoir 41 J6
Cedar Falls 40 D8
Cedar Key 43 L4
Cedar L. 36 C10
Cedar Rapids 40 E9
Cedartown 43 H3
Ceduna 30 G5
Cefalù 14 E6
Cegléd 16 E10
Celaya 44 C4
Celebes = Sulawesi □ 23 D4
Celebes Sea 23 C4
Celina 42 E3
Celje 16 E8
Celle 16 B5
Celtic Sea 7 F3
Center, N. Dak., U.S.A. 40 B4
Center, Tex., U.S.A. 41 K7
Centerville, Iowa, U.S.A. 40 E8
Centerville, Tenn., U.S.A. 43 H2
Central, Cordillera, Colombia 46 C4
Central, Cordillera, Puerto Rico 45 d
Central African Rep. ■ 28 C4
Central City, Colo., U.S.A. 38 G11
Central City, Nebr., U.S.A. 40 E6
Central Makran Range 24 C5
Central Point 38 E2
Centralia, Ill., U.S.A. 40 F10
Centralia, Wash., U.S.A. 38 C2
Cephalonia = Kefalliniá 15 E9
Ceram = Seram 23 D4
Ceram Sea = Seram Sea 23 D4
Ceredigion □ 9 E3
Ceres 29 L3
České Budějovice 16 D7
Českomoravská Vrchovina 16 D8
Ceuta 13 E3
Cévennes 12 D5
Ceylon = Sri Lanka ■ 25 L11
Chad ■ 27 E8
Chad, L. = Tchad, L. 27 F7
Chagos Arch. 5 E13

Chäh Bahar 24 C5
Chai Wan 21 G11
Chalky Inlet 33 M1
Challis 38 D6
Chalmette 41 L10
Chalon-sur-Saône 12 C6
Châlons-en-Champagne 12 B6
Chama 39 H10
Chambal → 25 C6
Chamberlain 40 D5
Chamberlain L. 43 B11
Chambersburg 42 F7
Chambéry 12 D6
Champaign 42 E1
Champlain 42 C9
Champlain, L. 42 C9
Chandigarh 25 B6
Chandler, Australia 32 A1
Chandler, Ariz., U.S.A. 39 K8
Chandler, Okla., U.S.A. 41 H6
Chang Jiang → 21 C7
Changane → 29 J6
Changchun 21 B7
Changde 21 D6
Changhua 21 D7
Changsha 21 D6
Changzhi 21 C6
Changzhou 21 C6
Channel Is., U.K. 9 H5
Channel Is., U.S.A. 39 K4
Channel Islands Nat. Park 39 K4
Channel-Port aux Basques 37 D14
Channing 41 H3
Chantrey Inlet 36 B10
Chanute 41 G7
Chao Phraya → 23 B2
Chaoyang 21 B7
Chapala, L. de 44 C4
Chapel Hill 43 H6
Chapleau 37 D11
Chappell 40 E3
Chardzhou = Chärjew 18 F7
Chari → 27 F8
Chärjew 18 F7
Charleroi 14 C6
Charles, C. 42 G8
Charles City 40 D8
Charles Town 42 F7
Charleston, Ill., U.S.A. 42 F1
Charleston, Miss., U.S.A. 41 H9
Charleston, S.C., U.S.A. 43 J6
Charleston, W. Va., U.S.A. 42 F5
Charlestown, Ireland 11 C3
Charlestown, St. Kitts 44 a
Charleville 32 A4
Charleville-Mézières 12 B6
Charlevoix 42 C3
Charlotte, Mich., U.S.A. 42 D3
Charlotte, N.C., U.S.A. 43 H5
Charlotte Amalie 45 d
Charlotte Harbor 43 M4
Charlottesville 42 F6
Charlottetown 37 D13
Charlton, Australia 32 C3
Charolles 12 C6
Charters Towers 30 E8
Chartres 12 B4
Châteaubriant 12 C3
Châteaulin 12 B1
Châteauroux 12 C4
Château, Pte. des 44 b
Châtellerault 12 C4
Chatham = Miramichi 37 D13
Chatham, U.K. 9 F8
Chatham Is. 34 M10
Chattahoochee 43 K3
Chattahoochee → 43 K3
Chattanooga 43 H3
Chatteris 9 E8
Chaumont 12 B6
Cheb 16 C7
Cheboksary 18 D5
Cheboygan 42 C3
Chech, Erg 26 D5
Cheduba I. 25 K18
Cheepie 32 A4
Cheju do 21 C7
Chelan 38 C4
Chelan, L. 38 B3
Chelmsford 9 F8
Cheltenham 9 F5
Chelyabinsk 18 D7
Chelyuskin, C. 19 B11
Chemnitz 16 C6
Chengde 21 B6
Chengdu 20 C5
Chengjiang 20 D5
Chennai 25 N12
Chepstow 9 F5
Chequamegon B. 40 B9
Cher → 12 C4
Cheraw 43 H6
Cherbourg 12 B3
Cherdyn 18 C6
Cheremkhovo 19 D11
Cherepovets 18 D4
Cherkasy 19 E4? 17 D10
Chernihiv 18 D4
Chernivtsi 17 D13
Chernobyl = Chornobyl 17 C10
Chernyakhovsk 7 J12
Cherokee, Iowa, U.S.A. 40 D7
Cherokee, Okla., U.S.A. 41 G5
Cherokee Village 41 G9
Cherokees, Grand Lake O'The 41 G7
Cherwell → 9 F6
Chesapeake 42 G7
Chesapeake B. 42 F7
Cheshire □ 8 D5
Chesil Beach 9 G5
Chester, U.K. 8 D5
Chester, Calif., U.S.A. 38 F3
Chester, Ill., U.S.A. 41 G10
Chester, Mont., U.S.A. 38 B8
Chester, Pa., U.S.A. 42 F8
Chester, S.C., U.S.A. 43 H5
Chester-le-Street 8 C6
Chesterfield 8 D6
Chesterfield Inlet 36 B10
Chesterton Ra. 32 A4
Chetumal 44 D7
Chetwynd 36 C7
Cheviot, The 8 B5
Cheviot Hills 8 B5
Chew Bahir 28 D7
Cheyenne, Okla., U.S.A. 41 H5
Cheyenne, Wyo., U.S.A. 40 E2
Cheyenne → 40 C4
Cheyenne Wells 40 F3
Chhapra 25 G14
Chiai 21 D7
Chiang Mai 23 A1
Chiba 22 F7
Chibougamau 37 D12
Chicago 42 E2

Chicago Heights 42 E2
Chichagof I. 36 C6
Chichester 9 G7
Chickasha 41 H6
Chiclayo 46 E3
Chicopee 42 D9
Chicoutimi 37 D12
Chidley, C. 37 B13
Chiengmai = Chiang Mai 23 A1
Chieti 14 C6
Chihli, G. of = Bo Hai 21 C6
Chihuahua 44 B3
Chilapa 44 D5
Childers 32 A5
Childress 41 H4
Chile ■ 48 D2
Chile Rise 35 L18
Chillán 48 D2
Chillicothe, Ill., U.S.A. 40 E10
Chillicothe, Mo., U.S.A. 40 F8
Chillicothe, Ohio, U.S.A. 42 F4
Chilliwack 36 D7
Chiloé, I. de 48 E2
Chilpancingo 44 D5
Chiltern Hills 9 F7
Chilton 42 C1
Chilung 21 D7
Chimbay 18 E6
Chimborazo 46 D3
Chimbote 46 E3
Chimkent = Shymkent 18 E7
Chimoio 29 H6
China ■ 20 C6
Chinandega 44 E7
Chincha Alta 46 F3
Chinchilla 32 A5
Chincoteague 42 G8
Chindwin → 25 C10
China Lake 39 J5
Chino 39 J5
Chino Valley 39 J7
Chinon 12 C4
Chinook 38 B9
Chióggia 14 B5
Chíos 15 E12
Chipata 29 G6
Chipley 43 K3
Chippenham 9 F5
Chippewa → 40 C8
Chippewa Falls 40 C9
Chipping Norton 9 F6
Chiquinquirá 46 B4
Chirchiq 18 E7
Chiricahua Peak 39 L9
Chisholm 40 B8
Chita 19 D12
Chitral 24 B8
Chittagong 25 H17
Chitungwiza 29 H6
Choiseul, St. Lucia 44 b
Choiseul, Solomon Is. 34 H7
Choix 44 B3
Chojnice 16 B9
Choluteca 44 E7
Chon Buri 23 B2
Chongjin 21 B8
Chongqing 20 D5
Chongqing Shi □ 20 C5
Chonos, Arch. de los 48 F2
Chorley 8 D5
Chornobyl 17 C10
Chorzów 16 C9
Choybalsan 21 B6
Christchurch, N.Z. 33 K4
Christchurch, U.K. 9 G6
Christmas I. = Kiritimati 35 G12
Chubbuck 38 E7
Chudskoye, Ozero 7 F9
Chugwater 40 E2
Chukchi Sea 19 C19
Chukotskoye Nagorye 19 C18
Chula Vista 39 K5
Chulman 19 D13
Chuquicamata 48 A3
Chur 16 E5
Churchill 36 C10
Churchill →, Man., Canada 36 C10
Churchill →, Nfld., Canada 37 C13
Churchill Falls 37 C13
Churchill Pk. 36 C7
Chuska Mts. 39 H9
Cicero 42 E2
Ciego de Ávila 45 C9
Ciénaga 46 A4
Cienfuegos 45 C8
Cincinnati 42 F3
Cinto, Mte. 12 E8
Circle, Mont., U.S.A. 40 B2
Circleville 42 F4
Cirebon 23 D2
Cirencester 9 F6
Citlaltépetl = Orizaba, Pico de 44 D5
Ciudad Bolívar 46 B6
Ciudad del Carmen 44 D6
Ciudad Delicias = Delicias 44 B3
Ciudad Guayana 46 B6
Ciudad Guzmán 44 D4
Ciudad Juárez 44 A3
Ciudad Madero 44 C5
Ciudad Mante 44 C5
Ciudad Obregón 44 B3
Ciudad Real 13 C4
Ciudad Trujillo = Santo Domingo 45 D11
Ciudad Victoria 44 C5
Clackmannanshire □ 10 E5
Clacton-on-Sea 9 F9
Claire, L. 36 C8
Clanton 43 J2
Clanwilliam 29 L3
Clara 11 C4
Clare, Australia 32 B2
Clare □ 11 D3
Clare → 11 C2
Clare I. 11 C1
Claremont 42 D9
Claremore 41 G7
Claremorris 11 C3
Clarence →, Australia 32 A5
Clarence →, N.Z. 33 K4
Clarendon 41 H4
Clarinda 40 E7
Clarion, Iowa, U.S.A. 40 D8
Clarion, Pa., U.S.A. 42 E6
Clark 40 C6
Clark Fork 38 B6
Clark Fork → 38 B5
Clark Hill L. 43 J4
Clarksburg 42 F5
Clarksdale 41 H9
Clarksville, Tenn., U.S.A. 43 G2
Clarksville, Tex., U.S.A. 41 J7

Claypool 39 K8
Clayton, N. Mex., U.S.A. 41 G3
Clayton, N.Y., U.S.A. 42 C8
Clear, C. 11 E2
Clear L. 38 G2
Clear Lake, Iowa, U.S.A. 40 D8
Clear Lake, S. Dak., U.S.A. 40 C6
Clear Lake Reservoir 38 F3
Clearfield, Pa., U.S.A. 42 E6
Clearfield, Utah, U.S.A. 38 F7
Clearlake 38 G2
Clearwater 43 M4
Clearwater Mts. 38 C6
Cleburne 41 J6
Clee Hills 9 E5
Cleethorpes 8 D7
Cleeve Cloud 9 F6
Clemson 43 H4
Clermont 32 C4
Clermont-Ferrand 12 D5
Clevedon 9 F5
Cleveland, Miss., U.S.A. 41 J9
Cleveland, Ohio, U.S.A. 42 E5
Cleveland, Tenn., U.S.A. 43 H3
Cleveland, Tex., U.S.A. 41 K7
Clew B. 11 C2
Clewiston 43 M5
Clifden, Ireland 11 C1
Clifden, N.Z. 33 M1
Cliffdell 38 C3
Clifton, Australia 32 A5
Clifton, Ariz., U.S.A. 39 K9
Clifton, Colo., U.S.A. 38 G9
Clifton, Tex., U.S.A. 41 K6
Clinch → 43 H3
Clingmans Dome 43 H4
Clint 39 L10
Clinton, Canada 36 C7
Clinton, Ark., U.S.A. 41 H8
Clinton, Ill., U.S.A. 40 E10
Clinton, Ind., U.S.A. 42 F2
Clinton, Iowa, U.S.A. 40 E9
Clinton, Miss., U.S.A. 41 J9
Clinton, Mo., U.S.A. 40 F8
Clinton, N.C., U.S.A. 43 H6
Clinton, Okla., U.S.A. 41 H5
Clinton, S.C., U.S.A. 43 H5
Clinton, Tenn., U.S.A. 43 G3
Clinton Colden L. 36 B9
Clintonville 40 C10
Clipperton, I. 35 F17
Clitheroe 8 D5
Clogher Hd. 11 C5
Clonakilty 11 E3
Clonakilty B. 11 E3
Clones 11 B4
Clonmel 11 D4
Cloquet 40 B8
Cloud Peak 38 D10
Cloverdale 38 G2
Clovis, Calif., U.S.A. 39 H4
Clovis, N. Mex., U.S.A. 41 H3
Cluj-Napoca 17 E12
Clunes 32 C3
Clutha → 33 M2
Clwyd → 8 D4
Clyde, Firth of 10 F3
Clyde River 37 A13
Clydebank 10 F4
Coachella 39 K5
Coachella Canal 39 K6
Coahoma 41 J4
Coalgate 41 H6
Coalinga 39 H3
Coalisland 11 B5
Coalville, U.K. 8 E6
Coari 46 D6
Coast Mts. 36 C7
Coast Ranges 38 F2
Coatbridge 10 F4
Coatesville 42 F8
Coats I. 37 B11
Coatzacoalcos 44 D6
Cobán 44 D6
Cobar 32 B4
Cóbh 11 E3
Cobija 46 F5
Cobleskill 42 D8
Coburg 16 C5
Cocanada = Kakinada 25 D7
Cochabamba 46 G5
Cochin 25 Q10
Cochran 43 J4
Cochrane, Canada 42 A5
Cockburn Canal 48 G2
Cockermouth 8 C4
Cockpit Country, The 44 a
Coco → 45 E8
Coco, I. del 35 G19
Cocoa 43 L5
Cocos B. 44 b
Cod, C. 43 D11
Codó 47 D10
Cody 38 D9
Coeur d'Alene 38 C5
Coeur d'Alene L. 38 C5
Coffeyville 41 G7
Coffin Bay 32 B2
Coffin Bay Peninsula 32 B2
Coffs Harbour 32 B5
Cognac 12 D3
Cohuna 32 C3
Coiba, I. 45 F8
Coig → 48 G3
Coigach, Rubha 10 C3
Coimbra 13 B1
Colac 32 C3
Colatina 47 G10
Colby 40 F4
Colchester 9 F8
Cold L. 36 C8
Coldstream 10 F6
Coldwater, Kans., U.S.A. 41 G5
Coldwater, Mich., U.S.A. 42 E3
Coleman 41 K5
Coleraine, Australia 32 C3
Coleraine, U.K. 11 A5
Coleridge, L. 33 K3
Colesberg 29 L5
Colfax, La., U.S.A. 41 K8
Colfax, Wash., U.S.A. 38 C5
Colima 44 D4
Coll 10 E2
College Station 41 K6
Collarenebri 32 A4
Collie 30 G2
Collier B. 30 D3
Collingwood 33 J4
Collinsville 32 C4
Collooney 11 B3
Colmar 12 B7
Colne 8 D5
Cologne = Köln 16 C3
Colombia ■ 46 C4
Colombo 25 R11
Colón, Cuba 45 C8
Colón, Panama 45 F9
Colonsay 10 E2
Colorado □ 39 G11
Colorado →, N. Amer. 39 L6
Colorado →, U.S.A. 41 L7
Colorado Plateau 39 H8
Colorado River Aqueduct 39 K6
Colorado Springs 40 F2
Colstrip 38 D10
Columbia, La., U.S.A. 41 J8

Columbia, Miss., U.S.A. 41 K10
Columbia, Mo., U.S.A. 40 F8
Columbia, Pa., U.S.A. 42 E7
Columbia, S.C., U.S.A. 43 H5
Columbia → 38 C1
Columbia, District of □ 42 F7
Columbia Basin 38 C4
Columbia Falls 38 B6
Columbia Plateau 38 D5
Columbus, Ga., U.S.A. 43 J3
Columbus, Ind., U.S.A. 42 F3
Columbus, Kans., U.S.A. 41 G7
Columbus, Miss., U.S.A. 43 J1
Columbus, Mont., U.S.A. 38 D9
Columbus, N. Mex., U.S.A. 39 L10
Columbus, Nebr., U.S.A. 40 E6
Columbus, Ohio, U.S.A. 42 F4
Columbus, Tex., U.S.A. 41 L6
Colusa 38 G2
Colville 38 B5
Colville → 36 A4
Colwyn Bay 8 D4
Comanche 41 K5
Comayagua 44 E7
Combahee → 43 J5
Comber 11 B6
Comeragh Mts. 11 D4
Comilla 25 H17
Commerce, Ga., U.S.A. 43 H4
Commerce, Tex., U.S.A. 41 J7
Committee B. 37 B11
Commoron Cr. → 32 A5
Communism Pk. = Kommunizma, Pik 18 F8
Como 12 D8
Como, Lago di 12 D8
Comodoro Rivadavia 48 F3
Comorin, C. 25 Q10
Comoros ■ 5 E12
Compiègne 12 B5
Conakry 26 G3
Concarneau 12 C2
Concepción, Chile 48 D2
Concepción del Oro 44 C4
Conception, Pt. 39 J3
Conchas Dam 41 H2
Concho 39 J9
Concho → 41 K5
Conchos → 44 B3
Concord, Calif., U.S.A. 38 H2
Concord, N.C., U.S.A. 43 H5
Concord, N.H., U.S.A. 42 D10
Concordia 48 C5
Concrete 38 B3
Condamine 32 A5
Condon 38 D3
Congleton 8 D5
Congo (Kinshasa) = Congo, Dem. Rep. of the ■ 28 E4
Congo ■ 28 E3
Congo, Dem. Rep. of the ■ 28 E4
Congo → 28 F2
Congo Basin 28 E4
Conn, L. 11 B2
Connacht □ 11 C2
Conneaut 42 E5
Connecticut □ 42 E9
Connecticut → 42 E9
Connell 38 C4
Connellsville 42 E6
Connemara 11 C2
Conran, C. 32 C4
Conroe 41 K7
Consett 8 C6
Constance, L. = Bodensee 12 C8
Constanța 15 B13
Constantine 26 A7
Contact 38 F6
Contwoyto L. 36 B8
Conway, Ark., U.S.A. 41 H8
Conway, N.H., U.S.A. 42 D10
Conway, S.C., U.S.A. 43 J6
Conwy 8 D4
Conwy → 8 D4
Coober Pedy 30 F5
Cook, Mount = Aoraki Mount Cook 33 J3
Cook Inlet 36 C4
Cook Is. ■ 35 J12
Cook Strait 33 J5
Cookeville 43 G3
Cookstown 11 B5
Cooktown 30 C8
Coolabah 32 B4
Cooladdi 32 A4
Coolah 32 B4
Coolamon 32 B4
Coolgardie 30 G3
Coolidge 39 K8
Coolidge Dam 39 K8
Coon Rapids 40 C8
Coonabarabran 32 B4
Coonamble 32 B4
Cooper → 43 J6
Cooper Cr. →, N. Terr., Australia 30 C5
Cooper Cr. →, S. Austral., Australia 30 B6
Coorong, The 32 C2
Cooroy 32 A5
Coosa → 43 J2
Cootamundra 32 B4
Cootehill 11 B4
Copenhagen = København 7 F6
Copiapó 48 B2
Copper Harbor 40 B2
Copperas Cove 41 K6
Coppermine → 36 B8
Coquet → 8 B6
Coquille 38 E1
Coquimbo 48 B2
Coracora 46 G4
Coral Gables 43 N5
Coral Sea 34 J8
Coral Springs 43 M5
Corbin 42 G3
Corby 9 E7
Corcaigh = Cork 11 E3
Cordele 43 K4
Cordell 41 H5
Córdoba, Argentina 48 C4
Córdoba, Mexico 44 D5
Córdoba, Spain 13 D3
Córdoba, Sierra de 48 C4
Cordova 36 B5
Corfu = Kérkira 15 E8
Corinth = Kórinthos 15 F10
Corinth 43 H1
Corinth, G. of = Korinthiakós Kólpos 15 E10
Cork 11 E3
Cork □ 11 E3
Cork Harbour 11 E3
Corner Brook 37 D14
Corning, Calif., U.S.A. 38 G2
Corning, Iowa, U.S.A. 40 E7
Corning, N.Y., U.S.A. 42 D7
Cornwall 37 D13

Cornwall □ 9 G3
Corny Pt. 32 B2
Coro 46 A5
Coromandel 33 G5
Coromandel Coast 25 D7
Corona, Calif., U.S.A. 39 K5
Corona, N. Mex., U.S.A. 39 J11
Coronation Gulf 36 B8
Corowa 43 C4
Corpus Christi 41 M6
Corpus Christi, L. 41 M6
Corraun Pen. 11 C2
Corrib, L. 11 C2
Corrientes 48 H5
Corrientes, C. 46 B3
Corrigan 41 K7
Corry 42 E6
Corse 12 E8
Corse, C. 12 E8
Corsica = Corse 12 E8
Corsicana 41 J6
Corte 12 E8
Cortez 39 H9
Cortland 42 D7
Corumbá 46 G7
Coruña = A Coruña 13 A1
Corvallis 38 D2
Corydon 40 E8
Cosenza 14 E7
Coshocton 42 E5
Costa Blanca 13 C5
Costa Brava 13 B7
Costa del Sol 13 D3
Costa Dorada 13 B6
Costa Rica ■ 45 F8
Cotabato 23 C4
Côte-d'Azur 12 E7
Côte d'Ivoire = Ivory Coast ■ 26 G4
Coteau des Prairies 40 C6
Coteau du Missouri 40 B4
Cotentin 12 B3
Cotonou 26 G6
Cotopaxi 46 D3
Cotswold Hills 9 F5
Cottage Grove 38 E2
Cottbus 16 C7
Cotulla 41 L5
Coudersport 42 E6
Couedic, C. du 43 F2
Coulee City 38 C4
Council 38 D5
Council Bluffs 40 E7
Council Grove 40 F6
Courantyne → 46 B7
Courtenay 36 D7
Courtrai = Kortrijk 10 D2
Coushatta 41 J8
Coventry 9 E6
Covington, Ga., U.S.A. 43 J4
Covington, Ky., U.S.A. 42 F3
Covington, Okla., U.S.A. 41 H10
Covington, Tenn., U.S.A. 41 H10
Covington, Va., U.S.A. 42 G5
Cowal, L. 32 B4
Cowangie 43 C3
Coward Springs 32 A2
Cowdenbeath 10 E5
Cowell 32 B2
Cowes 9 G6
Cowra 43 H3
Cozad 40 E5
Cozumel, Isla 44 C7
Crabhill 44 g
Cracow = Kraków 16 C9
Cracow 43 A5
Cradle Mt.-Lake St. Clair Nat. Park 32 D4
Cradock, Australia 32 B2
Cradock, S. Africa 29 L5
Craig 38 F10
Craiova 15 B10
Cranbrook 36 D8
Crandon 40 C10
Crane, Oreg., U.S.A. 38 E4
Crane, Tex., U.S.A. 41 K3
Crater L. 38 E2
Crater Lake Nat. Park 38 E2
Crawford 40 D3
Crawfordsville 42 E2
Crawley 9 F7
Crazy Mts. 38 C8
Cree →, Canada 36 C9
Cree →, U.K. 10 G4
Cree L. 36 C9
Creede 39 H10
Creighton 40 D6
Cremona 12 B4
Crescent City 38 F1
Creston 40 E7
Crestview 43 K2
Crete = Kríti 15 G11
Crete 40 E6
Creuse → 12 C4
Crewe 8 D5
Crewkerne 9 G5
Crianlarich 10 E4
Crimean Pen. = Krymskiy Pivostriv 17 B4
Crna Gora = Montenegro □ 15 C8
Croagh Patrick 11 C2
Croatia ■ 14 B7
Crocker, Banjaran 22 C3
Crocodile = Krokodil → 29 H6
Croker, C. 30 C5
Cromarty 10 D4
Cromer 8 E9
Cromwell 33 L2
Crook 8 C6
Crooked →, Canada 38 D3
Crooked I. 45 C10
Crookston, Minn., U.S.A. 40 B6
Crookston, Nebr., U.S.A. 40 D4
Crosby, U.K. 8 D4
Crosby, N. Dak., U.S.A. 40 A3
Crosbyton 41 J4
Cross City 43 L4
Cross Fell 8 C5
Cross Sound 36 C6
Crossett 41 J9
Crosshaven 11 E3
Crossville 43 H3
Crow Agency 38 D10
Crow Hd. 11 E1
Crowell 41 J5
Crowley 41 K8
Crown Point 42 E2
Crownpoint 39 J9
Crows Nest 43 A5
Crowsnest Pass 36 D8
Croydon 9 F7
Crozet, Is. 5 G12
Cruz Bay 45 C7
Cruzeiro do Sul 46 E4
Crystal Brook 32 B2
Crystal City 41 L5
Crystal Falls 42 B1
Crystal River 43 L4
Crystal Springs 41 K9
Cuamba 29 H4
Cuando → 29 H4
Cuango = Kwango → 28 F3
Cuanza → 28 F2
Cuauhtémoc 44 B3
Cuba ■ 45 C9
Cuba 39 J10
Cuballing 31 F2
Cubango → 29 H4
Cuckfield 9 F7
Cúcuta 46 B4
Cuenca, Ecuador 46 D3
Cuenca, Spain 13 B4
Cuernavaca 44 D5
Cuero 41 L6
Cuiabá 46 G7
Cuillin Hills 10 D2
Cuillin Sd. 10 D2
Culbertson 38 B11
Culcairn 32 C4

Culebra, Isla de 45 d
Culgoa → 32 A4
Culiacán 44 C3
Cullarin Ra. 32 B4
Cullen 10 D6
Cullera 43 H2
Cullman 43 H2
Culpeper 42 F7
Culuene → 46 F8
Culver, Pt. 31 F3
Culverden 33 K4
Cumaná 46 A6
Cumberland 42 F6
Cumberland →, U.S.A. 43 G2
Cumberland I. 43 K5
Cumberland Is. 30 J7
Cumberland Plateau 43 H3
Cumberland Sd. 37 B13
Cumbernauld 10 F5
Cumborah 32 A4
Cumbria □ 8 C5
Cumbrian Mts. 8 C5
Cumnock, Australia 32 B4
Cumnock, U.K. 10 F4
Cunene → 29 H2
Cúneo 12 D7
Cunnamulla 30 F8
Cupar 10 E5
Curaçao 45 E11
Curitiba 48 B7
Currabubula 32 B5
Currant 38 G6
Current → 41 G9
Current, Australia 32 C3
Currie 40 F4
Currie, U.S.A. 38 F6
Curtis Group 32 C4
Cushing 41 H6
Custer 40 D3
Cut Bank 38 B7
Cuthbert 43 K3
Cuttaburra → 32 A3
Cuttack 25 J14
Cuvier I. 33 G5
Cuxhaven 16 B4
Cuyahoga Falls 42 E5
Cuyuni → 46 B7
Cuzco 46 F4
Cwmbran 9 F4
Cynthiana 42 F3
Cyprus ■ 17 D4
Cyrenaica 27 C10
Czech Rep. ■ 16 D7
Częstochowa 16 C9

D

Da Hinggan Ling 21 B7
Da Lat 23 B2
Da Nang 23 B2
Da Qaidam 20 C4
Daba Shan 21 C5
Dacca = Dhaka 25 C8
Dade City 43 L4
Dagupan 23 A6
Dahlak Kebir 24 D3
Dahlonega 43 H4
Daingean 11 C4
Dajarra 30 C2
Dakar 26 F2
Dakhla 26 D2
Dakota City 40 D6
Dalandzadgad 20 B5
Dalap-Uliga-Darrit 34 G9
Dalbeattie 10 G5
Dalby 31 F2
Dale City 42 F7
Dale Hollow L. 43 G3
Dalhart 41 G3
Dali 20 D5
Dalian 21 C7
Dalkeith 10 F5
Dallas, Oreg., U.S.A. 38 D2
Dallas, Tex., U.S.A. 41 J6
Dalmacija 14 C7
Dalmatia = Dalmacija 14 C7
Dalmellington 10 F4
Daloa 26 G3
Dalry 10 F4
Dalton, Ga., U.S.A. 43 H3
Dalton, Nebr., U.S.A. 40 E3
Dalton-in-Furness 8 C4
Daly → 30 B5
Daly L. 36 C9
Daly Waters 30 B5
Damanhûr 27 B12
Damaraland 29 J2
Damascus = Dimashq 24 B2
Dámavand, Qolleh-ye 24 B4
Damietta = Dumyât 27 B12
Dammam = Ad Dammām 24 C4
Dampier 30 D2
Danbury 42 E9
Danby L. 39 J6
Dandenong 32 C4
Dandong 21 C7
Danger Is. = Pukapuka 35 J11
Dannemora 42 C9
Dannevirke 33 J6
Dansville 42 D7
Danube = Dunărea → 15 B13
Danville, Ill., U.S.A. 42 E2
Danville, Ky., U.S.A. 42 G3
Danville, Va., U.S.A. 43 G6
Danzig = Gdańsk 16 A9
Dar es Salaam 28 F7
Darbhanga 25 F14
Dardanelle 41 H8
Dardanelles = Çanakkale Boğazı 15 D12
Dargaville 33 F4
Darién, G. del 46 B3
Darjeeling = Darjiling 25 F16
Darjiling 25 F16
Darling → 32 A3
Darling Downs 31 F2
Darling Ra. 31 F2
Darlington, U.K. 8 C6
Darlington, Wis., U.S.A. 40 D9
Darlot, L. 31 E3
Darmstadt 16 D4
Darnley, C. 5 C6
Darnley B. 36 B7
Dart → 9 G4
Dartford 9 F8
Dartmoor 9 G4
Dartmouth, Canada 37 D13
Dartmouth, U.K. 9 G4
Dartmouth Res. 32 A4
Darwin 30 B5
Dashen, Ras 24 D2
Dauphin 36 C10
Dauphiné 12 D6
Davangere 25 D6
Davao 23 C4
Davao G. 23 C4
Davenport, Iowa, U.S.A. 40 E9
Davenport, Wash., U.S.A. 38 C4
David 45 F8
David City 40 E6
Davis 38 G5
Davis Mts. 41 K2
Davis Sea 5 C8
Davis Str. 37 B14
Dawei = Tavoy 23 B1
Dawlish 9 G4
Dawson 36 B6
Dawson →, Australia 30 C7
Dawson Creek 36 C7

Daxian 20 C5
Daxue Shan 20 C5
Dayr az Zawr 24 B3
Dayton, Ohio, U.S.A. 42 F3
Dayton, Tenn., U.S.A. 43 H3
Dayton, Wash., U.S.A. 38 C4
Dayton, Wyo., U.S.A. 38 D10
Daytona Beach 43 L5
Dayville 38 D4
De Aar 29 L4
De Funiak Springs 43 K2
De Kalb 40 E10
De Land 43 L5
De Leon 41 J5
De Pere 42 C1
De Queen 41 H7
De Quincy 41 K8
De Ridder 41 K8
De Smet 40 C6
De Soto 40 F9
De Tour Village 42 B4
De Witt 41 H9
Dead Sea 17 D5
Deadwood 40 C3
Deal 9 F9
Dean, Forest of 9 F5
Dease → 36 B6
Dease Lake 36 C6
Death Valley 39 H5
Death Valley Junction 39 H5
Death Valley Nat. Park 39 H5
Debrecen 17 A2
Decatur, Ala., U.S.A. 43 H2
Decatur, Ga., U.S.A. 43 J3
Decatur, Ill., U.S.A. 40 F10
Decatur, Ind., U.S.A. 42 E3
Decatur, Tex., U.S.A. 41 J6
Deccan 25 D6
Deception Bay 32 A5
Decorah 40 D8
Dee →, Aberds., U.K. 10 D6
Dee →, Dumf. & Gall., U.K. 10 G4
Dee →, Wales, U.K. 8 D4
Deepwater 32 A5
Deer Lake 37 D14
Deer Lodge 38 C7
Deer Park 38 C5
Deer River 40 B8
Defiance 42 E3
Dehra Dun 25 B6
Del Norte 39 H10
Del Rio 41 L4
Delano 39 J4
Delano Peak 39 G7
Delavan 40 D10
Delaware 42 E4
Delaware □ 42 F8
Delaware → 42 F8
Delaware B. 42 F8
Delegate 32 C4
Delgado, C. 28 G8
Delhi, India 25 E6
Delhi, U.S.A. 41 J9
Delicias 44 B3
Déline 36 B7
Dell City 39 L11
Dell Rapids 40 C6
Delmenhorst 16 B4
Delphi 42 E2
Delphos 42 E3
Delray Beach 43 M5
Delta, Colo., U.S.A. 39 G9
Delta, Utah, U.S.A. 38 G7
Delta Junction 36 B5
Deltona 43 L5
Delungra 32 A5
Demavend = Dámávand, Qolleh-ye 24 B4
Deming 39 K10
Demopolis 43 J2
Den Haag = 's-Gravenhage 16 B2
Den Helder 16 B2
Denbigh 8 D4
Denbighshire □ 8 D4
Denham, Mt. 44 a
Deniliquin 32 C3
Denison, Iowa, U.S.A. 40 E7
Denison, Tex., U.S.A. 41 J6
Denizli 15 F13
Denmark ■ 7 F6
Denmark 31 F2
Denmark Str. 6 C5
Dennery 45 f
Denny 10 E5
Denpasar 22 D3
Denton, Mont., U.S.A. 38 C9
Denton, Tex., U.S.A. 41 J6
D'Entrecasteaux Is. 30 B8
Denver 39 ...
Denver City 41 J3
Dera Ismail Khan 25 ...
Derby, Australia 30 C3
Derby, U.K. 8 E6
Derby, Conn., U.S.A. 42 E9
Derby, N.Y., U.S.A. 42 D6
Derbyshire □ 8 D6
Derg → 11 B4
Derg, L. 11 D3
Dermott 41 J9
Derry = Londonderry 11 B4
Derryveagh Mts. 11 B3
Derwent →, Cumb., U.K. 8 C4
Derwent →, Derby, U.K. 8 E6
Derwent →, N. Yorks., U.K. 8 D7
Des Moines, Iowa, U.S.A. 40 E8
Des Moines, N. Mex., U.S.A. 41 G3
Des Moines → 40 E9
Deschutes → 38 D3
Dese 24 E2
Desert Center 39 K6
D'Estrees B. 32 C2
Detour, Pt. 42 C2
Detroit 42 D4
Detroit Lakes 40 B7
Deutsche Bucht 16 A4
Deventer 16 B3
Devils Lake 40 A5
Devils Tower Junction 40 C2
Devine 41 L5
Devizes 9 F6
Devon □ 9 G4
Devon I. 4 B3
Devonport, Australia 30 G4
Devonport, N.Z. 33 G5
Dewey 45 d
Dexter, Maine, U.S.A. 43 C11
Dexter, Mo., U.S.A. 41 G10
Dexter, N. Mex., U.S.A. 41 J2
Dezfúl 24 B3
Dezhneva, Mys 19 C19
Dhaka 25 C8
Dharwad 25 D6
Dhaulagiri 25 E13
Dhodhekánisos 15 F12
Dhule 25 ...
Diamantina 46 G10
Diamond Mts. 38 G6
Dibrugarh 25 D18
Dickens 41 J4
Dickinson 40 B3
Dickson 43 G2
Diefenbaker, L. 36 C9
Diego Garcia 3 E13
Dieppe 12 B4
Dierks 41 H7
Digby 37 D13
Dighè-Ines-Bains ...
Dijlah, Nahr → 24 D5
Dili 23 D4
Dilley 41 L5
Dillingham 36 C4
Dillon, Mont., U.S.A. 38 D7
Dillon, S.C., U.S.A. 43 H6
Dimashq 24 B2
Dimbokro 26 G4
Dimboola 32 C3
Dimitrovgrad 15 C11

Dimmitt 41 H3
Dinan 12 B2
Dinant 16 C2
Dinara Planina 14 C7
Dinaric Alps = Dinara Planina 14 C7
Dingle 11 D1
Dingle B. 11 D1
Dingwall 10 D4
Dinosaur Nat. Monument 38 F9
Dinuba 39 H4
Dipolog 23 C4
Dirranbandi 32 A4
Disappointment, C. 38 C2
Disappointment, L. 30 D3
Disaster B. 32 C4
Discovery B., Australia 32 C3
Discovery B., China 21 G11
Diss 9 E9
Dixon 40 E10
Diyarbakır 17 C6
Djakarta = Jakarta 22 D2
Djerid, Chott 26 B7
Djibouti 24 D3
Djibouti ■ 24 D3
Dnepr = Dnipro → 17 A4
Dneprodzerzhinsk = Dniprodzerzhynsk 17 A4
Dnepropetrovsk = Dnipropetrovsk 17 A5
Dnestr = Dnister → 18 E4
Dnieper = Dnipro → 17 A4
Dniester = Dnister → 18 E4
Dnipro → 17 A4
Dniprodzerzhynsk 17 A5
Dnipropetrovsk 17 A5
Dnister → 17 A4
Dno 18 D4
Doberai, Jazirah 23 D5
Dobrich 15 C12
Dodecanese = Dhodhekánisos 15 F12
Dodge City 41 G5
Dodgeville 40 D9
Dodoma 28 F7
Dodson 38 B9
Doha = Ad Dawḩah 24 C4
Dole 12 C6
Dolgellau 8 E4
Dolomites = Dolomiti 14 A4
Dolomiti 14 A4
Dolores 39 H9
Dolphin and Union Str. 36 B8
Dominica ■ 45 D12
Dominican Rep. ■ 45 D10
Domville, Mt. 32 A5
Don →, Russia 18 E4
Don →, Aberds., U.K. 10 D6
Don →, S. Yorks., U.K. 8 D7
Don Figuero Mts. 44 a
Donaghadee 11 B6
Donaldsonville 41 K9
Donalsonville 43 K3
Donau = Dunărea → 15 B13
Doncaster 8 D6
Dondra Head 25 E7
Donegal 11 B3
Donegal □ 11 B4
Donegal B. 11 B3
Donetsk 17 A5
Dong Hoi 23 B2
Dongbei 21 B7
Dongchuan 20 D5
Dongola 27 C12
Dongting Hu 21 D6
Donington, C. 32 B2
Doniphan 41 G9
Donna 41 M5
Donnelly's Crossing 33 F4
Donner Pass 38 G3
Donostia-San Sebastián 13 A4
Doon → 10 F4
Dorchester 9 G5
Dorchester, C. 37 B12
Dordogne → 12 D3
Dordrecht 16 C2
Dornie 10 D3
Dornoch 10 D4
Dornoch Firth 10 D5
Döröö Nuur 20 B4
Dorris 38 F2
Dorset □ 9 G5
Dortmund 16 C3
Dothan 43 K3
Douai 16 C2
Douala 28 D1
Double Island Pt. 31 ...
Double Mountain Fork → 41 J4
Doubs → 12 C6
Doubtful Sd. 33 L1
Doubtless B. 33 F4
Douglas, U.K. 8 C3
Douglas, Ariz., U.S.A. 39 L9
Douglas, Ga., U.S.A. 43 K4
Douglas, Wyo., U.S.A. 40 D2
Douglasville 43 J3
Dounreay 10 C5
Dourados 46 H8
Douro → 13 B1
Dove → 8 E6
Dove Creek 39 H9
Dover, Australia 32 ...
Dover, U.K. 9 F9
Dover, Del., U.S.A. 42 F8
Dover, N.H., U.S.A. 42 D10
Dover, Ohio, U.S.A. 42 E5
Dover, Str. of 9 G9
Dover-Foxcroft 43 C11
Dovey = Dyfi → 9 E4
Dowagiac 42 E2
Down □ 11 B6
Downham Market 9 E8
Downieville 38 G3
Downpatrick 11 B6
Downpatrick Hd. 11 B2
Draguignan 12 E7
Drain 38 E2
Drake Passage 5 B17
Drakensberg 29 K6
Drama 15 D11
Drammen 7 F6
Drava → 14 B8
Dráva → 15 B8
Dresden 16 C7
Dreux 12 B4
Driffield 8 C7
Drina → 15 B8
Drobeta-Turnu Severin 15 B10
Drogheda 11 C5
Droichead Nua 11 C5
Droitwich 9 E5
Dromore 11 B5
Dromore West 11 B3
Dronfield 8 D6
Drumheller 36 C8
Drummond 38 C7
Drummond I. 42 B4
Drummond Pt. 32 B2
Drumright 41 H6
Drygalski I. 5 C7
Du Bois 42 E6
Du Quoin 40 G10
Dubawnt → 36 B9
Dubawnt, L. 36 B9
Dubayy 24 C4
Dubbo 31 E8
Dublin, Ireland 11 C5
Dublin, Ga., U.S.A. 43 J4
Dublin, Tex., U.S.A. 41 J5
Dublin □ 11 C5
Dubois 38 E8
Dubrovnik 15 C8
Dubuque 40 D9

Duchesne 38 F8
Duck → 43 H2
Dudinka 19 C9
Dudley 9 E5
Dufftown 10 D5
Duisburg 16 C3
Duluth 40 B8
Dumaguete 23 C4
Dumai 22 C2
Dumas, Ark., U.S.A. 41 J9
Dumas, Tex., U.S.A. 41 H4
Dumbarton 10 F4
Dumfries 10 F5
Dumfries & Galloway □ 10 F5
Dumyât 27 B12
Dún Laoghaire 11 C5
Duna = Dunărea → 15 B13
Dunaj = Dunărea → 15 B13
Dunărea → 15 B14
Dunav = Dunărea → 15 B13
Dunback 33 L3
Dunbar 10 E6
Dunblane 10 E5
Duncan, Ariz., U.S.A. 39 K9
Duncan, Okla., U.S.A. 41 H6
Duncansby Head 10 C5
Dundalk 11 B5
Dundalk Bay 11 C5
Dundee, U.K. 10 E6
Dundee, U.S.A. 42 D5
Dundrum 11 B6
Dundrum B. 11 B6
Dunedin 33 L3
Dunedin 43 L4
Dunfermline 10 E5
Dungannon 11 B5
Dungarvan 11 D4
Dungarvan Harbour 11 D4
Dungeness 9 G8
Dunhuang 20 B4
Dunkeld, Australia 32 C3
Dunkeld, U.K. 10 E5
Dunkerque 12 A5
Dunkery Beacon 9 F4
Dunkirk = Dunkerque 12 A5
Dunkirk 42 D6
Dunmanus B. 11 E2
Dunmanway 11 E2
Dunmarra 30 B5
Dunmore 42 E8
Dunmore Hd. 11 D1
Dunn 43 H6
Dunnellon 43 L4
Dunnet Hd. 10 C5
Dunning 40 E4
Dunolly 32 C3
Dunoon 10 F4
Dunphy 38 F5
Duns 10 F6
Dunseith 40 A4
Dunsmuir 38 F2
Dunstable 9 F7
Dunstan Mts. 33 L2
Dupree 40 C4
Dupuyer 38 B7
Durance → 12 E6
Durango, Mexico 44 C4
Durango, U.S.A. 39 H10
Durant, Miss., U.S.A. 41 J10
Durant, Okla., U.S.A. 41 J6
Durban 29 K6
Düren 16 C3
Durham, U.K. 8 C6
Durham, N.C., U.S.A. 43 H6
Durham □ 8 C6
Durness 10 C4
Durrës 15 D8
Durrow 11 D4
D'Urville I. 33 J4
Dushanbe 18 F7
Dusky Sd. 33 L1
Düsseldorf 16 C3
Dutch Harbor 36 C2
Duyun 20 D5
Dvina, Severnaya → 18 C5
Dvinsk = Daugavpils 7 F8
Dwight 42 E1
Dyer, C. 37 B13
Dyersburg 41 G10
Dyfi → 9 E4
Dzhambul = Taraz 18 E8
Dzhugdzhur, Khrebet 19 D14
Dzungaria = Junggar Pendi 20 B3
Dzungarian Gates 20 B3
Dzuumod 20 B5

E

Eads 40 F3
Eagar 39 J9
Eagle, Alaska, U.S.A. 36 B5
Eagle, Colo., U.S.A. 38 G10
Eagle Butte 40 C4
Eagle Grove 40 D8
Eagle L., Calif., U.S.A. 38 F3
Eagle L., Maine, U.S.A. 43 B11
Eagle Lake, Tex., U.S.A. 41 L6
Eagle Nest 39 H11
Eagle Pass 41 L4
Eagle River, Mich., U.S.A. 42 B1
Eagle River, Wis., U.S.A. 40 C10
Eaglehawk 32 C3
Ealing 9 F7
Earlimart 39 J4
Earn → 10 E5
Earn, L. 10 E4
Earnslaw, Mt. 33 L2
Earth 41 H3
Easley 43 H4
East Anglia 9 E9
East Ayrshire □ 10 F4
East C. 33 G7
East Chicago 42 E2
East China Sea 21 C7
East Dereham 8 E8
East Dunbartonshire □ 10 F4
East Falkland 48 G5
East Grand Forks 40 B6
East Grinstead 9 F7
East Helena 38 C8
East Kilbride 10 F4
East Lansing 42 D3
East Liverpool 42 E5
East London 29 L5
East Lothian □ 10 F6
East Orange 42 E8
East Pacific Ridge 35 J17
East Point 43 J3
East Renfrewshire □ 10 F4
East Retford = Retford 8 D7
East Riding of Yorkshire □ 8 D7
East St. Louis 40 F9
East Sea = Japan, Sea of 20 D4
East Siberian Sea 19 B17
East Sussex □ 9 G8
East Tawas 42 C4
East Timor ■ 23 D4
East Toorale 32 A4
Eastbourne, N.Z. 33 J5
Eastbourne, U.K. 9 G8
Easter I. = Pascua, I. de 35 K17
Eastern Ghats 25 D6

Eastland 41 J5
Eastleigh 9 G6
Eastmain 37 C12
Eastmain → 37 C12
Eastman 43 J4
Easton, Md., U.S.A. 42 F7
Easton, Pa., U.S.A. 42 E8
Eastport 43 C12
Eau Claire 40 C9
Eau Claire, L. à l' 37 C12
Ebbw Vale 9 F4
Ebro → 13 B6
Ech Chéliff 26 A6
Echo Bay 36 B8
Echuca 32 C3
Eclipse Sd. 37 A11
Ecuador ■ 46 D3
Eday 10 B6
Eddystone Pt. 32 D4
Eden, Australia 32 C4
Eden, N.C., U.S.A. 43 G6
Eden, Tex., U.S.A. 41 K5
Eden → 8 C5
Edenderry 11 C4
Edenton 43 G7
Edgar 40 E6
Edge Hill 9 E6
Edgefield 43 J5
Edgeley 40 B5
Edgemont 40 D3
Edina 40 E8
Edinburg 41 M5
Edinburgh 10 F5
Edirne 15 D12
Edithburgh 32 C2
Edmond 41 H6
Edmonds 38 C2
Edmonton 36 C8
Edmundston 43 B11
Edna 41 L6
Edremit 15 E12
Edson 36 C8
Edward, L. 28 E5
Edward VII Land 5 E15
Edwards Plateau 41 K4
Effingham 42 F1
Égadi, Ísole 14 F5
Eganville 42 C7
Eger = Cheb 16 C6
Egersund 7 G5
Egmont, C. 33 H4
Egmont, Mt. = Taranaki, Mt. 33 H5
Egypt ■ 27 C12
Eidsvold 31 F9
Eifel 16 C3
Eigg 10 E2
Eil, L. 10 E3
Eildon 32 C4
Eildon, L. 32 C4
Eindhoven 16 C3
Eire = Ireland ■ 11 C4
Eivissa 13 C6
Ekalaka 40 B2
Eketahuna 33 J5
El Aaiún 26 C2
El Asnam = Ech Chéliff 26 A6
El Cajon 39 K5
El Centro 39 K6
El Djouf 26 D3
El Dorado, Ark., U.S.A. 41 J8
El Dorado, Kans., U.S.A. 41 G6
El Faiyûm 27 C12
El Fâsher 27 F11
El Gîza 27 C12
El Iskandarîya 27 B11
El Khârga 27 C12
El Mahalla el Kubra 27 B12
El Mansûra 27 B12
El Minyâ 27 C12
El Obeid 27 F12
El Paso 39 L10
El Qâhira 27 B12
El Reno 41 H6
El Salvador ■ 44 E7
El Suweis 27 C12
Elâzığ 17 C6
Elba, Italy 14 C4
Elba, U.S.A. 43 K2
Elbasan 15 D9
Elbe → 16 B5
Elbert, Mt. 39 G10
Elberton 43 H4
Elbeuf 12 B4
Elblag 16 A9
Elbrus 18 E5
Elburz Mts. = Alborz, Reshteh-ye Kühhâ-ye 24 B4
Elche 13 C5
Eldon 40 F8
Eldora 40 D8
Eldorado, Ill., U.S.A. 42 G1
Eldorado, Tex., U.S.A. 41 K4
Eldorado Springs 40 G7
Eldoret 28 D7
Elephant Butte Reservoir 39 K10
Elephant I. 5 C18
Eleuthera 45 B9
Elgin, U.K. 10 D5
Elgin, Ill., U.S.A. 42 D1
Elgin, N. Dak., U.S.A. 40 B4
Elgin, Oreg., U.S.A. 38 D5
Elgon, Mt. 28 D6
Elizabeth, Australia 32 B2
Elizabeth, U.S.A. 42 E8
Elizabeth City 43 G7
Elizabethton 43 G4
Elizabethtown 42 G3
Elk City 41 H5
Elk River, Idaho, U.S.A. 38 C5
Elk River, Minn., U.S.A. 40 C8
Elkhart, Ind., U.S.A. 42 E3
Elkhart, Kans., U.S.A. 41 G4
Elkhorn → 40 E6
Elkin 43 G5
Elkins 42 F6
Elko 38 F6
Ellendale 40 B5
Ellensburg 38 C3
Ellenville 42 E8
Ellery, Mt. 32 C4
Ellesmere, L. 33 M4
Ellesmere I. 4 B4
Ellesmere Port 8 D5
Ellice Is. = Tuvalu ■ 35 H9
Elliot Lake 37 D11
Ellis 40 F5
Elliston 32 B1
Ellisville 41 K10
Ellon 10 D6
Ellsworth, Kans., U.S.A. 40 F5
Ellsworth, Maine, U.S.A. 43 C11
Ellsworth Land 5 D16
Ellwood City 42 E5
Elma 38 C2
Elmhurst 42 D2
Elmira 42 D7
Elmore 32 C3
Elmshorn 16 B5
Eloy 39 K8
Eltham 33 H5
Elvas 13 C2
Elwell, L. 38 B8
Elwood, Ind., U.S.A. 42 E3
Elwood, Nebr., U.S.A. 40 E5
Ely, U.K. 9 E8
Ely, Minn., U.S.A. 40 B9
Ely, Nev., U.S.A. 38 G6
Elyria 42 E5
Emámrud 24 B4
Emden 16 B3
Emerald 30 C8
Emmeloord 16 B3
Emmetsburg 40 D7
Emmett 38 E5
Emmonak 36 B3
Empalme 44 B2
Empangeni 29 K6
Emperor Seamount Chain 34 D9
Emporia, Kans., U.S.A. 40 F6
Emporia, Va., U.S.A. 42 G7
Emporium 42 E6
Empty Quarter = Rub' al Khâlî 24 D4
Ems → 16 B3
Enard B. 10 C3
Encampment 38 F10
Encounter B. 32 C2
Enderby Land 5 C5
Enderlin 40 B6
Endicott 42 D7
Enewetak Atoll 34 F8
Enfer, Pte. d' 45 f
Engels 18 D5
Enggano 22 D2
England 41 J9
England □ 7 F6
Englewood 40 F2
English Channel 9 G6
Enid 41 G6
Ennadai 36 B9
Ennedi 27 E10
Ennis, Ireland 11 D3
Ennis, Mont., U.S.A. 38 D8
Ennis, Tex., U.S.A. 41 J6
Enniscorthy 11 D5
Enniskillen 11 B4
Ennistimon 11 D2
Enns → 16 D7
Enschede 16 B3
Ensenada 44 A1
Enshi 21 C5
Enterprise, Ala., U.S.A. 43 K3
Enterprise, Oreg., U.S.A. 38 D5
Enugu 26 G7
Eólie, Ísole 14 E6
Épernay 12 B5
Ephraim 38 G8
Ephrata 38 C4
Épinal 12 B7
Epsom 9 F7
Equatorial Guinea ■ 28 D1
Erbil = Arbil 24 B3
Erdenet 20 B5
Erebus, Mt. 5 E15
Erfurt 16 C5
Erie 42 D5
Erie, L. 42 D4
Eriboll, L. 10 C4
Erigavo 24 E4
Eriskay 10 D1
Eritrea ■ 24 D2
Erlangen 16 D5
Erne → 11 B3
Erne, Lower L. 11 B4
Erne, Upper L. 11 B4
Erode 25 D6
Errigal 11 A3
Erris Hd. 11 B1
Erzgebirge 16 C6
Erzincan 17 C6
Erzurum 17 C6
Es Saffâ' Esh Sharqîya 27 C12
Esbjerg 7 F5
Escalante 39 H8
Escalante → 39 H8
Escanaba 42 C2
Esch-sur-Alzette 16 D3
Escondido 39 K5
Escuinapa 44 C3
Escuintla 44 E6
Eşfahân 24 B4
Esha Ness 10 A7
Esk →, Cumb., U.K. 8 C4
Esk →, N. Yorks., U.K. 8 C7
Esker 37 C13
Eskilstuna 7 F7
Eskimo Pt. 36 B10
Eskişehir 17 C5
Esla → 13 B2
Esmeraldas 46 C3
Esperance 30 G3
Esperanza 5 C18
Espichel, C. 13 C1
Espinhaço, Serra do 47 G10
Espoo 7 F8
Essaouira 26 B4
Essen 16 C3
Essequibo → 46 B7
Essex □ 9 F8
Estância, Brazil 47 F11
Estância, U.S.A. 39 J11
Estelí 44 E7
Estevan 36 D9
Estherville 40 D7
Estonia ■ 7 F8
Estrela, Serra da 13 B2
Etawah 25 F8
Ethiopia ■ 24 F2
Ethiopian Highlands 22 F7
Etive, L. 10 E3
Etna 14 F6
Etolin I. 36 C6
Etosha Pan 29 H3
Etowah 43 H3
Ettrick Water 10 F5
Euboea = Évvoia 15 E11
Euclid 42 E5
Eucumbene, L. 32 C4
Eudora 41 J9
Eudunda 32 B2
Eufaula, Ala., U.S.A. 43 K3
Eufaula, Okla., U.S.A. 41 H7
Eufaula L. 41 H7
Eugene 38 E2
Eugowra 32 B4
Eulo 32 A4
Eunice, La., U.S.A. 41 K8
Eunice, N. Mex., U.S.A. 41 J3
Euphrates = Furât, Nahr al → 24 D5
Eure → 12 B4
Eureka, Calif., U.S.A. 38 F1
Eureka, Mont., U.S.A. 38 B6
Eureka, Nev., U.S.A. 38 G6
Eureka, S. Dak., U.S.A. 40 C5
Europa, Île 29 J8
Eustis 43 L5
Evanston, Ill., U.S.A. 42 D2
Evanston, Wyo., U.S.A. 38 F8
Evansville 42 G2
Everard, L. 32 B1
Everest, Mt. 25 E15
Everett 38 C2
Everglades, The 43 N5
Everglades City 43 N5
Everglades Nat. Park 43 N5
Evergreen, Ala., U.S.A. 43 K2
Evergreen, Mont., U.S.A. 38 B6
Evesham 9 E6
Évora 13 C2
Évreux 12 B4
Évvoia 15 E11
Ewe, L. 10 D3
Ewing 40 D5
Excelsior Springs 40 F7
Exeter, U.K. 9 G4
Exeter, Calif., U.S.A. 39 H4
Exeter, Nebr., U.S.A. 40 E6
Exmoor 9 F4
Exmouth 9 G4
Extremadura □ 13 C2
Exuma Sound 45 C9
Eyemouth 10 F6
Eyre (North), L. 32 A2
Eyre (South), L. 32 A2
Eyre Mts. 33 L2
Eyre Pen. 32 B2

F

F.Y.R.O.M. = Macedonia ■ 15 D9
Fabens 39 L10
Faeroe Is. = Føroyar 6 C4
Fair Haven 42 D9
Fair Hd. 11 A5
Fairbanks 36 B5
Fairbury 40 E6
Fairfield, Ala., U.S.A. 43 J2
Fairfield, Calif., U.S.A. 38 G3
Fairfield, Idaho, U.S.A. 38 E6
Fairfield, Ill., U.S.A. 42 F1
Fairfield, Iowa, U.S.A. 40 E9
Fairfield, Tex., U.S.A. 41 K7
Fairhope 43 K2
Fairlie 33 L3
Fairmont, Minn., U.S.A. 40 D7
Fairmont, W. Va., U.S.A. 42 F5
Fairplay 39 G11
Fairview 41 G5
Fairweather, Mt. 36 C6
Faisalabad 25 B4
Faith 40 C3
Fajardo 45 d
Fakenham 8 E8
Fakfak 23 D5
Falcon Reservoir 41 M5
Falfurrias 41 M5
Falkirk 10 F5
Falkland 10 E5
Falkland Is. □ 48 G5
Fall River 42 E10
Fallon 38 G4
Falls City 40 E7
Falmouth, Jamaica 44 a
Falmouth, U.K. 9 G2
Falmouth, U.S.A. 42 F3
Falun 7 F7
Fanad Hd. 11 A4
Fannich, L. 10 D3
Farah 24 B5
Farasân, Jazâ'ir 24 D3
Fareham 9 G6
Farewell, C. 33 J4
Farewell, C. = Farvel, Kap 4 D5
Farghona 18 E8
Fargo 40 B6
Faribault 40 C8
Farina 32 A2
Farmerville 41 J8
Farmington, Maine, U.S.A. 43 C10
Farmington, Mo., U.S.A. 40 G9
Farmington, N. Mex., U.S.A. 39 H9
Farmington, Utah, U.S.A. 38 F8
Farmington → 42 E9
Farmville 42 G6
Farnborough 9 F7
Farne Is. 8 B6
Farnham 9 F7
Faro 36 B6
Faro, Brazil 46 D7
Faro, Portugal 13 D2
Faroe Is. = Føroyar 6 C4
Farquhar, C. 30 D1
Farsala 15 E10
Fartak, Ra's 24 D4
Farvel, Kap 4 D5
Farwell 41 H3
Faulkton 40 C5
Favignana 14 F5
Fawn → 37 C11
Faya-Largeau 27 E9
Fayette, Ala., U.S.A. 43 J2
Fayette, Mo., U.S.A. 40 F8
Fayetteville, Ark., U.S.A. 41 G7
Fayetteville, N.C., U.S.A. 43 H6
Fayetteville, Tenn., U.S.A. 43 H2
Fdérik 26 D3
Feale → 11 D2
Fear, C. 43 J7
Feather → 38 G3
Featherston 33 J5
Fécamp 12 B4
Feira de Santana 47 F11
Felipe Carrillo Puerto 44 D7
Felixstowe 9 F9
Fengjie 21 C6
Fenton 42 D4
Fenyang 21 C6
Fergana = Farghona 18 E8
Fergus Falls 40 B6
Fermanagh □ 11 B4
Fermoy 11 D3
Fernandina Beach 43 K5
Ferndale 38 B2
Fernie 36 D8
Fernlees 30 C8
Ferriday 41 K9
Fertile 40 B6
Fès 26 B5
Fessenden 40 B5
Fetlar 10 A8
Feuilles → 37 C12
Fezzan 27 C8
Fianarantsoa 29 J9
Figeac 12 D5
Fiji ■ 35 D8
Filey 8 C7
Filey B. 8 C7
Fillmore 39 G7
Findhorn → 10 D5
Findlay 42 E4
Finger Lakes 42 D7
Finisterre, C. = Fisterra, C. 13 A1
Finland ■ 7 E9
Finland, G. of 7 F8
Finlay → 36 C7
Finley, Australia 32 C3
Finley, U.S.A. 40 B6
Finn → 11 B4
Finniss, C. 32 B1
Firat = Furât, Nahr al → 24 D5
Firenze 14 C4
Firozabad 25 F8
Fish → 29 K3
Fishguard 9 F3
Fitchburg 42 D10
Fitzgerald 43 K4
Fitzroy →, Queens., Australia 30 C9
Fitzroy →, W. Austral., Australia 30 C3
Fiume = Rijeka 14 B6
Flagstaff 39 J8
Flaming Gorge Reservoir 38 F9
Flanders = Flandre 16 C2
Flandreau 40 C6
Flathead L. 38 C6
Flattery, C. 38 B1
Flatwoods 42 F4
Fleetwood 8 D4
Flensburg 16 A5
Flers 12 B3
Fleurieu Pen. 32 C2
Flin Flon 36 C9
Flinders → 30 B7
Flinders Group 30 A7
Flinders I., S. Austral., Australia 32 B1
Flinders I., Tas., Australia 30 G4
Flinders Ranges 32 B2
Flinders Reefs 30 B9
Flint, U.K. 8 D4
Flint, U.S.A. 42 D4
Flint → 43 K3
Flint I. 35 J12
Flintshire □ 8 D4
Flodden 8 B5
Floodwood 40 B8
Flora 42 F1
Florala 43 K2
Florence = Firenze 14 C4
Florence, Ala., U.S.A. 43 H2
Florence, Ariz., U.S.A. 39 K8
Florence, Colo., U.S.A. 40 F2
Florence, Oreg., U.S.A. 38 E1
Florence, S.C., U.S.A. 43 H6
Florence, L. 32 A2
Flores 44 D6
Flores Sea 23 D4
Floresville 41 L5
Florianópolis 48 B7
Florida, Cuba 45 B9
Florida □ 43 L5
Florida, Straits of 45 N5
Florida Keys 43 N5
Floydada 41 J4
Fly → 30 B7
Focşani 15 B12
Fóggia 14 D6
Foix 12 E4
Foley 43 K2
Folkestone 9 F9
Fond-du-Lac, Canada 36 C9
Fond du Lac, U.S.A. 42 D1
Fontainebleau 12 B5
Fontenay-le-Comte 12 C3
Foochow = Fuzhou 21 D6
Forbes 32 B4
Ford's Bridge 32 A4
Fordyce 41 J8
Forel, Mt. 4 C6
Forest 41 J10
Forest City, Iowa, U.S.A. 40 D8
Forest City, N.C., U.S.A. 43 H5
Forest Grove 38 D2
Forestier Pen. 32 D4
Forfar 10 E6
Forks 38 C1
Forlì 14 B5
Formby Pt. 8 D4
Formentera 13 C6
Formia 14 D5
Formosa = Taiwan ■ 21 D7
Formosa 48 B5
Føroyar 6 C4
Forres 10 D5
Forrest City 41 H9
Forsayth 30 B7
Forsyth 38 C10
Fort Albany 37 C11
Fort Augustus 10 D4
Fort Benton 38 C8
Fort Bragg 38 G2
Fort Bridger 38 F8
Fort Chipewyan 36 C8
Fort Collins 40 E2
Fort Davis 41 K3
Fort-de-France 45 c
Fort Defiance 39 J9
Fort Dodge 40 D7
Fort Fairfield 43 B12
Fort Good-Hope 36 B7
Fort Kent 43 B11
Fort Klamath 38 E2
Fort Laramie 40 D2
Fort Lauderdale 43 M5
Fort Liard 36 B7
Fort Lupton 40 E2
Fort Mackay 36 C8
Fort Macleod 36 D8
Fort McMurray 36 C8
Fort Madison 40 E9
Fort Meade 43 M5
Fort Morgan 40 E3
Fort Myers 43 M5
Fort Nelson 36 C7
Fort Nelson → 36 C7
Fort Payne 43 H3
Fort Peck 38 B10
Fort Peck Dam 38 C10
Fort Peck L. 38 C10
Fort Pierce 43 M5
Fort Pierre 40 C4
Fort Providence 36 B8
Fort St. John 36 C7
Fort Scott 41 G7
Fort Simpson 36 B7
Fort Smith, Canada 36 B8
Fort Smith, U.S.A. 41 H7
Fort Stockton 41 K3
Fort Sumner 41 H2
Fort Thompson 40 C5
Fort Walton Beach 43 K2
Fort Wayne 42 E3
Fort William 10 E3
Fort Worth 41 J6
Fort Yates 40 B4
Fort Yukon 36 B5
Fortaleza 47 D11
Forth → 10 E5
Forth, Firth of 10 E6
Fortrose 10 D4
Fortuna, Calif., U.S.A. 38 F1
Fortuna, N. Dak., U.S.A. 40 A3
Foshan 21 D6
Fossano 12 D7
Fosston 40 B7
Fostoria 42 E4
Fougères 12 B3
Foula 10 B6
Foulness I. 9 F8
Fountain 40 F2
Fouta Djalon 26 F3
Foveaux Str. 33 M2
Fowey 9 G3
Fowler 40 F2
Fowlers B. 31 F5
Foxe Basin 37 B12
Foxe Chan. 37 B11
Foxe Pen. 37 B12
Foxton 33 J5
Foyle, Lough 11 A4
Foynes 11 D2
France ■ 12 C5
Franche-Comté 12 C6
Francis Case, L. 40 D5
Francistown 29 J5
Frankfort, Ky., U.S.A. 42 F3
Frankfort, Kans., U.S.A. 40 F6
Frankfurt, Brandenburg, Germany 16 B7
Frankfurt, Hessen, Germany 16 C4
Franklin, Ky., U.S.A. 43 G2
Franklin, La., U.S.A. 41 L9
Franklin, N.H., U.S.A. 42 D10
Franklin, Nebr., U.S.A. 40 E5
Franklin, Pa., U.S.A. 42 E6
Franklin, Tenn., U.S.A. 43 H2
Franklin, Va., U.S.A. 42 G7
Franklin, W. Va., U.S.A. 42 F6
Franklin B. 36 B7
Franklin D. Roosevelt L. 38 B4
Franklin Mts. 36 B7
Franklin Str. 36 A10
Franz Josef Land = Frantsa Iosifa, Zemlya 18 A6
Frantsa Iosifa, Zemlya 18 A6
Fraser → 36 D7
Fraserburgh 10 D6
Frederick, Md., U.S.A. 42 F7
Frederick, Okla., U.S.A. 41 H5
Frederick, S. Dak., U.S.A. 40 C5
Fredericksburg, Tex., U.S.A. 41 K5

Fredericksburg, Va., U.S.A. 42 F7
Fredericktown 41 G9
Fredericton 7 F6 (?)
Frederikshavn 7 F6
Fredonia, Ariz., U.S.A. 39 H7
Fredonia, Kans., U.S.A. 41 G6
Fredonia, N.Y., U.S.A. 42 D6
Fredrikstad 7 F6
Free State □ 29 K5
Freeman 40 D6
Freeport, Bahamas 45 B9
Freeport, Ill., U.S.A. 40 D10
Freeport, N.Y., U.S.A. 42 E9
Freeport, Tex., U.S.A. 41 L7
Freetown 26 G3
Fréjus 12 E7
Fremont, Calif., U.S.A. 38 H3
Fremont, Mich., U.S.A. 42 D3
Fremont, Nebr., U.S.A. 40 E6
Fremont, Ohio, U.S.A. 42 E4
Fremont → 39 G8
French Guiana ■ 46 C8
French Polynesia ■ 35 K13
Frenchman Cr. →, N. Amer. 38 B10
Frenchman Cr. →, U.S.A. 40 E4
Fresnillo 44 C4
Fresno 39 H4
Fresno Reservoir 38 B9
Freycinet Pen. 32 D4
Fria, C. 29 H2
Friendly Is. = Tonga ■ 35 D9
Frio → 41 L5
Friona 41 H3
Fritch 41 H4
Frobisher B. 37 B13
Frobisher L. 36 C9
Frome 9 F5
Frome → 9 G5
Frome, L. 32 B2
Front Royal 42 F6
Frosinone 14 D5
Frostburg 42 F6
Frunze = Bishkek 18 E8
Frýdek-Místek 16 D9
Fuengirola 13 D3
Fuerte → 44 B3
Fuhai 20 B3
Fujian □ 21 D6
Fujin 21 B8
Fukui 22 F6
Fukuoka 21 C7
Fukushima 22 F7
Fukuyama 21 C7
Fulda 16 C4
Fulda → 16 C4
Fullerton 40 E6
Fulton, Mo., U.S.A. 40 F9
Fulton, N.Y., U.S.A. 42 D7
Fundy, B. of 37 D13
Furāt, Nahr al → 24 D5
Furneaux Group 30 G4
Fürth 16 D5
Fury and Hecla Str. 37 B11
Fushun 21 B7
Futian 21 F11
Futuna 35 J9
Fuxin 21 B7
Fuyang 21 C6
Fuyu 21 B7
Fuzhou 21 D6
Fylde 8 D5
Fyne, L. 10 F3

G

Gabès 27 B8
Gabès, G. de 27 B8
Gaborone 29 J5
Gabrovo 15 C11
Gadag 25 D6
Gadsden 43 H3
Gaffney 43 H5
Gagnon 37 C13
Gaillimh = Galway 11 C2
Gainesville, Fla., U.S.A. 43 L4
Gainesville, Ga., U.S.A. 43 H4
Gainesville, Tex., U.S.A. 41 J6
Gainsborough 8 D7
Gairdner, L. 32 B2
Gairloch, L. 10 D3
Galapagos = Colón, Arch. de 35 H18
Galashiels 10 F6
Galați 15 B13
Galdhøpiggen 7 E5
Galena 36 B4
Galesburg 40 E9
Galicia □ 13 A2
Galle 25 E7
Galley Hd. 11 E3
Gallatin 43 G2
Gallipoli = Gelibolu 15 D12
Gallipolis 42 F4
Gällivare 6 B10
Galloway 10 G4
Galloway, Mull of 10 G4
Gallup 39 J9
Galty Mts. 11 D3
Galtymore 11 D3
Galva 40 E9
Galveston 41 L7
Galveston B. 41 L7
Galway 11 C2
Galway □ 11 C2
Galway B. 11 C2
Gambia ■ 26 F2
Gambia → 26 F2
Gambier, C. 30 B5
Gambier Is. 32 C2
Gan Jiang → 21 D6
Ganado 39 J9
Gand = Gent 16 C2
Gander 37 D14
Ganga → 25 G8
Ganganagar 25 E4
Ganges = Ganga → 25 G8
Gangtok 25 F16
Gannett Peak 38 E9
Gansu □ 20 C5
Ganzhou 21 D6
Gao 26 E5
Gap 12 D7
Garberville 38 F2
Garda, L. di 12 B4
Garden City, Kans., U.S.A. 41 G4
Garden City, Tex., U.S.A. 41 K4
Gardiner, Maine, U.S.A. 43 C11
Gardiner, Mont., U.S.A. 38 D8
Garforth 8 D6
Garland, Tex., U.S.A. 41 J6
Garland, Utah, U.S.A. 38 F7
Garmo, Qullai = Kommunizma, Pik 18 F8
Garnett 40 F7
Garoe 24 F4

Garonne → 12 D3
Garrison, Mont., U.S.A. 38 C7
Garrison, N. Dak., U.S.A. 40 B4
Garron Pt. 11 A6
Garry → 10 E5
Garry, L. 36 B9
Garvie Mts. 33 L2
Garzê 20 C5
Garzón 12 E4
Gascogne 12 E4
Gascogne, G. de 12 D2
Gascony = Gascogne 12 E4
Gaspé 37 D13
Gaspé, Pén. de 37 D13
Gasteiz = Vitoria-Gasteiz 13 A4
Gastonia 43 H5
Gatehouse of Fleet 10 G4
Gateshead 8 C6
Gatesville 32 A5
Gatton 33 D8
Gau 33 D8
Gävle 7 E7
Gawler 32 B2
Gaxun Nur 20 B5
Gaylord 42 C3
Gaylord 32 A5
Gaza 17 D4
Gaziantep 17 C5
Gcuwa 29 L5
Gdańsk 16 A9
Gdańska, Zatoka 16 A9
Gdynia 16 A9
Gebe 23 C4
Gedser 7 G6
Geelong 30 H7
Gejiu 21 D5
Geita 28 E6
Gelibolu 15 D12
Gelsenkirchen 16 C3
General Santos 23 C4
Genesee 42 D7
Geneseo, Ill., U.S.A. 40 E9
Geneseo, N.Y., U.S.A. 42 D7
Geneva, Ala., U.S.A. 43 K3
Geneva = Genève 12 C7
Geneva, N.Y., U.S.A. 42 D7
Geneva, Ohio, U.S.A. 42 E5
Geneva, L. = Léman, ... 12 C7
Geneva, L. 42 D7
Genève 12 C7
Gennargentu, Mti. di 14 D3
Genoa = Génova 12 D8
Genoa, Australia 32 C4
Genoa, U.S.A. 40 E6
Génova 12 D8
Gent 16 C1
George 29 L4
George → 37 C13
George, L., N.S.W., Australia 32 C4
George, L., S. Austral., Australia 32 C4
George, L., Fla., U.S.A. 43 L5
George, L., N.Y., U.S.A. 42 D9
George Sound 33 L1
George Town, Australia 32 C4
George Town, Malaysia 23 C2
George V Land 1 D14
George West 41 L5
Georgetown, Guyana 46 B7
Georgetown, Colo., U.S.A. 38 G11
Georgetown, Ky., U.S.A. 42 F3
Georgetown, Ohio, U.S.A. 42 F4
Georgetown, S.C., U.S.A. 43 J6
Georgetown, Tex., U.S.A. 41 K6
Georgia □ 43 K5
Georgia ■ 37 D11
Gera 16 C6
Geraldine 33 K3
Geraldton 30 F1
Gereshk 24 B5
Gering 38 F4
Gerlach 38 F4
Germantown 41 M10
Germany ■ 16 C6
Germiston 29 K5
Gerona = Girona 13 B7
Getafe 13 B4
Gettysburg, Pa., U.S.A. 42 F7
Gettysburg, S. Dak., U.S.A. 40 C5
Geyser 38 C8
Ghana ■ 26 G5
Ghanzi 29 J4
Ghawdex = Gozo 14 F6
Ghazâl, Bahr el → 27 G12
Ghazni 24 B5
Ghent = Gent 16 C1
Giants Causeway 11 A5
Gibbon 40 E5
Gibraltar 13 E3
Gibraltar, Str. of 13 E3
Gibson Desert 30 E4
Giddings 41 K6
Gifu 19 B5
Gigha 10 F3
Gijón 13 A3
Gila → 39 K6
Gila Bend 39 K7
Gila Bend Mts. 39 K7
Gilbert Is. 34 G9
Gilgandra 32 B4
Gilgit 25 B6
Gillam 36 B10
Gilles, L. 32 B2
Gillette 40 C2
Gillingham 9 F8
Gilroy 39 H3
Gimie, Mt 44 f
Gin Gin 32 A5
Girard 41 G7
Girdle Ness 10 D6
Girona 13 B7
Gironde → 12 D3
Girvan 10 F4
Gisborne 31 H14
Gisenyi 28 E5
Giza = El Gîza 27 C12
Gizhiga 19 C17

Glendo 40 D2
Gleneig → 10 D3
Glengarriff 11 E2
Glenmorgan 32 A4
Glennallen 36 B5
Glennamaddy 11 C3
Glenns Ferry 38 E6
Glenreagh 32 B5
Glenrothes 10 E5
Glens Falls 42 D9
Glenties 11 B3
Glenville 38 C4
Glenwood, Ark., U.S.A. 41 H8
Glenwood, Iowa, U.S.A. 40 E7
Glenwood, Minn., U.S.A. 40 C7
Glenwood Springs 38 G10
Gliwice 16 C9
Głogów 16 C8
Glomma → 7 F6
Glossop 8 D6
Gloucester, Australia 32 B5
Gloucester, U.K. 9 F5
Gloucester Point 42 G7
Gloucestershire □ 9 F5
Goa □ 25 D6
Goalen Hd. 32 C5
Goat Fell 10 F3
Gobabis 29 J3
Gobi 21 B6
Godavari → 25 D7
Godhra 24 H8
Gods → 36 B10
Gods L. 36 C10
Godthåb = Nuuk 37 B14
Goeie Hoop, Kaap die = Good Hope, C. of 29 L3
Gogebic, L. 40 B10
Goiânia 47 G9
Goio-Erê 48 A6
Golconda 38 F5
Gold Beach 38 E1
Gold Coast, Australia 30 F9
Gold Coast, W. Afr. 26 H5
Gold Hill 38 E2
Golden 36 C8
Golden Gate 38 H2
Golden Vale 11 D3
Goldendale 38 D3
Goldfield 39 H5
Goldsboro 43 H7
Goldsmith 41 K3
Goldthwaite 41 K5
Goliad 41 L6
Golspie 10 D5
Gomel = Homyel 18 D4
Gómez Palacio 44 B4
Gonâbad 24 B4
Gonaïves 45 D10
Gonbei 21 G10
Gonghe 20 C5
Gonghe 21 F10
Gongolgon 32 B4
Gonzales, Calif., U.S.A. 39 H3
Gonzales, Tex., U.S.A. 41 L6
Good Hope, C. of 29 L3
Gooding 38 E6
Goodland 40 F4
Goodooga 32 A4
Goole 8 D7
Goolgowi 32 B4
Goomalling 30 F2
Goondiwindi 30 A5
Goose Creek 38 F7
Goose L. 38 F3
Gorakhpur 25 C7
Gordon 40 D3
Gordon → 32 G4
Gore 33 M2
Gorey 11 D5
Gorgān 24 B4
Gorgān 24 B4
Gorki = Nizhniy Novgorod 18 C5
Gorkiy = Nizhniy Novgorod 18 C5
Görlitz 16 C7
Gorlovka = Horlivka 19 E6
Gorontalo 23 C4
Gort 11 C3
Gorzów Wielkopolski 16 B7
Gosford 32 B5
Goshen 42 E3
Gosport 9 G6
Göta kanal 7 F6
Göteborg 7 F6
Gotha 16 C5
Gothenburg = Göteborg 7 F6
Gothenburg 40 E4
Gotland 7 F7
Göttingen 16 C4
Gottwaldov = Zlín 16 D8
Gouda 16 B2
Gough I. 2 G9
Gouin, Rés. 37 D12
Goulburn 32 B4
Goulimine 26 C3
Gourock 32 A4
Gove 30 C6
Governador Valadares 47 G10
Gowanda 42 D6
Gower 9 F3
Gowna, L. 11 C4
Goyder Lagoon 32 A2
Gozo 14 F6
Graaff-Reinet 29 L4
Gracias a Dios, C. 45 D8
Grady 41 H3
Grafham Water 9 E7
Grafton, Australia 30 F9
Grafton, N. Dak., U.S.A. 40 A6
Grafton, W. Va., U.S.A. 42 F5
Graham 41 J5
Graham Land 6 D3
Grahamstown 29 L4
Grain Coast 26 H3
Grampian Mts. 10 E5
Grampians, The 32 C3
Gran Canaria 26 C2
Gran Chaco 48 B3
Gran Sasso d'Italia 14 C5
Granada, Nic. 45 E7
Granada, Spain 13 D4
Granard 11 C4
Granbury 41 J5
Granby, Canada 37 D12
Granby, U.S.A. 38 F11
Grand → 40 C4
Grand Bahama 45 B9
Grand Bourg 44 b
Grand Canyon 39 H7
Grand Canyon Nat. Park 39 H7
Grand Centre 36 C6
Grand Coulee 38 C4
Grand Coulee Dam 38 C4
Grand Falls 37 D14
Grand Falls-Windsor 37 D14
Grand Forks 40 B6
Grand Haven 42 D2
Grand I. 42 D6
Grand Island 40 E5
Grand Isle 41 L10
Grand Junction 38 G9
Grand L. 42 C4
Grand Lake 38 F11
Grand Marais, Canada 42 B3
Grand Marais, U.S.A. 40 B9
Grand Portage 42 B3
Grand Prairie 41 J6
Grand Rapids, Canada 36 C10
Grand Rapids, Mich., U.S.A. 42 D2
Grand Rapids, Minn., U.S.A. 40 B8

Grand St-Bernard, Col du 12 D7
Grand Teton 38 E8
Grand Teton Nat. Park 38 E8
Grand Union Canal 9 E7
Grand-Vigie, Pte. de la 44 a
Grande, Rio → 41 N6
Grande Baleine, R. de la → 37 C12
Grande Prairie 36 B5
Grande-Terre, I. 44 b
Grandfalls 41 K3
Grandview 38 C4
Grangemouth 10 E5
Granger 38 F9
Grangeville 38 D5
Granite City 40 F9
Granite Falls 40 C7
Granite Pk. 38 D9
Grant 40 E4
Grant, Mt. 38 G4
Grant City 40 E7
Grant Range 39 G6
Grantham 8 E7
Grantown-on-Spey 10 D5
Grants 39 J10
Grants Pass 38 E2
Grantsville 38 F7
Granville, N. Dak., U.S.A. 40 A4
Granville, N.Y., U.S.A. 42 D9
Grass Range 38 C9
Grass Valley, Calif., U.S.A. 38 G3
Grass Valley, Oreg., U.S.A. 38 D3
Grasse 12 E7
Grassflat 42 E6
Graulhet 12 E4
Gravelbourg 36 D9
Gravenhurst 42 B5
's-Gravenhage 16 B2
Gravesend, Australia 32 A5
Gravesend, U.K. 9 F8
Grayling 42 C3
Grays Harbor 38 C1
Grays L. 38 E8
Graz 16 E8
Great Abaco I. 45 B9
Great Australian Bight 30 G5
Great Barrier I. 31 G5
Great Barrier Reef 30 C4
Great Basin 38 G5
Great Basin Nat. Park 38 G6
Great Bear → 36 B7
Great Bear L. 36 B7
Great Bend 40 F5
Great Blasket I. 11 D1
Great Camanoe 45 e
Great Channel 25 E8
Great Driffield = Driffield 8 C7
Great Exuma I. 45 C9
Great Falls 38 C8
Great Inagua I. 45 C10
Great Karoo 29 L4
Great Lake 32 G4
Great Malvern 9 E5
Great Miami → 42 F3
Great Ormes Head 8 D4
Great Ouse → 8 E8
Great Pedro Bluff 44 a
Great Plains 35 A6
Great Salt L. 38 F7
Great Salt Lake Desert 38 F7
Great Salt Plains L. 41 G5
Great Sandy Desert 30 E3
Great Skellig 11 E1
Great Slave L. 36 B8
Great Smoky Mts. Nat. Park 43 H4
Great Snow Mt. 36 B4
Great Stour → 9 F9
Great Victoria Desert 30 F4
Great Wall 21 C5
Great Whernside 8 C6
Great Yarmouth 8 E9
Greater Antilles 45 D10
Greater London □ 9 F7
Greater Manchester □ 8 D5
Greater Sunda Is. 23 D3
Greece ■ 15 E9
Greeley, Colo., U.S.A. 40 E2
Greeley, Nebr., U.S.A. 40 E5
Green → 38 G9
Green → Ky., U.S.A. 42 G2
Green → Utah, U.S.A. 38 G9
Green B. 42 C2
Green Bay 42 C2
Green Cove Springs 43 L5
Green River, Utah, U.S.A. 38 G8
Green River, Wyo., U.S.A. 38 F9
Green Valley 39 L8
Greenbush 40 A6
Greencastle 42 F2
Greenfield, Ind., U.S.A. 42 F3
Greenfield, Iowa, U.S.A. 40 E7
Greenfield, Mass., U.S.A. 42 D9
Greenfield, Mo., U.S.A. 41 G8
Greenland ■ 6 C4
Greenland Sea 6 B6
Greenock 11 B5
Greenore 11 B5
Greenore Pt. 11 D5
Greensboro, Ga., U.S.A. 43 J4
Greensboro, N.C., U.S.A. 43 G6
Greensburg, Ind., U.S.A. 42 F3
Greensburg, Kans., U.S.A. 41 G5
Greensburg, Pa., U.S.A. 42 E6
Greenstone Pt. 10 D3
Greenville, Maine, U.S.A. 43 C11
Greenville, Mich., U.S.A. 42 D3
Greenville, Miss., U.S.A. 41 J9
Greenville, N.C., U.S.A. 43 H7
Greenville, Ohio, U.S.A. 42 E3
Greenville, Tenn., U.S.A. 43 G4
Greenville, Tex., U.S.A. 41 J6
Greenwich □ 9 F8
Greenwood, Ark., U.S.A. 41 H7
Greenwood, S.C., U.S.A. 43 J5
Gregory 40 D5
Gregory → 30 D6
Grenada 44 H4
Grenada ■ 44 H4
Grenfell 32 B4
Grenoble 12 D6
Grenville, C. 30 A7
Gresham 38 D2
Gretna 10 F5
Grey → 33 K3
Grey Ra. 32 A3
Greymouth 31 K3
Greystones 11 C5
Gridley 38 G3
Griffin 43 J3
Griffith 32 B4
Grimsby 8 D7
Grimsey 7 C5
Grinnell 40 E8
Gris-Nez, C. 12 A4
Grodno = Hrodna 7 B13

Groesbeck 41 K6
Groningen 16 B3
Groom 41 H4
Groote Eylandt 30 C6
Gros Islet 45 f
Gros Piton 45 f
Gros Piton Pt. 45 f
Groton 42 D7
Grove Hill 43 K2
Groveton 42 C10
Groznyy 19 F8
Grudziądz 16 B9
Grundy Center 40 D8
Gryazi 18 D6
Guadalajara, Mexico 44 C4
Guadalajara, Spain 13 B4
Guadalcanal 35 B8
Guadalete → 13 D2
Guadalquivir → 13 D2
Guadalupe = Guadeloupe ■ 44 b
Guadalupe, Sierra de 13 C3
Guadalupe Mts. Nat. Park 41 K2
Guadalupe Peak 41 K2
Guadarrama, Sierra de 13 B4
Guadeloupe ■ 44 b
Guadiana → 13 D2
Guadix 13 D4
Guajará-Mirim 46 F5
Gualeguaychú 48 C5
Guam ■ 34 F6
Guamúchil 44 B3
Guanabacoa 45 C8
Guanajuato 44 C4
Guane 45 C8
Guangdong □ 21 D6
Guangxi Zhuangzu Zizhiqu □ 21 D5
Guangzhou 21 D6
Guánica 45 d
Guantánamo 45 C9
Guaporé → 46 F5
Guaqui 46 G5
Guarapuava 48 B6
Guarda 13 B2
Guardafui, C. = Asir, Ras 24 E5
Guatemala 44 E6
Guatemala ■ 44 D6
Guaviare → 46 C5
Guayama 45 d
Guayaquil 46 D3
Guayaquil, G. de 46 D2
Guaymas 44 B2
Güeret 12 C4
Guernsey, U.K. 9 H5
Guernsey, U.S.A. 40 D2
Guildford 9 F7
Guilin 21 D6
Guinea ■ 26 F3
Guinea, Gulf of 5 D10
Guinea-Bissau ■ 26 F3
Güines 45 C8
Guingamp 12 B2
Guiyang 20 D5
Guizhou □ 20 D5
Gujarat □ 25 C6
Gujranwala 24 G8
Gujrat 24 G8
Gulbarga 25 D6
Gulf, The 24 C4
Gulfport 41 K10
Gulgong 32 B4
Gull L. 40 B7
Gümüshane 17 F6
Gunisao → 36 C10
Gunnbjørn Fjeld 6 C5
Gunnedah 32 B5
Gunnewin 32 A4
Gunningbar Cr. → 32 B4
Gunnison, Colo., U.S.A. 38 G10
Gunnison, Utah, U.S.A. 38 G8
Gunnison → 38 G9
Guntakal 25 D6
Guntersville 43 H2
Guntur 25 D7
Gurley 32 A4
Gürün 17 G6
Guryev = Atyrau 19 E9
Gusinoozersk 19 D11
Gustine 39 H3
Guthrie, Okla., U.S.A. 41 H6
Guthrie, Tex., U.S.A. 41 J4
Guttenberg 40 D9
Guyana ■ 46 C7
Guyenne 12 D4
Guymon 41 G4
Guyra 32 B5
Gwa 25 D8
Gwabegar 32 B4
Gwādar 24 C5
Gwalior 24 G11
Gweebarra B. 11 B3
Gweedore 11 A3
Gweru 29 H5
Gwinn 42 B2
Gwydir → 32 A4
Gwynedd □ 8 E4
Gyandzha = Gäncä 19 F8
Gympie 30 F9
Győr 16 E8
Gyumri 17 B6

H

Ha Tinh 23 B2
Ha'apai Group 31 D16
Haarlem 16 B3
Haast → 33 K2
Hab Nadi Chauki 24 H5
Hadejia 27 F7
Haden 32 A5
Hadhramaut = Hadramawt 24 D4
Hadrian's Wall 8 B5
Haeju 21 C7
Hafar al Bāţin 24 C3
Hafizabad 24 G8
Hafnarfjörður 7 D2
Hagen 16 C3
Hagerman 41 J2
Hagerstown 42 F7
Hags Hd. 11 D2
Hague, C. de la 12 B3
Hague, The = 's-Gravenhage 16 B2
Haguenau 12 B7
Haifa = Hefa 17 D4
Haikou 21 D6
Ha'il 24 C3
Hailar 21 B6
Hailey 38 E6
Hailuoto 7 D8
Hainan □ 21 E5
Haines 36 C6
Haines City 43 L5
Haines Junction 36 B6
Haiphong 20 D5
Haiti ■ 45 D10
Hajdúböszörmény 16 E10
Hakodate 18 F12
Halab 17 C5
Halberstadt 16 C5
Halcombe 33 J5
Halden 7 F6
Haldia 25 C7
Haldwani 25 C7
Hale → 30 C5
Haleakala Crater 45 H16
Halesowen 9 E5
Halfmoon Bay 33 M2
Haliburton 42 A6
Halifax, Australia 30 C7
Halifax, Canada 37 D13
Halifax, U.K. 8 D6
Halifax B. 30 C7
Hall Pen. 37 B13
Halle 16 C5
Hallett 32 B2
Hallettsville 41 L6
Halls Creek 30 C4
Halmahera 23 C4
Halmstad 7 F6
Halstad 40 B6
Hälsingborg = Helsingborg 7 F6
Halti 7 B8
Halton □ 8 D5
Haltwhistle 8 C5
Hamā 17 D5
Hamadān 24 B3
Hamāh 17 D5
Hamamatsu 19 B5
Hamar 7 E6
Hamburg, Germany 16 B5
Hamburg, Ark., U.S.A. 41 J9
Hamburg, N.Y., U.S.A. 42 D6
Häme 7 E8
Hämeenlinna 7 E8
Hameln 16 B4
Hamersley Ra. 30 E2
Hami 20 B4

Hamilton, Australia 32 C3
Hamilton, Canada 37 D12
Hamilton, N.Z. 31 H14
Hamilton, U.K. 10 F4
Hamilton, Ala., U.S.A. 43 H1
Hamilton, Mont., U.S.A. 38 C6
Hamilton, N.Y., U.S.A. 42 D8
Hamilton, Ohio, U.S.A. 42 F3
Hamilton, Tex., U.S.A. 41 K5
Hamilton → 32 C3
Hamley Bridge 32 B2
Hamlin 41 J4
Hamm 16 C3
Hammerfest 7 C8
Hammond, Ind., U.S.A. 42 E2
Hammond, La., U.S.A. 41 K9
Hammonton 42 F8
Hampden 33 L3
Hampshire □ 9 F6
Hampshire Downs 9 F6
Hampton, Ark., U.S.A. 41 J8
Hampton, Iowa, U.S.A. 40 D8
Hampton, S.C., U.S.A. 43 J5
Hampton, Va., U.S.A. 42 G7
Hancock 42 B10
Handa 19 B5
Handan 21 C6
Hangayn Nuruu 20 B4
Hangchou = Hangzhou 21 C7
Hangzhou 21 C7
Hangzhou Wan 21 C7
Hankinson 40 B6
Hanko 7 F7
Hanna, Canada 36 C6
Hanna, U.S.A. 38 F10
Hannah B. 37 C12
Hannibal 40 F9
Hannover 16 B4
Hanoi 20 D5
Hanover = Hannover 16 B4
Hanover, N.H., U.S.A. 42 D9
Hanover, Pa., U.S.A. 42 F7
Hans Lollik I. 45 e
Hanson 32 A2
Hanzhong 20 C5
Haparanda 7 D8
Happy 41 H4
Happy Camp 38 F2
Happy Valley-Goose Bay 37 C13
Har Hu 20 C4
Har Us Nuur 20 B4
Harare 29 H6
Harbin 21 B7
Harbor Beach 42 D4
Hardangerfjorden 7 E5
Hardin 38 D10
Harding 29 K6
Hardwar = Haridwar 25 C6
Harer 24 D3
Hargeisa 24 E3
Hari → 23 D2
Haridwar 25 C6
Harirūd → 24 B5
Harlem 38 B9
Harlingen 41 M6
Harlow 9 F8
Harlowton 38 C9
Harney Basin 38 E4
Harney L. 38 E4
Harney Peak 40 D3
Härnösand 7 E7
Haroldswick 10 A8
Harp → 37 C12
Harris 10 D2
Harris, Sd. of 10 D1
Harrisburg, Ill., U.S.A. 41 G10
Harrisburg, Nebr., U.S.A. 40 E3
Harrisburg, Pa., U.S.A. 42 E7
Harrison, Ark., U.S.A. 41 G8
Harrison, Nebr., U.S.A. 40 D3
Harrison, C. 37 C14
Harrisonville 40 F7
Harriston 42 D4
Harrisville 42 C4
Harrogate 8 D6
Harrow □ 9 F7
Harry S. Truman Reservoir 40 F7
Hart 42 D2
Hart, L. 32 B2
Hartford, Conn., U.S.A. 42 E9
Hartford, Ky., U.S.A. 42 G2
Hartford, S. Dak., U.S.A. 40 D6
Hartford, Wis., U.S.A. 40 D10
Hartford City 42 E3
Hartland Pt. 9 F3
Hartlepool 8 C6
Hartney 40 A8
Hartselle 43 H2
Hartshorne 41 H7
Hartsville 43 H5
Hartwell 43 H4
Harvey, Ill., U.S.A. 42 E2
Harvey, N. Dak., U.S.A. 40 B5
Harwich 9 F9
Haryana □ 25 C6
Harz 16 C5
Hasa □ 24 C3
Haskell 41 J5
Haslemere 9 F7
Hassan 25 D6
Hasselt 16 C3
Hastings 32 C4
Hastings, N.Z. 31 H6
Hastings, U.K. 9 G8
Hastings, Mich., U.S.A. 42 D3
Hastings, Minn., U.S.A. 40 C8
Hastings, Nebr., U.S.A. 40 E5
Hastings Ra. 32 B5
Hat Yai 23 C2
Hatay = Antalya 17 G5
Hatch 39 K10
Hatfield P.O. 32 B3
Hatgal 20 A5
Hathras 25 C6
Hatteras, C. 43 H8
Hattiesburg 41 K10
Haugesund 7 F5
Haukipudas 7 D8
Hauraki G. 33 G5
Haut Atlas 26 B4
Hauts Plateaux 26 B5
Havana = La Habana 45 C8
Havana 40 E9
Havant 9 G7
Havasu, L. 39 J6
Havel → 16 B6
Havelock, N.Z. 33 J4
Havelock, Canada 42 B7
Haverford 42 D10
Haverhill 42 D10
Havering □ 9 F8
Havırga 21 B6
Havre 38 B9
Havre-Aubert 37 C13
Havre-St-Pierre 37 C13
Haw → 43 H6
Hawaii □ 45 H17
Hawaii I. 45 J17
Hawaiian Is. 45 H16
Hawaiian Ridge 35 E11
Hawarden 40 D6
Hawea, L. 33 L2
Hawera 33 H5
Hawick 10 F6
Hawke B. 31 H6
Hawker 32 B2
Hawkesbury 37 D12
Hawkesbury → 32 B5
Hawkinsville 43 J4
Hawley 40 B6
Haworth 8 D6
Hawran, W. → 24 B3
Hawthorne 38 G4
Hay 32 B3
Hay →, Australia 30 C6
Hay →, Canada 36 B6
Hay-on-Wye 9 E4
Hay River 36 B8
Hay Springs 40 D3
Hayden 38 F10
Hayes → 36 B10
Hayle 9 G2
Hays 40 F5
Hayward, Calif., U.S.A. 38 H2
Hayward, Wis., U.S.A. 40 B9
Hazard 42 G4
Hazaribag 25 C7
Hazelton 43 K4
Hazelton 42 E8

Hazleton 42 E8
Healdsburg 38 G2
Healdton 41 H6
Healesville 32 C4
Heard I. 5 G13
Hearne 41 K6
Hearst 37 D11
Heart → 40 B4
Heavener 41 H7
Hebbronville 41 M5
Hebei □ 21 C6
Hebel 32 A4
Heber Springs 41 H8
Hebgen L. 38 D8
Hebrides 10 D2
Hebrides, Sea of the 10 D2
Hebron = Al Khalīl 17 D4
Hebron, Canada 37 C13
Hebron, N. Dak., U.S.A. 40 B4
Hebron, Nebr., U.S.A. 40 E6
Hecate Str. 36 C6
Hechi 20 D5
Hechuan 20 C5
Hecla 40 C5
Hecla I. 36 C10
Heerenveen 16 B3
Heerlen 16 C3
Hefa 17 D4
Hefei 21 C6
Hegang 21 B8
Heidelberg 16 D4
Heidenheim 16 D5
Heilbron 29 K5
Heilbronn 16 D4
Heilongjiang □ 21 B7
Heimaey 7 E3
Hejaz = Ḥijāz □ 24 C2
Hekou 20 D5
Helena, Ark., U.S.A. 41 H9
Helena, Mont., U.S.A. 38 C7
Helensburgh 10 E4
Helensville 33 G5
Helgeland 7 C6
Helgoland 16 A4
Heligoland B. = Deutsche Bucht 16 A4
Hellespont = Çanakkale Boğazı 15 D12
Helmand → 24 B5
Helmsdale 10 C5
Helsingborg 7 F6
Helsingfors = Helsinki 7 E9
Helsingør 7 F6
Helsinki 7 E9
Helston 9 G2
Helvellyn 8 C4
Hemel Hempstead 9 F7
Hemet 39 K5
Hemingford 40 D3
Hempstead 41 K6
Henan □ 21 C6
Henares → 13 B4
Henderson, Ky., U.S.A. 42 G2
Henderson, N.C., U.S.A. 43 G6
Henderson, Nev., U.S.A. 39 J6
Henderson, Tenn., U.S.A. 43 H1
Henderson, Tex., U.S.A. 41 J7
Hendersonville, N.C., U.S.A. 43 H4
Hendersonville, Tenn., U.S.A. 43 G2
Hengelo 16 B3
Hengyang 21 D6
Henlopen, C. 42 F8
Hennessey 41 G6
Henrietta 41 J5
Henrietta Maria, C. 37 C11
Henry 40 E10
Henryville 42 F3
Hentiyn Nuruu 21 B5
Heppner 38 D4
Hereford, U.K. 9 E5
Hereford, U.S.A. 41 H3
Herefordshire □ 9 E5
Herford 16 B4
Herington 40 F6
Herkimer 42 D8
Herm 9 H5
Hermann 40 F9
Hermidale 32 B4
Hermosillo 44 B2
Hernád → 16 D11
Herne 16 C3
Herne Bay 9 F9
Herning 7 F5
Heroica Nogales = Nogales 44 A2
Herreid 40 C4
Herrin 41 G10
Hertford 9 F7
Hertfordshire □ 9 F7
's-Hertogenbosch 16 C3
Hesperia 39 J5
Hessen □ 16 C4
Hettinger 40 C3
Hewitt 41 K6
Heyfield 32 C4
Heysham 8 C5
Heywood 32 C3
Hialeah 43 N5
Hiawatha 40 F7
Hibbing 40 B8
Hibbs B. 32 G4
Hickman 41 G10
Hickory 43 H5
Hicks, Pt. 32 C4
Hidalgo del Parral 44 B3
Higashiōsaka 19 B4
High Island Res. 21 G11
High Level 36 B5
High Point 43 H6
High Prairie 36 B5
High River 36 C6
High Wycombe 9 F7
Highland □ 10 D4
Highland Park 42 D2
Highmore 40 C5
Hiiumaa 7 F8
Ḥijāz □ 24 C2
Hildesheim 16 B5
Hill City, Idaho, U.S.A. 38 E6
Hill City, S. Dak., U.S.A. 40 D3
Hillary 43 K5
Hillcrest 45 g
Hillsboro, Kans., U.S.A. 40 F6
Hillsboro, N. Dak., U.S.A. 40 B6
Hillsboro, N.H., U.S.A. 42 D10
Hillsboro, Ohio, U.S.A. 42 F4
Hillsboro, Oreg., U.S.A. 38 D2
Hillsboro, Tex., U.S.A. 41 J6
Hillsdale 42 E3
Hillside 30 E2
Hillston 32 B4
Hilo 45 J17
Hilton 42 C7
Hilton Head Island 43 J5
Hilversum 16 B3
Himachal Pradesh □ 25 C6
Himalaya 25 C7
Himeji 19 B4
Ḥimṣ 17 D5
Hinckley, U.K. 9 E6
Hinckley, U.S.A. 40 B8
Hindu Kush 24 B6
Hinesville 43 K5
Hingham 38 B8
Hinton 42 G5
Hirosaki 18 F12
Hiroshima 19 B3
Hispaniola 45 D10
Hitachi 19 A7
Hitchin 9 F7
Hjälmaren 7 F7
Ho Chi Minh City = Thanh Pho Ho Chi Minh 23 B2
Hoare B. 37 B13
Hobart, Australia 30 J8
Hobart, U.S.A. 41 H5
Hobbs 41 J3

Hobe Sound 43 M5
Hodgson 36 C10
Hōfu 19 B2
Hogan Group 32 C4
Hoggar = Ahaggar 26 D7
Hohhot 21 B6
Hoisington 40 F5
Hokianga Harbour 33 G4
Hokitika 33 K3
Hokkaidō □ 18 F12
Holbrook, Australia 32 C4
Holbrook, U.S.A. 39 J8
Holden 38 G7
Holdenville 41 H6
Holdrege 40 E5
Holguín 45 C9
Holland 42 D2
Hollandale 41 J9
Hollidaysburg 42 E6
Hollis 41 H5
Hollister, Calif., U.S.A. 39 H3
Hollister, Idaho, U.S.A. 38 E6
Holly Hill 43 L5
Holly Springs 41 H10
Hollywood 43 N5
Holman 36 A8
Holmen 40 D9
Holstebro 7 F5
Holton 40 F7
Holy I., Angl., U.K. 8 D3
Holy I., Northumb., U.K. 8 B6
Holyhead 8 D3
Holyoke, Colo., U.S.A. 40 E3
Holyoke, Mass., U.S.A. 42 D9
Homalin 25 C8
Hombori 26 E5
Home B. 37 B13
Homer, Alaska, U.S.A. 36 C4
Homer, La., U.S.A. 41 J8
Homestead 43 N5
Homs = Ḥimṣ 17 D5
Homyel 18 D4
Hon Chong 23 B2
Honda 46 B4
Hondo 41 L5
Honduras ■ 44 D7
Honduras, G. de 44 D7
Hønefoss 7 E6
Honey L. 38 F3
Hong Kong □ 21 D6
Hongjiang 20 D5
Hongshui He → 21 D5
Hongze Hu 21 C6
Honiara 35 B8
Honiton 9 G4
Honolulu 45 H16
Honshū 19 B6
Hood, Mt. 38 D3
Hood River 38 D3
Hoodsport 38 C2
Hook Hd. 11 D5
Hooper Bay 36 B3
Hoopeston 42 E2
Hoorn 16 B3
Hoover 43 J2
Hoover Dam 39 J6
Hopedale 37 C13
Hopetoun 32 C3
Hopetown 29 K4
Hopewell 42 G7
Hopkinsville 43 G2
Hopland 38 G2
Hoquiam 38 C2
Horlick Mts. 6 E15
Horlivka 19 E6
Hormoz, Str. of 24 C4
Horn, Cape = Hornos, C. de 48 H3
Horn Head 11 A3
Hornavan 7 C7
Hornbeck 41 K8
Hornbrook 38 F2
Horncastle 8 D7
Hornos, C. de 48 H3
Hornsea 8 D7
Horqin Youyi Qianqi 21 B6
Horse Creek 38 F2
Horsham, Australia 32 C3
Horsham, U.K. 9 F7
Horton → 36 B7
Hot Creek Range 38 G6
Hot Springs, Ark., U.S.A. 41 H8
Hot Springs, S. Dak., U.S.A. 40 D3
Hotan 20 C2
Hotchkiss 39 G10
Hou Hai 21 F10
Houghton 42 B10
Houghton L. 42 C3
Houhora Heads 33 F4
Houlton 43 B12
Houma 41 L9
Houston, Mo., U.S.A. 41 G9
Houston, Tex., U.S.A. 41 L7
Hove 9 G7
Hövsgöl Nuur 20 A5
Howard, Australia 32 A5
Howard, U.S.A. 40 C6
Howe, C. 32 C5
Howell 42 D3
Howland I. 34 G10
Hoy 10 C5
Høyanger 7 E5
Hoylake 8 D4
Hpungan Pass 25 C8
Hradec Králové 16 C8
Hrodna 7 B13
Hron → 16 D9
Hsinchu 21 D7
Hua Hin 23 B1
Huai He → 21 C6
Huaihua 20 D5
Huainan 21 C6
Huajuapan de León 44 D5
Hualapai Peak 39 J7
Huallaga → 46 E3
Huambo 29 G3
Huancavelica 46 F3
Huancayo 46 F3
Huang He → 21 C6
Huangshan 21 D6
Huánuco 46 E3
Huascarán 46 E3
Huatabampo 44 B3
Hubbard 41 K6
Hubei □ 21 C6
Hubli 25 D6
Hucknall 8 D6
Huddersfield 8 D6
Hudiksvall 7 E7
Hudson → 42 E8
Hudson, Mass., U.S.A. 42 D10
Hudson, N.Y., U.S.A. 42 D9
Hudson, Wis., U.S.A. 40 C8
Hudson, Wyo., U.S.A. 38 E9
Hudson B., Nunavut, Canada 37 C11
Hudson B., Sask., Canada 36 C9
Hudson Bay 37 C11
Hudson Falls 42 D9
Hudson Str. 37 B13
Hue 23 B2
Huelva 13 D2
Huesca 13 A5
Hugh → 30 D5
Hughenden 30 E7
Hughes 32 B2
Hugo, Colo., U.S.A. 40 F3
Hugo, Okla., U.S.A. 41 H7
Hugoton 41 G4
Hui Xian 21 C6
Huila, Nevado del 46 C3
Huize 20 D5
Hull = Kingston upon Hull 8 D7
Hull 37 D12
Hulun Nur 21 B6
Humaitá 46 E6
Humansdorp 29 L4
Humber → 8 D7
Humboldt, Canada 36 C9
Humboldt, Iowa, U.S.A. 40 D7
Humboldt, Tenn., U.S.A. 41 H10
Humboldt → 38 F4

Hume, L. 32 C4
Humenné 16 D11
Humphreys Peak 39 J8
Hūn 27 C9
Hunan □ 21 D6
Hungary ■ 16 E9
Hungarford 32 A3
Hüngnam 21 C7
Hunsrück 16 D3
Hunstanton 8 E8
Hunter I. 32 G3
Hunterville 33 H5
Huntingdon 9 E7
Huntingdon 42 F6
Huntington, Ind., U.S.A. 42 E3
Huntington, Oreg., U.S.A. 38 D5
Huntington, Utah, U.S.A. 38 G8
Huntington, W. Va., U.S.A. 42 F4
Huntington Beach 39 K5
Huntly, N.Z. 33 G5
Huntly, U.K. 10 D6
Huntsville, Canada 37 D12
Huntsville, Ala., U.S.A. 43 H2
Huntsville, Tex., U.S.A. 41 K7
Huon G. 32 B1
Hurd, C. 42 C4
Hure Qi 21 C6
Hurley, N. Mex., U.S.A. 39 K9
Hurley, Wis., U.S.A. 40 B9
Huron 42 E5
Huron, Ohio, U.S.A. 42 E4
Huron, S. Dak., U.S.A. 40 C5
Huron, L. 42 C4
Hurricane 39 H7
Hurunui → 33 K4
Húsavík 7 C5
Huşi 16 E12
Hutchinson, Kans., U.S.A. 40 F6
Hutchinson, Minn., U.S.A. 40 C7
Hutton, Mt. 32 A4
Huy 16 C3
Hwang Ho = Huang He → 21 C6
Hyannis, Mass., U.S.A. 42 E10
Hyannis, Nebr., U.S.A. 40 E4
Hyargas Nuur 20 B4
Hyderabad, India 25 D6
Hyderabad, Pakistan 24 G6
Hyères 12 E7
Hyères, Îs. d' 12 E7
Hyndman Peak 38 E6
Hyrum 38 F8
Hysham 38 C10
Hythe 9 F9

I

Ialomita → 15 B13
Iaşi 16 E12
Ibadan 26 G6
Ibagué 46 C3
Ibar → 15 C9
Ibaraki 19 B4
Iberian Peninsula 4 H5
Ibiza = Eivissa 13 C6
Ica 46 F3
Içel = Mersin 17 C4
Ichihara 19 B7
Ichinomiya 19 B5
Ida Grove 40 D7
Idabel 41 J7
Idaho □ 38 D7
Idaho Falls 38 E7
Idar-Oberstein 16 D3
Idi 22 C1
Idlib 17 C5
Ife 26 G6
Igarka 18 C9
Iglésias 14 E3
Igloolik 37 B11
Igluligaarjuk 36 B10
Iguaçu → 48 B7
Iguaçu, Cat. del 48 B7
Iguala 44 D5
Iguassu = Iguaçu → 48 B7
Iijoki → 7 D9
Iisalmi 7 E9
IJsselmeer 16 B3
Ikaluktutiak 36 B9
Ikeda 19 B4
Ilagan 23 B4
Ilām 24 B3
Iława 16 B9
Île-de-France □ 12 B5
Ilford 9 F8
Ilfracombe 9 F3
Ilhéus 47 F11
Ili → 18 E8
Iligan 23 C4
Iliamna L. 36 C4
Ilkeston 8 E6
Ilkley 8 D6
Illapel 48 C2
Iller → 16 D5
Illinois □ 40 E10
Illinois → 40 F9
Ilmen, Ozero 18 C4
Iloilo 23 B4
Ilorin 26 G6
Imabari 19 B3
Imandra, L. 18 A4
Imari 19 C1
Imbil 32 A5
imeni 26 Bakinskikh Komissarov = Neftçala 24 B4
Imola 12 D9
Imperatriz 47 E9
Imperial, Calif., U.S.A. 39 K6
Imperial, Nebr., U.S.A. 40 E4
Imperial Dam 39 K6
Imphal 25 C8
Imroz = Gökçeada 15 D11
Ina 19 B5
Inangahua 33 J3
Inari 7 C9
Inarijärvi 7 C9
Inca 13 C7
Inch'ŏn 21 C7
Incline Village 38 G4
Incomáti → 29 K6
Indalsälven → 7 E7
Independence, Calif., U.S.A. 39 H4
Independence, Iowa, U.S.A. 40 D9
Independence, Kans., U.S.A. 41 G7
Independence, Mo., U.S.A. 40 F7
India ■ 25 D6
Indian → 43 M5
Indian Ocean 5 E13
Indian Springs 39 J6
Indiana 42 E6
Indiana □ 42 E3
Indianapolis 42 F2
Indianola, Iowa, U.S.A. 40 E8
Indianola, Miss., U.S.A. 41 J9
Indigirka → 19 B15
Indonesia ■ 22 D4
Indore 24 H9
Indravati → 25 D7
Indre → 12 C4
Indus → 24 G5
Indus, Mouths of the 24 H5
Inebolu 17 F5
Inglewood, Queens., Australia 32 A5
Inglewood, Vic., Australia 32 C3
Inglewood, N.Z. 33 H5
Inglewood, U.S.A. 39 K4
Ingolstadt 16 D5
Ingomar 38 C10
Ingraj Bazar 25 C7
Ingulec = Inhulec 19 E5
Inhambane 29 J7
Inharrime 29 J7
Inhulec 19 E5
Ining = Yining 18 E9
Inírida → 46 C5
Inishbofin 11 C1
Inishmore 11 C2
Inishowen Pen. 11 A4
Inishshark 11 C1
Inishturk 11 C1
Inishvickillane 11 D1
Injune 32 A4
Inland Sea = Setonaikai 19 B3
Inn → 16 D6
Innamincka 32 A3
Inner Hebrides 10 E2

Inner Mongolia = Nei Monggol Zizhiqu □ 21 B6
Innisfail 30 C7
Inny → 11 C4
Inowrocław 16 B9
Inscription, C. 30 E1
Insein 25 D8
Interlaken 12 C7
International Falls 40 A8
Inukjuak 37 C12
Inuvik 36 B6
Inveraray 10 E3
Inverbervie 10 E6
Invercargill 33 M2
Inverclyde □ 10 F4
Invergordon 10 D4
Inverness, Canada 37 D14
Inverness, U.K. 10 D4
Inverness, U.S.A. 43 L4
Inverurie 10 D6
Investigator Group 32 B1
Investigator Str. 32 C2
Inyo Mts. 39 H5
Inyokern 39 K5
Iō-Jima 19 G7
Iona 10 E2
Ionia 42 D3
Ionian Is. = Iónioi Nísoi 15 E9
Ionian Sea 14 E7
Iónioi Nísoi 15 E9
Iowa □ 40 D8
Iowa → 40 E9
Iowa City 40 E9
Iowa Falls 40 D8
Ipameri 47 G9
Ipatinga 47 G10
Ipin = Yibin 20 D5
Ipoh 23 C2
Ipswich, Australia 30 F9
Ipswich, U.K. 9 E9
Ipswich, Mass., U.S.A. 42 D10
Ipswich, S. Dak., U.S.A. 40 C5
Iqaluit 37 B13
Iquique 46 H4
Iquitos 46 D4
Iráklion 15 G11
Iran ■ 24 B4
Iran Ra. = Iran, Pegunungan 22 C3
Irānshahr 24 C5
Irapuato 44 C4
Iraq ■ 24 B3
Ireland ■ 11 C4
Iringa 28 F7
Irish Republic ■ 11 C4
Irish Sea 8 D3
Irkutsk 18 D11
Iron Baron 32 B2
Iron Gate = Portile de Fier 15 B10
Iron Knob 32 B2
Iron Mountain 42 C1
Iron River 40 B10
Ironton, Mo., U.S.A. 41 G9
Ironton, Ohio, U.S.A. 42 F4
Ironwood 40 B9
Irrara Cr. → 32 A4
Irrawaddy → 25 D8
Irtysh → 18 C7
Irumu 28 D5
Irún = Pamplona 13 A5
Irvine, U.K. 10 F4
Irvine, U.S.A. 42 G4
Irvinestown 11 B4
Irwin → 30 E1
Isabel 40 C4
Isabela 45 d
İscehisar 17 C13
İsère → 12 D6
Isérnia 14 D6
Ishikari-Wan 18 F12
Ishim → 18 D8
Ishinomaki 18 G12
Ishpeming 42 B2
Iskenderun 17 G6
Isla → 10 E5
Islamabad 24 B8
Island L. 36 C10
Island Lagoon 32 B2
Island Pond 42 C10
Islay 10 F2
Isle → 12 D3
Isle of Wight □ 9 G6
Isle Royale Nat. Park 37 B11
Ismâ'ilîya 27 B12
Israel ■ 17 D4
Issoire 12 D5
İstanbul 17 B12
İstanbul Boğazı 15 D13
Istra 16 F7
Istres 12 E6
Itabira 47 G10
Itabuna 47 F11
Itaipú, Reprêsa de 48 B6
Itajaí 48 B7
Italy ■ 14 C5
Itaperuna 47 H10
Itapicuru → 47 F11
Itapipoca 47 D11
Ithaca 42 D7
Itháki 15 E9
Ivanava 7 B14
Ivanhoe, Australia 32 B3
Ivano-Frankivsk 16 D13
Ivanovo 18 C5
Ivory Coast ■ 26 G4
Ivujivik 37 B12
Ivybridge 9 G4
Iwaki 19 A7
Iwo 26 G6
Ixtapa 44 D4
Iyo 19 C3
İzmir 17 C12
İzmit = Kocaeli 17 B13

J

Jabalpur 25 C6
Jaboatão 47 E11
Jackman 43 C10
Jacksboro 41 J5
Jackson, Barbados 44 b
Jackson, Ala., U.S.A. 43 K2
Jackson, Calif., U.S.A. 38 G3
Jackson, Ky., U.S.A. 42 G4
Jackson, Mich., U.S.A. 42 D3
Jackson, Minn., U.S.A. 40 D7
Jackson, Miss., U.S.A. 41 J9
Jackson, Mo., U.S.A. 41 G10
Jackson, Ohio, U.S.A. 42 F4
Jackson, Tenn., U.S.A. 43 H1
Jackson, Wyo., U.S.A. 38 E8
Jackson B. 33 K2
Jacksonville, Ala., U.S.A. 43 J3
Jacksonville, Calif., U.S.A. 38 H2
Jacksonville, Fla., U.S.A. 43 K5
Jacksonville, Ill., U.S.A. 40 F9
Jacksonville, N.C., U.S.A. 43 H7
Jacksonville, Tex., U.S.A. 41 K7
Jacksonville Beach 43 K5
Jacmel 45 D10
Jacob Lake 39 H7
Jaén 13 D4
Jaffa = Tel Aviv-Yafo 17 D4
Jaffna 25 E7
Jagdalpur 25 D7
Jaguariaíva 48 A7
Jahrom 24 C4
Jaipur 24 F9
Jakarta 22 D3
Jalalabad 24 B7
Jalapa Enríquez = Xalapa 44 D5
Jalgaon 25 C6
Jalna 25 D6
Jalón → 13 B5
Jaluit I. 34 G8
Jamaica ■ 44 a
Jamalpur 25 C7
Jambi 22 D2
James →, S. Dak., U.S.A. 40 D6
James →, Va., U.S.A. 42 G7
James B. 37 C11
Jamestown, Australia 32 B2
Jamestown, N. Dak., U.S.A. 40 B5
Jamestown, N.Y., U.S.A. 42 D6
Jammu 25 B6
Jammu & Kashmir □ 25 B6
Jamnagar 24 H7
Jamshedpur 25 C7
Jan Mayen 4 B6
Jandowae 32 A5
Janesville 40 D10
Japan ■ 19 G11
Japan, Sea of 18 E14
Japan Trench 34 D6
Japurá → 46 D5
Jarvis I. 35 H12
Jāsk 24 C4
Jasper, Canada 36 C8
Jasper, Ala., U.S.A. 43 J2
Jasper, Fla., U.S.A. 43 K4
Jasper, Ind., U.S.A. 42 F2
Jászberény 16 E9
Jaunpur 25 C7
Java = Jawa 22 D3
Java Sea 22 D3
Java Trench 22 D2
Jawa 22 D3
Jaya, Puncak 23 D5
Jayton 41 J4
Jean 39 J6
Jeanerette 41 L9
Jebel, Bahr el → 27 G12
Jedburgh 10 F6
Jedda = Jiddah 24 C2
Jefferson, Iowa, U.S.A. 40 D7
Jefferson, Tex., U.S.A. 41 J7
Jefferson, Mt., Nev., U.S.A. 38 G5
Jefferson, Mt., Oreg., U.S.A. 38 D3
Jefferson City, Mo., U.S.A. 40 F8
Jefferson City, Tenn., U.S.A. 43 G4
Jeffersontown 42 F3
Jeffersonville 42 F3
Jeffrey City 38 E10
Jekyll I. 43 K5
Jelenia Góra 16 C8
Jelgava 7 F8
Jena, Germany 16 C5
Jena, U.S.A. 41 K8
Jenkins 42 G4
Jennings 41 K8
Jeparit 32 C3
Jequié 47 F10
Jérémie 45 D9
Jerez de la Frontera 13 D2
Jerid, Chott el = Djerid, Chott 26 B7
Jerilderie 32 C4
Jerome 38 E6
Jersey 9 H5
Jersey City 42 E8
Jersey Shore 42 E7
Jerseyville 40 F9
Jerusalem 17 D4
Jervis B. 32 C5
Jessore 25 C7
Jesup 43 K5
Jhang Maghiana 24 G8
Jhansi 25 C6
Jharkhand □ 25 C7
Jhelum 24 G8
Jhelum → 24 G8
Jiamusi 21 B8
Ji'an 21 D6
Jiangmen 21 D6
Jiangsu □ 21 C7
Jiangxi □ 21 D6
Jiaxing 21 C7
Jiddah 24 C2
Jihlava 16 D8
Jijiga 24 D3
Jilin 21 B7
Jima 28 D7
Jiménez 44 B4
Jin Xian 21 C7
Jinan 21 C6
Jinchang 20 C5
Jindabyne 32 C4
Jingdezhen 21 D6
Jinggu 20 D5
Jining, Shandong, China 21 C6
Jining, Nei Monggol Zizhiqu, China 21 B6
Jinja 28 D6
Jinsha Jiang → 20 D5
Jinzhou 21 B7
Jiujiang 21 D6
Jixi 21 B8
João Pessoa 47 E12
Jodhpur 24 F8
Joensuu 18 B4
Johannesburg 29 K5
John Crow Mts. 44 a
John Day 38 D4
John Day → 38 D3
John o' Groats 10 C5
Johnson 41 G4
Johnson City, Tenn., U.S.A. 43 G4
Johnson City, Tex., U.S.A. 41 K5
Johnston I. 35 F11
Johnstown, N.Y., U.S.A. 42 D8
Johnstown, Pa., U.S.A. 42 E6
Johor Baharu 23 C2
Joinville 48 B7
Joliet 42 E1
Joliette 37 D12
Jolo 23 C4
Jonesboro, Ark., U.S.A. 41 H9
Jonesboro, La., U.S.A. 41 J8
Jönköping 7 F6
Jonquière 37 D12
Joplin 41 G7
Jordan ■ 24 B2
Jordan → 17 D4
Jordan Valley 38 E5
Jos 26 G7
Joseph Bonaparte G. 30 B4
Joshua Tree Nat. Park 39 K6
Jost Van Dyke 45 e
Jotunheimen 7 E5
Jourdanton 41 L5
Juan de Fuca Str. 38 B2
Juan Fernández, Arch. de 35 L20
Juàzeiro 47 E10
Juàzeiro do Norte 47 E11
Juba = Giuba → 28 D8
Juba 28 D6
Júcar = Xúquer → 13 C5
Juchitán 44 D5
Judith → 38 C9
Judith Gap 38 C9
Jugoslavia = Yugoslavia ■ 15 B9
Juiz de Fora 47 H10
Julesburg 40 E3
Juliaca 46 G4
Julian 39 K5
Julianehåb = Qaqortoq 37 B14
Jullundur 25 C6
Junagadh 24 H7
Junction, Tex., U.S.A. 41 K5
Junction, Utah, U.S.A. 39 G7
Junction City, Kans., U.S.A. 40 F6
Junction City, Oreg., U.S.A. 38 D2
Jundiaí 48 A7
Juneau 36 C6
Junggar Pendi 20 B3
Juntura 38 E4
Jura 10 F3
Jura, Mts. du 12 C7
Jura, Sd. of 10 F3
Jurado 46 B3
Juruá → 46 D5
Juruena → 46 E7
Jutland = Jylland 7 F5
Juventud, I. de la 45 C8
Jylland 7 F5
Jyväskylä 7 E9

K

Kabaena	23	D4
Kabetogama	40	A8
Kabul	25	B5
Kābul □	25	B5
Kabwe	29	G5
Kachchh, Gulf of	25	C7
Kachin □	24	C4
Kadavu	31	E14
Kadina	31	F2
Kadoka	40	D4
Kaduna	26	F7
Kaesŏng	21	C7
Kagoshima	22	H2
Kahoka	40	F8
Kahramanmaraş	17	C5
Kai, Kepulauan	23	D5
Kaiapoi	33	K4
Kaifeng	21	C6
Kaikohe	33	F4
Kaikoura	33	K4
Kaikoura Mts.	33	K4
Kaipara Harbour	33	G5
Kaiserslautern	16	D3
Kaitaia	31	H13
Kaitangata	33	M2
Kajaani	7	E9
Kajabbi	32	H2
Kakanui Mts.	33	L3
Kakinada	25	D7
Kalaallit Nunaat = Greenland ■	6	C4
Kalahari	29	J4
Kalama	38	D2
Kalamazoo	42	D3
Kalamazoo →	42	D3
Kalemie	28	F5
Kalgoorlie-Boulder	30	G3
Kalimantan □	23	D3
Kalinin = Tver	18	C4
Kaliningrad	7	J7
Kalispell	38	B6
Kalisz	16	C9
Kalkaska	42	C3
Kalmar	7	F7
Kaluga	18	D4
Kama →	18	D6
Kamchatka, Poluostrov	19	D16
Kamchatka Pen. = Kamchatka, Poluostrov	19	D16
Kamensk Uralskiy	18	D7
Kamiah	38	C5
Kamina	28	F5
Kamloops	36	D7
Kampala	28	D6
Kampong Saom	23	B2
Kamyanets-Podilskyy	17	A3
Kamyshin	18	D5
Kanaaupscow →	37	C12
Kanab	39	H7
Kanab →	39	H7
Kananga	28	F4
Kanawha →	42	F4
Kanazawa	22	E5
Kandahar = Qandahār	24	B5
Kandanghaur	23	D2
Kandos	32	B4
Kandy	25	E7
Kane	42	E6
Kane Basin	6	B3
Kangaroo I.	31	F2
Kangean, Kepulauan	23	D3
Kangiqsualujjuaq	37	C13
Kangiqsujuaq	37	B12
Kangirsuk	37	B13
Kaniapiskau → = Caniapiscau →	37	C13
Kanin, Poluostrov	18	C5
Kanin Pen. = Kanin, Poluostrov	18	C5
Kaniva	32	C3
Kankakee	42	E2
Kankakee →	42	E1
Kankan	26	F4
Kannapolis	43	H5
Kano	26	F7
Kanpur	25	C7
Kansas □	40	F6
Kansas →	40	F7
Kansas City, Kans., U.S.A.	40	F7
Kansas City, Mo., U.S.A.	40	F7
Kansk	19	D10
Kanturk	11	D3
Kanye	29	J5
Kaohsiung	21	D7
Kaolack	26	F2
Kapiti I.	31	K8
Kaplan	41	K8
Kaposvár	16	E8
Kapuas →	23	D2
Kapuas Hulu, Pegunungan	23	C3
Kapunda	32	B2
Kapuni	33	H5
Kaputar	32	B5
Kara Kalpak Republic = Qoraqalpoghistan □	18	E7
Kara Kum	18	F6
Kara Sea	18	B7
Karachi	24	C5
Karaganda = Qaraghandy	18	E8
Karakalis = Vanadzor	17	B6
Karakoram Ra.	25	B6
Karaman	17	C3
Karamea Bight	33	J3
Karasburg	29	K3
Karbalā'	24	B3
Karimata, Kepulauan	23	D2
Karimata, Selat	23	D2
Karimunjawa, Kepulauan	23	D3
Karl-Marx-Stadt = Chemnitz	16	C6
Karlskrona	7	F7
Karlsruhe	16	D4
Karlstad, Sweden	7	F6
Karlstad, U.S.A.	40	A6
Karnal	25	C6
Karnataka □	25	D6
Karnes City	41	L6
Kärnten □	16	E6
Karoonda	32	C2
Karsakpay	18	E7
Karshi = Qarshi	18	F7
Kasai →	28	E3
Kasba L.	36	B9
Kāshān	24	B4
Kashi = Kashgar	20	C2
Kashmir	25	B6
Kaskaskia →	40	G10
Kassalā	27	E13
Kassel	16	C4
Kasson	40	C8
Katahdin, Mt.	43	C11
Katanga □	28	F4
Katha	24	C4
Katherine	30	C5
Kathiawar	25	C7
Kathmandu	25	C7
Katoomba	32	B5
Katowice	16	C9
Katrine, L.	10	E4
Katsina	26	F7
Kauai	40	H15
Kaufman	41	J6
Kaukauna	42	C1
Kavajë	15	D11
Kavīr, Dasht-e	24	B4
Kawagoe	22	F6
Kawaguchi	22	F6
Kawasaki	22	F6
Kawerau	33	H6
Kawhia Harbour	33	H5

Kaycee	38	E10
Kayenta	39	H8
Kayes	26	F3
Kayseri	17	C5
Kaysville	38	F8
Kazakstan ■	18	E7
Kazan	18	D5
Kazan-Rettō	34	E6
Kāzerūn	24	C4
Keady	11	B5
Kearney	40	E5
Kearny	39	K8
Kebnekaise	7	D7
Kebri Dehar	24	F3
Kebumen	23	D2
Kecskemét	16	E9
Kediri	23	D3
Keeling Is. = Cocos Is.	3	E14
Keene	42	D9
Keeper Hill	11	D3
Keetmanshoop	29	K3
Kefallinía	15	E9
Keighley	8	D6
Keila	32	G4
Keizer	38	D2
Kellogg	38	C5
Kelowna	36	D8
Kelso, N.Z.	33	L2
Kelso, U.K.	10	F6
Kelso, U.S.A.	38	C2
Keluang	23	C2
Kemerovo	18	D9
Kemi	7	D8
Kemijoki →	7	D8
Kemmerer	38	F8
Kemp Land	6	D9
Kemp, L.	41	J5
Kempsey	32	B5
Kempton	32	G4
Kenai	36	B4
Kendal	8	C5
Kendall, Australia	32	B5
Kendall, U.S.A.	43	N5
Kendallville	42	E3
Kendari	23	D4
Kenedy	41	L6
Keng Tung	24	D4
Kenmare, Ireland	11	E2
Kenmare, U.S.A.	40	A3
Kenmare River	11	E2
Kennebec →	43	D11
Kennebunk	43	D10
Kennedy	41	L9
Kennet →	9	F7
Kennett	41	G9
Kennewick	38	C4
Kenogami →	37	C11
Keno	36	D10
Kenosha	42	D2
Kent	41	K2
Kent □	9	F8
Kent Group	32	C4
Kent Pen.	36	B9
Kentland	42	E2
Kenton	42	E4
Kentucky □	42	G3
Kentucky →	42	F3
Kentucky L.	43	G2
Kentville	37	D13
Kentwood	41	K9
Kenya ■	28	D7
Kenya, Mt.	28	E7
Keokuk	40	E9
Kerala □	25	D6
Kerang	32	C3
Kerch	17	A5
Kerguelen	5	G13
Kericho	28	E7
Kerinci	23	D2
Kermadec Is.	34	L10
Kermadec Trench	34	L10
Kermān	24	B4
Kermānshāh = Bākhtarān	24	B3
Kermit	41	K3
Kern →	39	J4
Kerrera	10	E3
Kerrville	41	K5
Kerry □	11	D2
Kerry Hd.	11	D2
Kerulen →	21	B6
Keswick	8	C4
Ketchikan	36	C6
Ketchum	38	E6
Kettering, U.K.	9	E7
Kettering, U.S.A.	42	F3
Kettle Falls	38	B4
Kewanee	40	E10
Kewaunee	42	C2
Keweenaw B.	42	B1
Keweenaw Pen.	42	B2
Keweenaw Pt.	42	B2
Key Largo	43	N5
Keynsham	9	F5
Keyser	42	F6
Khabarovsk	19	E14
Khambhat, G. of	25	C6
Khaniá	15	G11
Khapcheranga	19	E12
Kharkiv	17	E4
Kharkov = Kharkiv	17	E4
Khartoum = El Khartûm	27	E12
Khaskovo	15	D11
Khatanga	19	B11
Kherson	17	E4
Khios	15	E12
Khodzent = Khŭjand	18	E7
Khon Kaen	23	B2
Khorramshahr	24	B3
Khouribga	26	B4
Khudzhand = Khŭjand	18	E7
Khŭjand	18	E7
Khulna	25	C7
Khuriya Muriya, Jazā'ir	24	D4
Khyber Pass	25	B5
Kiama	32	B5
Kicking Horse Pass	36	C8
Kidderminster	9	E5
Kidnappers, C.	33	H6
Kidsgrove	8	D5
Kiel	16	A5
Kiel Canal = Nord-Ostsee-Kanal	16	A4
Kielce	16	C10
Kielder Water	8	B5
Kiev = Kyyiv	17	B6
Kigali	28	E6
Kigoma-Ujiji	28	E5
Kikládhes	15	F11
Kikwit	28	E3
Kilbrannan Sd.	10	F3
Kilcoy	32	A5
Kilcorgin	11	C5
Kildare	11	C5
Kildare □	11	C5
Kilfinnane	11	D3
Kilimanjaro	28	E7
Kilkee	11	D2
Kilkenny	11	D4
Kilkenny □	11	D4
Kilkieran B.	11	C2
Killala	11	B2
Killala B.	11	B2
Killaloe	11	D3
Killarney, Australia	32	A5
Killarney, Ireland	11	D2
Killary Harbour	11	C2
Killdeer	40	B3
Killeen	41	K6
Killin	10	E4
Killorglin	11	D2
Killybegs	11	B3
Kilmarnock	10	F4
Kilmore	32	C3
Kilrush	11	D2
Kimba	31	E2
Kimball, Nebr., U.S.A.	40	E3
Kimball, S. Dak., U.S.A.	40	D5
Kimberley, Australia	30	D4
Kimberley, S. Africa	29	K4

Kimberly	38	E6
Kimmirut	37	B13
Kinabalu, Gunong	23	C3
Kinder Scout	8	D6
Kindersley	36	C9
Kindu	28	E5
King City	39	H3
King George I.	6	C18
King George Is.	37	C11
King I.	30	H7
Kingfisher	41	H6
Kingman, Ariz., U.S.A.	39	J6
Kingman, Kans., U.S.A.	41	G5
Kings →	39	H4
Kings Canyon Nat. Park	39	H4
King's Lynn	8	D8
Kings Mountain	43	H5
King's Peak	38	F8
Kingsbridge	9	G4
Kingscote	32	C2
Kingscourt	11	C5
Kingsford	42	C1
Kingsland	43	K5
Kingsport	43	G4
Kingston, Canada	42	C8
Kingston, Jamaica	44	a
Kingston, N.Y., U.S.A.	42	E8
Kingston, Pa., U.S.A.	42	E8
Kingston South East	32	C2
Kingston upon Hull	8	D7
Kingston-upon-Thames □	9	F7
Kingstown	45	E12
Kingstree	43	J6
Kingsville	41	M6
Kingussie	10	D4
Kingwood	41	K7
Kinleith	33	H5
Kinnairds Hd.	10	D6
Kinross	10	E5
Kinsale	11	E3
Kinsale, Old Hd. of	11	E3
Kinshasa	28	E3
Kinsley	41	G5
Kinston	43	H7
Kintyre	10	F3
Kintyre, Mull of	10	F3
Kiowa, Kans., U.S.A.	41	G5
Kiowa, Okla., U.S.A.	41	H7
Kirensk	19	D11
Kirghizia = Kyrgyzstan ■	18	E8
Kiribati ■	34	H10
Kırıkkale	17	C4
Kirinyaga = Kenya, Mt.	28	E7
Kiritimati	35	G12
Kirkby	8	D5
Kirkby Lonsdale	8	C5
Kirkcaldy	10	E5
Kirkcudbright	10	G4
Kirkland Lake	37	D11
Kirksville	40	E8
Kirkūk	24	B3
Kirkwall	10	C6
Kirov	18	D5
Kirovabad = Gäncä	17	B7
Kirovakan = Vanadzor	17	B6
Kirovohrad	17	A4
Kirriemuir	10	E5
Kiruna	7	D8
Kiryū	22	E6
Kisangani	28	D5
Kishinev = Chişinău	17	A3
Kislovodsk	17	A6
Kissimmee	43	L5
Kissimmee →	43	M5
Kisumu	28	E6
Kit Carson	40	F3
Kitakyūshū	22	G2
Kitami	22	B8
Kitchener	42	D4
Kíthira	15	F10
Kittanning	42	E6
Kittery	43	D10
Kitwe	29	G5
Kivu, L.	28	E5
Kiyev = Kyyiv	17	B6
Kizil Irmak →	17	B5
Kladno	16	C7
Klagenfurt	16	E7
Klaipeda	7	J8
Klamath →	38	F1
Klamath Falls	38	E3
Klamath Mts.	38	F2
Klarälven →	7	F6
Klerksdorp	29	K5
Klickitat	38	D3
Kluane L.	36	B6
Klyuchevskaya, Gora	19	D17
Knaresborough	8	C6
Knighton	9	E4
Knock	11	C3
Knockmealdown Mts.	11	D4
Knossós	15	G11
Knox	42	E2
Knoxville, Iowa, U.S.A.	40	E8
Knoxville, Tenn., U.S.A.	43	H4
Kōbe	22	F4
København	7	F6
Koblenz	16	C3
Kocaeli	17	B3
Kodiak	36	C4
Kodiak I.	36	C4
Koforidua	26	G5
Kōfu	22	F6
Kokand = Qŭqon	18	E8
Kokomo	42	E2
Kokshetaū	18	D7
Koksoak →	37	C13
Kokstad	29	L5
Kola Peninsula = Kolskiy Poluostrov	7	D11
Kolar Gold Fields	25	D6
Kolhapur	25	D6
Kolhapur	25	D6
Köln	16	C3
Kolomna	18	D4
Kolskiy Poluostrov	7	D11
Kolwezi	28	G5
Kolyma →	19	C17
Kolymskoye Nagorye	19	C16
Komandorskiye Ostrova	19	D17
Komatsu	22	E5
Kommunarsk = Alchevsk	17	A5
Kommunizma, Pik	18	F8
Kompong Cham	23	B2
Komsomolets, Ostrov	19	A10
Komsomolsk	19	D14
Kong Frederik VI Kyst	37	B15
Königsberg = Kaliningrad	7	J7
Konin	16	B9
Konya	17	C4
Koocanusa, L.	38	B6
Koolish	32	B4
Koorawatha	32	B4
Kootenai →	38	B5
Kootenay L.	36	D8
Kopeysk	18	D7
Koppeh Dāgh = Kopet Dagh	24	B4
Korçë	15	D9
Korea, North ■	21	C7
Korea, South ■	21	C7
Korea Bay	21	C7
Korea Strait	21	C7
Korinthiakós Kólpos	15	E10
Kōriyama	22	E7

Korla	20	B3
Koro	31	D8
Koro Sea	33	C9
Koror	34	G5
Körös →	16	E10
Kortrijk	16	C1
Kos	15	F12
Kosciusko	41	J10
Kosciusko, Mt.	30	H8
Kosovo □	15	C9
Kôstï	27	F12
Kostroma	18	D5
Koszalin	16	A8
Kota	25	C6
Kota Baharu	23	C2
Kota Kinabalu	23	C3
Kotabumi	23	D2
Kotka	7	F9
Kotuy →	19	B11
Kotzebue	36	B3
Kouroussa	26	F4
Kountze	41	K7
Kowloon	21	G11
Kozhikode = Calicut	25	D6
Kra, Isthmus of = Kra, Kho Khot	23	B1
Kra, Kho Khot	23	B1
Kragujevac	15	B9
Krakatau	23	D2
Kraków	16	C9
Kramatorsk	17	A5
Krasnodar	18	E4
Krasnyy Luch	17	A5
Krefeld	16	C3
Kremenchuk	17	A4
Kremmling	38	F10
Krishna →	25	D7
Kristiansand	7	F5
Kristiansund	7	E5
Kríti	15	G11
Krivoy Rog = Kryvyy Rih	17	A4
Kroonstad	29	K5
Krung Thep = Bangkok	23	B2
Kruševac	15	C9
Krymskyy Poluostrov	17	B4
Krymskyy Pivostriv	17	A4
Kryvyy Rih	17	A4
Kuala Belait	23	C3
Kuala Lumpur	23	C2
Kuala Terengganu	23	C2
Kualakapuas	23	D3
Kuandian	21	B7
Kuban →	17	A5
Kuching	23	C3
Kudat	23	C3
Kuglutuk	36	B8
Kuichong	21	F11
Kulwin	32	B3
Kumagaya	22	E6
Kumamoto	22	G2
Kumanovo	15	C9
Kumara	33	K3
Kumasi	26	G5
Kumayri = Gyumri	17	B6
Kumbakonam	25	D6
Kumbarilla	32	A5
Kumbia	32	A5
Kunlun Shan	20	C3
Kunming	20	D5
Kuopio	7	E9
Kupang	23	E4
Kür →	17	C7
Kura = Kür →	17	C7
Kurdistan	24	B3
Kure	22	F3
Kurgan	18	D7
Kuril Is. = Kurilskiye Ostrova	19	E15
Kuril Trench	34	C7
Kurilskiye Ostrova	19	E15
Kurnool	25	D6
Kuro Kurri	32	B5
Kuruktag	20	B3
Kuruman	29	K4
Kurume	22	G2
Kushiro	22	B9
Kuskokwim B.	36	C3
Kustanay = Qostanay	18	D7
Kütahya	17	C3
Kutaisi	17	B6
Kutujuaq	37	C13
Kuujjuarapik	37	C12
Kuwait = Al Kuwayt	24	C3
Kuwait ■	24	C3
Kuybyshev = Samara	18	D6
Kwangju	21	C7
Kwango →	28	E3
Kwangtung = Guangdong □	21	D6
Kwun Tong	21	G11
Kyabram	32	C4
Kyancutta	32	B2
Kyangin	32	B5
Kyaukse	25	D8
Kyle of Lochalsh	10	D3
Kyneton	32	C3
Kyōto	22	F4
Kyrgyzstan ■	18	E8
Kyūshū	22	G2
Kyyiv	17	B6
Kyzyl Kum	18	E7
Kyzyl-Orda = Qyzylorda	18	E7

L

La Barge	38	E8
La Belle	43	M5
La Ceiba	44	D7
La Coruña = A Coruña	13	A1
La Crescent	40	D9
La Crosse, Kans., U.S.A.	40	F5
La Crosse, Wis., U.S.A.	40	D9
La Désirade	44	b
La Fayette	43	H3
La Follette	43	G3
La Grande	38	D4
La Grande →	37	C12
La Grange, Ga., U.S.A.	43	J3
La Grange, Ky., U.S.A.	42	F3
La Grange, Tex., U.S.A.	41	L6
La Junta	41	F3
La Mancha	13	C4
La Mesa	39	K5
La Moure	40	B5
La Paz, Bolivia	46	D3
La Paz, Mexico	44	C2
La Perouse Str.	22	A8
La Pine	38	E3
La Plata	47	D5
La Porte, Ind., U.S.A.	42	E2
La Porte, Tex., U.S.A.	41	L7
La Rioja	47	B3
La Roche-sur-Yon	12	C3
La Rochelle	12	C3
La Romana	45	D11
La Ronge	36	C9
La Spézia	14	B3
La Trinité	44	c
La Tuque	37	D12
La Vega	45	D10
Labasa	33	C8
Labe = Elbe →	16	B5
Labé	26	F3
Laborie	45	f
Labrador	37	C13
Labrador City	37	C13
Labrador Sea	37	C14

Labyrinth, L.	32	B2
Lac La Biche	36	C8
Laccadive Is. = Lakshadweep Is.	25	E6
Lacepede B.	32	C2
Lachlan →	32	B3
Lacombe	36	C8
Laconia	42	D10
Ladoga, L. = Ladozhskoye Ozero	7	E10
Ladozhskoye Ozero	7	E10
Ladysmith, S. Africa	29	K5
Lae	34	H6
Lafayette, Colo., U.S.A.	40	F2
Lafayette, Ind., U.S.A.	42	E2
Lafayette, La., U.S.A.	41	K9
Lafayette, Tenn., U.S.A.	43	G2
Lagan →	11	B6
Lagos, Nigeria	26	G6
Lagos, Portugal	13	D1
Laguna	23	J10
Lahad	23	D2
Lahore	25	B6
Lahti	7	E9
Lairg	10	C4
Lajosmizse	16	E9
Lake Andes	40	D5
Lake Cargelligo	32	B4
Lake Charles	41	K8
Lake City, Colo., U.S.A.	39	G10
Lake City, Fla., U.S.A.	43	K4
Lake City, Mich., U.S.A.	42	C3
Lake City, Minn., U.S.A.	40	C8
Lake City, S.C., U.S.A.	43	J6
Lake District	8	C4
Lake Havasu City	39	J6
Lake Jackson	41	L7
Lake Junction	38	B8
Lake Mead Nat. Recr. Area	39	J6
Lake Mills	40	D8
Lake Providence	41	J9
Lake Village	41	J9
Lake Wales	43	M5
Lake Worth	43	M5
Lakeba	33	D9
Lakeland	43	M5
Lakeport	38	G2
Lakes Entrance	32	C4
Lakeside, Ariz., U.S.A.	39	J9
Lakeside, Nebr., U.S.A.	40	D3
Lakeview	38	E3
Lakewood, Colo., U.S.A.	40	F2
Lakewood, Ohio, U.S.A.	42	E5
Lakin	41	G4
Lakota	40	A5
Lakshadweep Is.	25	E6
Lamar, Colo., U.S.A.	40	F3
Lamar, Mo., U.S.A.	41	G7
Lambay I.	11	C5
Lame Deer	38	D10
Lameroo	32	C3
Lamesa	41	J4
Lamía	15	E10
Lammermuir Hills	10	F6
Lamon B.	23	B4
Lampasas	41	K5
Lampeter	9	E3
Lanai	40	H16
Lanark	10	F5
Lancang Jiang →	20	D5
Lancashire □	8	D5
Lancaster, U.K.	8	C5
Lancaster, Calif., U.S.A.	39	J4
Lancaster, Ky., U.S.A.	42	G3
Lancaster, Ohio, U.S.A.	42	F4
Lancaster, Pa., U.S.A.	42	E7
Lancaster, Wis., U.S.A.	40	D9
Lancaster Sd.	37	A11
Landes	12	D3
Land's End	9	G2
Lanett	43	J3
Langton	40	A5
Langkawi	23	C1
Langon	12	D3
Langres	12	C6
Langres, Plateau de	12	C6
Langsa	23	C1
Langtry	41	L4
Languedoc	12	E5
Lannion	12	B2
L'Anse	42	B1
L'Anse au Loup	37	C14
L'Anse la Raye	45	f
Lansing	42	D3
Lanzhou	20	C5
Laoag	23	B4
Laois □	11	D4
Laon	12	B5
Laona	42	C1
Laos ■	23	B2
Lapeer	42	D4
Lapland = Lappland	7	D8
Lappland	7	D8
Laptev Sea	19	B13
Laramie	38	F11
Laramie Mts.	38	E11
Larder Lake	42	A6
Laredo	41	M5
Largs	10	F4
Lárisa	15	E10
Larkana	24	C5
Larne	11	B6
Larned	40	F5
Larvik	7	F6
Las Animas	40	F3
Las Cruces	39	K10
Las Palmas	26	C2
Las Vegas, N. Mex., U.S.A.	39	J11
Las Vegas, Nev., U.S.A.	39	H6
Lashio	24	D4
Lassen Pk.	38	F3
Lassen Volcanic Nat. Park	38	F3
Latakia = Al Lādhiqīyah	24	B2
Latina	14	D5
Latrobe	32	D4
Lau Fau Shan	21	G10
Lau Group	33	D9
Laune →	11	D2
Launceston, Australia	30	J8
Launceston, U.K.	9	G3
Laurel, Miss., U.S.A.	41	K10
Laurel, Mont., U.S.A.	38	D9
Laurencekirk	10	E6
Laurens	43	H5
Laurinburg	43	H6
Lausanne	14	A2
Laut, Pulau	23	D3
Laut Kecil, Kepulauan	23	D3
Lauvaï Mure	11	B3
Laval	12	B3
Lavenham	9	E8
Lawrence, N.Z.	33	L2
Lawrence, Kans., U.S.A.	40	F7
Lawrence, Mass., U.S.A.	42	D10
Lawrenceburg, Ind., U.S.A.	42	F3

Lawrenceburg, Tenn., U.S.A.	43	H2
Lawrenceville	43	H4
Lawton	41	H5
Laxford, L.	10	C3
Layla	24	C3
Laytonville	38	F7
Lazio □	14	C5
Le Creusot	12	C6
Le François	44	c
Le Havre	12	B4
Le Mans	12	C4
Le Marin	44	c
Le Mont-Dore	44	D6
Le Prêcheur	44	c
Le Puy-en-Velay	12	D5
Le Robert	44	c
Le St-Esprit	44	c
Le Sueur	40	C8
Lea →	9	F8
Lead	40	C3
Leadville	39	G10
Leaf →	41	K10
Leamington Spa = Royal Leamington Spa	9	E6
Leane, L.	11	D2
Leavenworth, Kans., U.S.A.	40	F7
Leavenworth, Wash., U.S.A.	38	C3
Lebanon, Ind., U.S.A.	42	E2
Lebanon, Kans., U.S.A.	40	F5
Lebanon, Ky., U.S.A.	42	G3
Lebanon, Mo., U.S.A.	41	G8
Lebanon, N.H., U.S.A.	42	D9
Lebanon, Oreg., U.S.A.	38	D2
Lebanon, Pa., U.S.A.	42	E7
Lebanon, Tenn., U.S.A.	43	G2
Lebanon ■	24	B2
Lebec	39	J4
Lecce	14	D8
Lecco	14	B3
Leech L.	40	B7
Leeds, U.K.	8	D6
Leeds, U.S.A.	40	A5
Leek	8	D5
Leesburg	43	L5
Leesville	41	K8
Leeton	32	B4
Leeuwarden	16	B2
Leeuwin, C.	30	G2
Leeward Is.	45	D12
Leganés	13	B4
Legazpi	23	B4
Legnica	16	C8
Leh	25	B6
Lehigh Acres	43	M5
Leicester	9	E6
Leicestershire □	9	E6
Leiden	16	B2
Leine →	16	B4
Leinster □	11	C4
Leinster, Mt.	11	D5
Leipzig	16	C6
Leith	10	F5
Leith Hill	9	F7
Leitrim	11	B3
Leitrim □	11	B4
Leizhou Bandao	21	D6
Leland, Miss., U.S.A.	41	J9
Léman, L.	14	A2
Lemhi Ra.	38	D7
Lemmon	40	C3
Lemoore	39	H4
Lena →	19	B13
Leninabad = Khŭjand	18	E7
Leninakan = Gyumri	17	B6
Leningrad = Sankt-Peterburg	18	D4
Leninogorsk	18	D9
Leninsk-Kuznetskiy	18	D9
Lennox	40	D6
Lenoir	43	H5
Lenoir City	43	H3
Lens	12	A5
Leodhas = Lewis	10	C2
Leola	40	C5
Leominster, U.K.	9	E5
Leominster, U.S.A.	42	D10
León, Mexico	44	C4
León, Nic.	44	E7
León, Spain	13	A3
Leonardtown	42	F7
Leongatha	32	C4
Leonora	30	F3
Leoti	40	F4
Lérida = Lleida	13	B6
Lerwick	10	A7
Les Cayes	45	D10
Les Sables-d'Olonne	12	C3
Lesbos = Lésvos	15	E12
Leshan	20	D5
Leskovac	15	C9
Lesotho ■	29	K5
Lesser Antilles	45	E12
Lesser Slave L.	36	C8
Lesser Sunda Is.	23	D4
Lésvos	15	E12
Leszno	16	C8
Letchworth	9	F7
Lethbridge	36	D8
Letterkenny	11	B4
Leti, Kepulauan	23	D4
Leuven = Louvain	16	C2
Leveland	41	J3
Leven	10	E6
Leven, L.	10	E5
Levin	33	J5
Levittown	42	E8
Levkás	15	E9
Levkôsia = Nicosia	17	C4
Lewellen	40	E3
Lewes, U.K.	9	G8
Lewes, U.S.A.	42	F8
Lewis	10	C2
Lewis, Butt of	10	C2
Lewis Range	38	B7
Lewisburg, Tenn., U.S.A.	43	H2
Lewisburg, W. Va., U.S.A.	42	G5
Lewiston, Idaho, U.S.A.	38	C5
Lewiston, Maine, U.S.A.	43	C11
Lewistown, Mont., U.S.A.	38	C9
Lewistown, Pa., U.S.A.	42	E7
Lexington, Ky., U.S.A.	42	F3
Lexington, N.C., U.S.A.	43	H5
Lexington, Nebr., U.S.A.	40	E5
Lexington, Tenn., U.S.A.	43	H1
Lexington Park	42	F7
Leyburn	8	C6
Leyte	23	B4
Lhasa	20	D4
L'Hospitalet de Llobregat	13	B7
Lianyungang	21	C6
Liaoning □	21	B7
Liaoyang	21	B7
Liard →	36	B7
Libby	38	B6
Liberal	41	G4
Liberia ■	26	G4
Liberty, Mo., U.S.A.	40	F7

Liberty, N.Y., U.S.A.	42	E8
Liberty, Tex., U.S.A.	41	K7
Lichtenburg	29	K5
Lichinga	29	G7
Licking →	42	F3
Liechtenstein ■	14	C8
Liège	16	C2
Liepāja	7	F8
Liffey →	11	C5
Lifford	11	B4
Lightning Ridge	32	A4
Liguria □	14	B3
Ligurian Sea	14	C3
Lijiang	20	D5
Likasi	28	G5
Lille	12	A5
Lillehammer	7	E6
Lilongwe	29	G6
Lima, Mont., U.S.A.	38	D7
Lima, Ohio, U.S.A.	42	E3
Lima, Peru	46	D2
Limavady	11	A5
Limbe	28	D1
Limerick	11	D3
Limerick □	11	D3
Límnos	15	E11
Limoges	12	D4
Limón, Costa Rica	44	E8
Limón, U.S.A.	40	F3
Limousin	12	D4
Limoux	12	E5
Limpopo →	29	K6
Linares, Mexico	44	C5
Linares, Spain	13	C4
Lincoln, U.K.	8	D7
Lincoln, Ill., U.S.A.	40	E10
Lincoln, Kans., U.S.A.	40	F5
Lincoln, Maine, U.S.A.	43	C11
Lincoln, N. Mex., U.S.A.	39	K11
Lincoln, Nebr., U.S.A.	40	E6
Lincoln City	38	D1
Lincoln Sea	6	A5
Lincolnshire □	8	D7
Lincolnton	43	H5
Lindsborg	40	F6
Linden, Ala., U.S.A.	43	J2
Linden, Tex., U.S.A.	41	J7
Lindesnes	7	F5
Lindsay, Calif., U.S.A.	39	H4
Lindsay, Okla., U.S.A.	41	H6
Linfen	21	C6
Lingayen	23	B4
Lingga, Kepulauan	23	D2
Lingle	40	D2
Linhai	21	D7
Linhares	47	G10
Linköping	7	F7
Linnhe, L.	10	E3
Linstead	44	a
Linton, Ind., U.S.A.	42	F2
Linton, N. Dak., U.S.A.	40	B4
Linxia	20	C5
Lion, G. du	12	E6
Lions, G. of = Lion, G. du	12	E6
Lipari	14	E6
Lipetsk	18	D4
Lippe →	16	C3
Liptrap C.	32	C4
Liria = Llíria	13	C5
Lisala	28	D4
Lisboa	13	C1
Lisbon = Lisboa	13	C1
Lisbon	40	B6
Lisbon Falls	43	D10
Lisburn	11	B5
Liscannor B.	11	D2
Lisianski I.	34	E10
Lisichansk	17	A5
Lisieux	12	B4
Lismore, Australia	30	F9
Lismore, Ireland	11	D4
Listowel	11	D2
Litchfield, Ill., U.S.A.	40	F10
Litchfield, Minn., U.S.A.	40	C7
Lithgow	32	B5
Líthinon, Ákra	15	G11
Lithuania ■	7	J8
Little Andaman I.	25	D8
Little Barrier I.	33	G5
Little Blue →	40	E6
Little Colorado →	39	H8
Little Falls, Minn., U.S.A.	40	C7
Little Falls, N.Y., U.S.A.	42	D8
Little Fork →	40	A8
Little Humboldt →	38	F5
Little Minch	10	D2
Little Missouri →	40	B3
Little Red →	41	H9
Little River	33	K4
Little Rock	41	H8
Little Sable Pt.	42	D2
Little Snake →	38	F9
Little Wabash →	42	G1
Little White →	40	D4
Littlefield	41	J3
Littlehampton	9	G7
Liuzhou	20	D5
Live Oak	43	K4
Livermore, Mt.	41	K2
Livermore Falls	43	C11
Liverpool, Canada	37	D13
Liverpool, U.K.	8	D4
Liverpool Plains	32	B5
Liverpool Ra.	32	B5
Livingston, Ala., U.S.A.	43	J1
Livingston, Mont., U.S.A.	38	D8
Livingston, S.C., U.S.A.	43	J5
Livingston, Tenn., U.S.A.	43	G3
Livingstone	29	H5
Livny	18	D4
Livonia	42	D4
Livorno	14	C4
Lizard Pt.	9	H2
Ljubljana	14	A6
Llandeilo	9	F3
Llandovery	9	F4
Llandrindod Wells	9	E4
Llandudno	8	D4
Llanelli	9	F3
Llanes	13	A3
Llangollen	8	E4
Llanidloes	9	E4
Llano	41	K5
Llano →	41	K5
Llano Estacado	41	J3
Llanos	46	B3
Llanwrtyd Wells	9	E4
Lleida	13	B6
Llíria	13	C5
Lloret de Mar	13	B7
Lluchmayor	13	C7
Llullaillaco, Volcán	47	A3

Lawrenceburg, Tenn., U.S.A.	43	H2
Lawrenceville	43	H4
Lo → = Lô →	20	D5
Loa	39	G8
Loa →	47	A2
Lobito	29	G2
Loc Ninh	23	B2
Loch Garman = Wexford	11	D5
Lochaber	10	E3
Lochboisdale	10	D1
Lochgilphead	10	E3
Lochinver	10	C3
Lochmaddy	10	D1
Lochnagar	10	E5
Lochy, L.	10	E4
Lock	32	B2
Lock Haven	42	E7

Lockerbie	10	F5
Lockhart	41	L6
Lockney	41	H4
Lockport	42	D10
Lodge Grass	38	D10
Lodgepole Cr. →	40	E2
Lodi	38	G3
Łódź	16	C9
Lofoten	7	D6
Logan, Iowa, U.S.A.	40	E7
Logan, Ohio, U.S.A.	42	F4
Logan, Utah, U.S.A.	38	F8
Logan, W. Va., U.S.A.	42	G5
Logan, Mt.	36	B5
Logansport, Ind., U.S.A.	42	E2
Logroño	13	A4
Loir →	12	C3
Loire →	12	C2
Loja	46	D2
Lokoja	26	G7
Lolland	7	G6
Lom	15	C10
Loma	38	C8
Lombárdia □	14	B3
Lomblen	23	D3
Lombok	23	D3
Lomé	26	G6
Lomond, L.	10	E4
London, Canada	37	D11
London, Ky., U.S.A.	42	G3
London, Ohio, U.S.A.	42	F4
London, Greater □	9	F7
Londonderry	11	B4
Londonderry □	11	B4
Londonderry, C.	30	C4
Londrina	47	A6
Lone Pine	39	H4
Long B.	43	J6
Long Beach, Calif., U.S.A.	39	K4
Long Beach, Wash., U.S.A.	38	C1
Long Branch	42	E8
Long Creek	38	D4
Long Eaton	8	E6
Long I., Bahamas	45	C9
Long I., Ireland	11	E2
Long Island Sd.	42	E9
Long Prairie →	40	C7
Long Xuyen	23	B2
Longboat Key	43	M4
Longford, Australia	32	D4
Longford, Ireland	11	C4
Longford □	11	C4
Longhua	21	B6
Longido	28	E7
Longlac	37	D11
Longmont	40	E2
Longnawan	23	C3
Longview, Tex., U.S.A.	41	J7
Longview, Wash., U.S.A.	38	C2
Longxue Dao	21	F10
Lonoke	41	H9
Lons-le-Saunier	12	C6
Loop Hd.	11	D2
Lop Nur	20	B4
Lopez, C.	28	E1
Lora →	32	A2
Lorain	42	E4
Loraine	41	J4
Lorca	13	D5
Lord Howe I.	34	K8
Lord Howe Ridge	34	L8
Lordsburg	39	K9
Lorient	12	C2
Lorn	10	E3
Lorn, Firth of	10	E3
Lorraine	12	B7
Los Alamos	39	J10
Los Angeles, Chile	47	D2
Los Angeles, U.S.A.	39	K4
Los Angeles Aqueduct	39	J5
Los Banos	39	H3
Los Lunas	39	J10
Los Mochis	44	B3
Lossiemouth	10	D5
Lostwithiel	9	G3
Lot →	12	D4
Lota	47	D2
Loughborough	8	E6
Loughrea	11	C3
Loughros More B.	11	B3
Louis XIV, Pte.	37	C12
Louisa	42	F4
Louisiade Arch.	34	J7
Louisiana □	41	K9
Louisville, Ky., U.S.A.	42	F3
Louisville, Miss., U.S.A.	41	J10
Loup City	40	E5
Lourdes	12	E3
Louth, Australia	32	B4
Louth, Ireland	11	C5
Louth, U.K.	8	D7
Louth □	11	C5
Louvain = Leuven	16	C2
Lovech	15	C11
Loveland	40	E2
Lovell	38	D9
Lovelock	38	F4
Loving	41	J2
Lovington	41	J3
Lowell	42	D10
Lower Alkali L.	38	F3
Lower California = Baja California	44	A1
Lower Hutt	33	J5
Lower Saxony = Niedersachsen □	16	B4
Lowestoft	9	E9
Łowicz	16	B9
Loyalty Is. = Loyauté, Îs.	34	K8
Loyauté, Îs.	34	K8
Lu Wo	21	F11
Lualaba →	28	D5
Luanda	28	F2
Luang Prabang	23	B2
Luangwa →	29	G6
Luanshya	29	G5
Lubango	29	G2
Lubbock	41	J4
Lübeck	16	B5
Lublin	16	C11
Lubumbashi	29	G5
Lucca	14	C4
Lucedale	43	K1
Lucena	23	B4
Lucerne = Luzern	14	C8
Luckenwalde	16	B6
Lucknow	25	C7
Lüda = Dalian	21	C7
Lüderitz	29	K3
Ludhiana	25	C6
Ludington	42	D2
Ludlow	9	E5
Ludwigshafen	16	D4
Lufira →	28	F5
Lufkin	41	K7
Lugano	14	C8
Lugansk = Luhansk	17	A5
Lugnaquilla	11	D5
Lugo	13	A2
Luhansk	17	A5
Luing	10	E3
Luleå	7	D8
Luleälven →	7	D8
Lüneburger Heide	16	B5
Lünéville	12	B7
Luni →	25	C6
Luofu	28	E5
Luoyang	21	C6
Lupanshui	20	D5
Luray	42	F6

Lurgan	11	B5
Lusaka	29	H5
Lushnjë	15	D8
Lüt, Dasht-e	24	B4
Luton	9	F7
Lutselke	36	B8
Lutsk	17	D3
Luverne, Ala., U.S.A.	43	K2
Luverne, Minn., U.S.A.	40	D6
Luxembourg	12	B7
Luxembourg ■	12	B7
Luxor = El Uqsur	27	C12
Luza	18	C5
Luzern	14	C8
Luzhou	20	D5
Luzon	23	B4
Lviv	17	A3
Lvov = Lviv	17	A3
Lyakhovskiye, Ostrova	19	B15
Lybster	10	C5
Lydenburg	29	K6
Lyell	33	J4
Lyme B.	9	G4
Lyme Regis	9	G5
Lymington	9	G6
Lynchburg	42	G6
Lynd Ra.	32	A4
Lynden	38	B2
Lyndonville	42	C9
Lynn Lake	36	C9
Lynton	9	F4
Lyon	12	D6
Lyonnais	12	D6
Lyons, Kans., U.S.A.	40	F5
Lysychansk	17	A5
Lytham St. Anne's	8	D4
Lyttelton	33	K4

M

Ma'ān	24	B2
Ma'anshan	21	C6
Maas →	16	C2
Maastricht	16	C2
Mablethorpe	8	D8
McAlester	41	H7
McAllen	41	M5
McAlpine L.	36	B9
Macapá	46	B4
McCall	38	D5
McCamey	41	K3
McCammon	38	E7
McClesney	43	K4
Macclesfield	8	D5
M'Clintock Chan.	36	A9
M'Clure Str.	6	B1
McComb	41	K9
McConaughy, L.	40	E4
McCook	40	E4
McDermitt	38	F5
MacDonnell Ranges	30	E5
Macduff	10	D6
Macedonia = Makedonía	15	D10
Macedonia ■	15	D9
Maceió	46	C6
Macfarlane, L.	32	B2
McGehee	41	J9
McGill	38	G6
Macgillycuddy's Reeks	11	E2
McGregor	40	D9
McGregor Ra.	32	A3
Machakos	28	E7
Machala	46	C2
Machias	43	C12
Machynlleth	9	E4
McIntosh	40	C4
Macintyre →	32	A5
Mackay, Australia	30	E8
Mackay, U.S.A.	38	E7
Mackay, L.	30	E4
McKeesport	42	E6
Mackenzie	36	B6
McKenzie	43	G1
Mackenzie →	36	B6
Mackenzie Mts.	36	B6
Mackinaw City	42	C3
McKinley, Mt.	36	B4
McKinley Sea	6	A7
McKinney	41	J6
Mclean	41	H4
McLeansboro	40	F10
Maclear	29	L5
McLennan	36	C8
McLoughlin, Mt.	38	E2
McMinnville, Oreg., U.S.A.	38	D2
McMinnville, Tenn., U.S.A.	43	H3
McMurdo Sd.	6	E15
McPherson	40	F6
McPherson Ra.	32	A5
Macon, Ga., U.S.A.	43	J4
Mâcon, France	12	C6
Macon, Miss., U.S.A.	43	J1
Macon, Mo., U.S.A.	40	F8
Macquarie Harbour	30	J8
Macquarie Is.	34	N7
Macroom	11	E3
Madagascar ■	29	J9
Madera	39	H3
Madeira →	46	C4
Madeleine, Îs. de la	37	D13
Madha Pradesh □	25	C6
Madison, Ind., U.S.A.	42	F3
Madison, S. Dak., U.S.A.	40	C6
Madison, Wis., U.S.A.	40	D10
Madison →	38	D8
Madison Heights	42	G6
Madisonville, Ky., U.S.A.	42	G2
Madisonville, Tex., U.S.A.	41	K7
Madras = Chennai	25	D7
Madre de Dios →	46	D3
Madre Occidental, Sierra	44	B3
Madre Oriental, Sierra	44	C5
Madrid	13	B4
Madurai	25	E6
Maesteg	9	F4
Mafeking	29	K5
Maffra	32	C4
Magadan	19	D16
Magallanes, Estrecho de	48	G2
Magangué	46	B2
Magdalena, Bolivia	46	D4
Magdalena, U.S.A.	39	J10
Magdeburg	16	B5
Magee	41	K10
Magelang	23	D3
Magellan's Str. = Magallanes, Estrecho de	48	G2
Maggiore, Lago	14	B3

Maggotty	44	a
Magherafelt	11	B5
Magnitogorsk	18	D6
Magnolia, Ark., U.S.A.	41	J8
Magnolia, Miss., U.S.A.	41	K9
Mahajanga	29	G9
Mahanadi →	25	C7
Maharashtra □	25	D6
Maheno	33	L3
Mahia Pen.	33	H6
Mahon	13	C8
Mahnomen	40	B7
Maiduguri	27	F8
Maidstone	9	F8
Maine □	43	C11
Maine →	11	D2
Main → , Germany	16	D4
Mainland, Orkney, U.K.	10	C5
Mainland, Shet., U.K.	10	A7
Mainz	16	C4
Maitland, N.S.W., Australia	32	B5
Maitland, S. Austral., Australia	32	B2
Majorca = Mallorca	13	C7
Makalu	23	D3
Makasar = Ujung Pandang	23	D3
Makasar, Selat	23	D3
Makedonía □	15	D10
Makeyevka = Makiyivka	17	A5
Makgadikgadi Salt Pans	29	J5
Makhachkala	17	A5
Makiyivka	17	A5
Makkah	24	C2
Mal B.	11	D2
Malabar Coast	25	D6
Malabo = Rey Malabo	28	D1
Malacca, Str. of	23	C2
Malad City	38	E7
Málaga	13	D3
Malahide	11	C5
Malaita	31	B11
Malakula	31	D12
Malang	23	D3
Malanje	28	F3
Mälaren	7	F7
Malatya	17	C6
Malawi ■	29	G6
Malawi, L. = Nyasa, L.	29	G6
Malaysia ■	23	C3
Malbooma	32	A1
Malden	41	G10
Malden I.	35	H12
Maldives ■	24	E5
Maldon	32	A5
Malheur →	38	D5
Malheur L.	38	E4
Mali ■	26	E5
Malin Hd.	11	A4
Malin Pen.	11	A4
Malines = Mechelen	16	C2
Mallacoota Inlet	32	C4
Mallaig	10	E3
Mallorca	13	C7
Mallow	11	D3
Malmö	7	F6
Malone	42	C8
Malpelo, I. de	35	G19
Malta, Idaho, U.S.A.	38	E7
Malta, Mont., U.S.A.	38	B10
Malta ■	14	G6
Maltby	8	D6
Malton	8	C7
Maluku	23	D4
Malvern, U.K.	9	E5
Malvern Hills	9	E5
Malvinas, Is. = Falkland Is. □	48	G5
Mamoré →	46	D3
Man, I. of	8	C3
Manado	23	C4
Manapouri	33	L1
Manapouri, L.	33	L1
Manas	20	B3
Manassa	39	H11
Manaus	46	C4
Manchester, U.K.	8	D5
Manchester, Ga., U.S.A.	43	J3
Manchester, Iowa, U.S.A.	40	D9
Manchester, Ky., U.S.A.	42	G4
Manchester, N.H., U.S.A.	42	D10
Manchester, Tenn., U.S.A.	43	H2
Manchuria = Dongbei	21	B7
Mandalay	24	D4
Mandan	40	B4
Mandsaur	25	C6
Mandurah	30	G2
Maneroo	32	A3
Mangaweka	33	H5
Mango	26	F6
Mangonui	33	F4
Manhattan	40	F6
Manicouagan, Rés.	37	C13
Manihiki	35	J11
Manila, Phil.	23	B4
Manila, U.S.A.	38	F9
Manistee	42	C2
Manistee →	42	C2
Manitoba □	36	C10
Manitoba, L.	36	C10
Manitou Is.	42	C2
Manitou Springs	40	F2
Manizales	46	B2
Mankato, Kans., U.S.A.	40	F5
Mankato, Minn., U.S.A.	40	C8
Mannar	25	E6
Mannar, G. of	25	E6
Mannheim	16	D4
Manning, Canada	36	C8
Manning, U.S.A.	43	J5
Mansel I.	37	B11
Mansfield, Australia	32	C4
Mansfield, U.K.	8	D6
Mansfield, Ohio, U.S.A.	42	E4
Mansfield, Mt.	42	C9
Mantalingajan, Mt.	23	C3
Manteca	38	H3
Manteo	43	H8
Mantes-la-Jolie	12	B4
Mántova	14	B4
Mantua = Mántova	14	B4
Manui	23	D4
Manukau	33	G5

Maputo 29 K6
Maquan He 20 D3
Maquoketa 40 D9
Mar Chiquita, L. 47 F4
Mar del Plata 48 D5
Marabá 46 C4
Maracaibo 46 A4
Maracaibo, L. de 46 B4
Maracay 46 A5
Marajó, I. de 46 C4
Marana 39 K8
Maranhão = São Luís 47 D10
Marañón → 46 C4
Marão 32 A4
Maraş = Kahramanmaraş 17 C5
Marathon 42 E1
Marbella 13 D3
Marble Falls 41 K5
March 9 E8
Marche 13 D3
Marco 43 N5
Marcus I. = Minami-Tori-Shima 34 E7
Marcus Necker Ridge 34 F9
Maree, L. 10 D3
Marengo 40 E8
Marfa 41 K2
Margarita, I. de 46 A6
Margate 9 F9
Margow, Dasht-e 24 D3
Maria I. 32 G4
Maria van Diemen, C. 31 F4
Mariana Trench 34 F6
Marianna, Ark., U.S.A. 41 J9
Marianna, Fla., U.S.A. 43 K3
Marias → 38 C8
Maribor 14 A6
Maricopa, Ariz., U.S.A. 39 K7
Maricopa, Calif., U.S.A. 39 J4
Marie Byrd Land 5 D14
Marie-Galante 44 b
Mariental 29 J3
Marietta, Ga., U.S.A. 43 J3
Marietta, Ohio, U.S.A. 42 F5
Marília 47 H9
Marinette 40 A6
Maringá 47 A6
Marion, Ill., U.S.A. 41 G10
Marion, Ind., U.S.A. 42 E3
Marion, Iowa, U.S.A. 40 D9
Marion, Kans., U.S.A. 40 F6
Marion, N.C., U.S.A. 43 H5
Marion, Ohio, U.S.A. 42 E4
Marion, S.C., U.S.A. 43 G5
Marion, Va., U.S.A. 43 G5
Mariposa 39 H4
Maritimes, Alpes 13 D7
Mariupol 17 A5
Marked Tree 41 H9
Market Drayton 8 E5
Market Harborough 9 E7
Market Rasen 8 D7
Markham, Mt. 6 F15
Marks 41 K9
Marksville 41 K8
Marla 32 A1
Marlborough 9 F6
Marlborough Downs 41 K6
Marlin 41 K6
Marlow 9 F7
Marmara Denizi 15 D13
Marmara, Sea of = Marmara Denizi 15 D13
Maroochydore 32 A5
Maroona 32 C3
Marquesas Is. = Marquises, Is. 35 H14
Marquette 42 B2
Marquis 45 f
Marquises, Is. 35 H14
Marrakech 26 B4
Marrawah 32 D3
Marree 32 A2
Marrero 41 L9
Marrowie Cr. → 32 B4
Mars Hill 43 C14
Marsden 32 B4
Marseille 13 E6
Marsh I. 41 L9
Marshall, Ark., U.S.A. 41 H8
Marshall, Mich., U.S.A. 42 D3
Marshall, Minn., U.S.A. 40 C7
Marshall, Mo., U.S.A. 40 F8
Marshall, Tex., U.S.A. 41 J7
Marshall Is. ■ 34 G9
Marshalltown 40 D8
Marshfield, Mo., U.S.A. 40 G8
Marshfield, Wis., U.S.A. 40 C9
Mart 41 K6
Martaban, G. of 25 D8
Martapura 22 D3
Martha's Vineyard 42 E10
Martigues 13 E6
Martin, S. Dak., U.S.A. 40 D4
Martin, Tenn., U.S.A. 41 G10
Martinborough 31 J5
Martinez 39 G3
Martinique ■ 44 c
Martin's Bay 45 g
Martins Ferry 42 F7
Martinsburg 42 F7
Martinsville, Ind., U.S.A. 42 F2
Martinsville, Va., U.S.A. 43 G6
Marton 31 J5
Maryborough = Port Laoise 10 E3
Maryborough, Queens., Australia 30 F9
Maryborough, Vic., Australia 32 C3
Maryland □ 42 F7
Maryport 8 C4
Marystown 37 D14
Marysville, Calif., U.S.A. 38 G3
Marysville, Kans., U.S.A. 40 F6
Marysville, Ohio, U.S.A. 42 E4
Maryville, Mo., U.S.A. 40 E7
Maryville, Tenn., U.S.A. 43 H4
Masan 21 C7
Masaya 44 E7
Masbate 23 B6
Maseru 29 K5
Mashhad 24 B4
Maşīrah 24 C4
Mask, L. 10 C2
Mason 41 K5
Mason City 40 D8
Masqat 24 C4
Massachusetts □ 42 D10
Massena 42 C8
Massawa = Mitsiwa 28 D2
Massiah Street 45 g
Massif Central 12 D5
Massillon 42 E5
Masterton 31 J5
Masvingo 29 J6
Mata Utu 35 C15
Matadi 26 G6
Matagalpa 44 E7
Matagami 37 D12
Matagami, L. 37 D12
Matagorda B. 41 L6
Matamoros, Coahuila, Mexico 44 B5
Matamoros, Tamaulipas, Mexico 44 B5
Matanzas 37 D13
Matapan, C. = Taínaron, Ákra 15 F10
Matara 25 C5
Mataró 13 B7
Mataura 31 M2
Matehuala 44 C4
Matera 14 D7
Mathis 41 L6
Mathura 25 C5
Mati 23 C7
Matiri Ra. 33 J4

Matlock 8 D6
Mato Grosso □ 47 F8
Mato Grosso, Planalto do 47 G8
Matsue 22 F3
Matsumoto 22 E6
Matsusaka 22 F5
Matsuyama 22 G3
Mattagami → 37 C11
Mattancheri 25 G6
Mattawa 37 D12
Matterhorn 12 E4
Matthew, I. 31 E13
Matún 12 A6
Maubeuge 12 A6
Maud 41 H6
Maude 32 B3
Maughold Hd. 8 C3
Maumee 42 E4
Maumee → 42 E4
Maumere 23 F6
Maun 29 H4
Maupin 38 D3
Maupas, L. 41 K9
Maupas, L. 41 K9
Mauritania ■ 26 E3
Mauritius ■ 5 F12
Mauston 40 D9
Mauston 40 D9
May, C. 42 F8
May Pen 44 a
Mayaguana 45 C10
Mayagüez 45 d
Maybell 38 F9
Maybole 10 F4
Maydena 32 D4
Mayenne 12 B3
Mayfield 43 G1
Mayhill 39 K11
Maykop 17 B6
Maynard 38 C2
Maynooth 10 E5
Mayo 36 B6
Mayo □ 10 C2
Mayor I. 31 G6
Maysville 42 F4
Mayville 40 B6
Mazār-e Sharīf 24 B5
Mazatlán 44 C3
Mazurian Lakes = Mazurski, Pojezierze 16 B10
Mazurski, Pojezierze 16 B10
Mbabane 29 K6
Mbandaka 26 D3
Mbanza Ngungu 26 F2
Mbeya 28 F6
Mbini = Río Muni □ 28 D2
Mbuji-Mayi 28 F4
Mead, L. 39 H6
Meade 41 G4
Meadow Lake 36 C9
Meadow Valley Wash → 39 H6
Meadville 42 E5
Meares, C. 38 D2
Meath □ 10 C5
Meaux 12 B5
Mecca = Makkah 16 C2
Mechelen 11 C4
Mecklenburg 16 B5
Medan 22 D1
Médéa 26 A6
Medellín 46 B3
Medford, Oreg., U.S.A. 38 E2
Medford, Wis., U.S.A. 40 C9
Medicine Bow 38 F10
Medicine Bow Pk. 38 F10
Medicine Bow Ra. 38 F10
Medicine Hat 36 D8
Medicine Lake 40 A2
Medicine Lodge 41 G5
Medina = Al Madīnah 24 C2
Medina, N. Dak., U.S.A. 40 B5
Medina, N.Y., U.S.A. 42 D6
Medina, Ohio, U.S.A. 42 E5
Medina → 41 L5
Mediterranean Sea 12 D3
Médoc 12 D3
Medway → 9 F8
Medway □ 9 F8
Meekatharra 30 F2
Meeker 38 F10
Meerut 25 C6
Meghalaya □ 25 C8
Mehlville 40 F9
Meizhou 21 D6
Mejillones 48 A2
Mekele 28 C3
Mekvari = Kür → 24 B3
Mekong → 25 D5 (Mekong → 23 C2)
Melaka 22 C2
Melanesia 34 H7
Melbourne, Australia 32 C4
Melbourne, U.S.A. 43 L5
Melekeok 23 C8
Melfort 36 C9
Melilla 13 E4
Melitopol 17 A5
Mellen 40 B9
Mellette 40 C5
Melolo 23 F6
Melrose, Minn., U.S.A. 40 C7
Melrose, N. Mex., U.S.A. 41 H3
Melstone 38 C10
Melton Mowbray 9 E7
Melun 12 B5
Melville 36 C9
Melville, L. 37 C14
Melville I., Australia 30 C5
Melville I., Canada 4 B2
Melville Pen. 4 B11
Memel = Klaipėda 18 D3
Memmingen 16 E6
Memphis, Tenn., U.S.A. 41 H10
Memphis, Tex., U.S.A. 41 H4
Mena 41 H7
Menai Strait 8 D3
Ménaka 26 E6
Mendip Hills 9 F5
Mendocino 38 F1
Mendocino, C. 38 F1
Mendota, Calif., U.S.A. 39 H3
Mendota, Ill., U.S.A. 40 E10
Mendoza 48 C3
Menemen 15 E12
Menominee 42 C2
Menominee → 42 C2
Menomonie 40 C9
Menorca 13 C8
Mentawai, Kepulauan 22 E1
Mentor 42 E5
Merbein 32 B3
Merced 39 H3
Merced → 39 H3
Mercedes 48 C4
Mercury, Nev., U.S.A. 37 B13
Mere 9 F5
Meredith, L. 41 H4
Mergui 23 B1
Mergui Arch. = Myeik Kyunzu 23 B1
Mérida, Mexico 44 C7
Mérida, Spain 13 C2
Mérida, Venezuela 46 B4
Mérida, Cord. de 46 B4
Meriden, U.K. 9 E6
Meriden, U.S.A. 42 E9
Meridian, Idaho, U.S.A. 38 E5
Meridian, Miss., U.S.A. 43 J1
Merkel 41 J4
Merkel 41 J4
Merredin 30 G2
Merrick 10 F4
Merrill, Oreg., U.S.A. 38 E3
Merrill, Wis., U.S.A. 40 C10
Merriman 40 D4
Merritt 36 C7
Merritt Island 43 L5
Merriwa 32 B5
Merriwagga 32 B4
Merry Hill 33 M2
Mersea I. 9 F8
Merseburg 16 C6
Mersey → 8 D4
Merseyside □ 8 D4
Mersin 17 C4

Merthyr Tydfil 9 F4
Mertzon 41 K4
Mesa 39 K8
Mesa Verde Nat. Park 39 H9
Mesilla 39 K10
Mesopotamia = Al Jazīrah 24 B3
Mesquite 39 H6
Messina, Italy 14 E6
Messina, S. Africa 14 E6
Messina, Str. di 14 F6
Meta → 46 B5
Meta Incognita Peninsula 37 B13
Metairie 41 L9
Metaline Falls 38 B5
Methven 33 K3
Metlakatla 36 C6
Metropolis 41 G10
Metz 12 B7
Meuse → 11 C5
Mexia 41 K6
Mexiana, I. 46 C4
Mexicali 44 A1
Mexican Water 39 H9
México, Mexico 44 D5
Mexico, Maine, U.S.A. 42 C10
Mexico, Mo., U.S.A. 40 F9
Mexico ■ 44 C4
Mexico, G. of 44 B7
Meymaneh 24 B4
Mezen 18 A5
Mezen → 18 A5
Mglin 18 C4
Mhow 25 C6
Miami, Fla., U.S.A. 43 N5
Miami, Okla., U.S.A. 41 G7
Miami, Tex., U.S.A. 41 H4
Miami Beach 43 N5
Mianwali 25 B6
Mianyang 20 C5
Miarinarivo 29 H9
Miass 18 D10
Michigan □ 42 C3
Michigan, L. 42 D2
Michigan City 42 E2
Michurinsk 18 D5
Micoud 45 f
Micronesia 34 G7
Micronesia, Federated States of ■ 34 G7
Middelburg 11 C3
Middelburg 11 C3
Middle Alkali L. 38 F3
Middle Loup → 40 E5
Middlebury 42 C9
Middleport 42 F4
Middlesboro 43 G4
Middlesbrough 8 C6
Middlesbrough □ 8 C6
Middleton 42 E8
Middletown, U.K. 11 B5
Middletown, N.Y., U.S.A. 42 E8
Middletown, Ohio, U.S.A. 42 F3
Midhurst 9 G7
Midi, Canal du → 12 E4
Midland, Mich., U.S.A. 42 D3
Midland, Tex., U.S.A. 41 K3
Midlothian 41 J6
Midlothian □ 10 F5
Midway Is. 34 E10
Midwest 38 E10
Midwest City 41 H6
Mieres 13 A3
Mikkeli 6 F13
Milaca 40 C8
Milan = Milano 12 D8
Milan, Tenn., U.S.A. 43 H1
Milano 12 D8
Milâs 15 F12
Milbank 40 C6
Mildenhall 9 E8
Mildura 32 B3
Miles 32 A5
Miles City 40 B2
Milford, Del., U.S.A. 42 F8
Milford, Utah, U.S.A. 39 G7
Milford Haven 9 F2
Milford Sd. 33 L1
Milford Sound 33 L1
Milh, Baḩr al 38 B10
Milk → 38 B10
Mill City 38 D2
Millau 12 D5
Mille Lacs L. 40 B8
Milledgeville 43 J4
Millen 43 J5
Millennium I. = Caroline I. 35 H12
Miller 40 C5
Millicent 32 A3
Millinocket 43 C11
Millmerran 32 A5
Millom 8 C4
Mills 41 H10
Milltown Malbay 10 D2
Millville 42 F8
Millwood L. 41 J8
Milo 43 C11
Milparinka 32 A3
Milton, N.Z. 33 M2
Milton, Fla., U.S.A. 43 K2
Milton-Freewater 38 D4
Milton Keynes 9 E7
Milton Keynes □ 9 E7
Milwaukee 42 D2
Milwaukee → 38 D2
Min Jiang →, Fujian, China 21 D6
Min Jiang →, Sichuan, China 20 D5
Minami-Tori-Shima 34 E7
Minas Gerais □ 47 G9
Minatitlán 44 D6
Minbu 25 C8
Mindanao 23 C6
Mindanao Trench 23 B7
Minden, La., U.S.A. 41 J8
Minden, Nev., U.S.A. 38 G4
Mindoro 23 B6
Mindoro Str. 23 B6
Mineral Wells 41 J5
Minehead 9 F4
Mineola 41 J7
Minersville 39 G7
Minidoka 38 E7
Minna 26 G7
Minneapolis, Kans., U.S.A. 40 F6
Minneapolis, Minn., U.S.A. 40 C8
Minnesota □ 40 B7
Minnewaukan 40 A5
Minnipa 32 B2
Minorca = Menorca 13 C8
Minot 40 A4
Minsk 17 B4
Mintabie 32 A1
Minto, L. 37 C12
Minturn 38 G10
Minzhong 21 D6
Miramichi 37 D13
Mirbāṭ 24 D4
Mirjāveh 24 C5
Mirpur Khas 25 C5
Mirzapur 25 C7
Mishan 21 B8
Mishawaka 42 E2
Mishmi Hills 25 C9
Miṣrātah 27 B9
Mississippi □ 41 J10
Mississippi → 41 L10
Mississippi River Delta 41 L10
Mississippi Sd. 41 K10
Missoula 38 C6
Missouri □ 40 F8
Missouri → 40 F9
Missouri City 41 L7
Missouri Valley 40 E7
Mistassini, L. 37 C12
Misurata = Miṣrātah 27 B9
Mitchell, Australia 32 A4
Mitchell, Oreg., U.S.A. 38 D3
Mitchell, S. Dak., U.S.A. 40 D6
Mitchell, Mt. 43 H4
Mitchell → 30 D7
Mitchelstown 10 D3

Mitiwa 24 D2
Mittagong 32 B5
Mitumba, Mts. 28 F5
Miyakonojō 22 H2
Miyazaki 22 H2
Mizen Hd., Cork, Ireland 10 E2
Mizen Hd., Wick., Ireland 10 D5
Mizoram □ 25 C8
Mjösa 6 F11
Mkomazi → 29 K6
Mo i Rana 6 C9
Moab 39 G9
Moala 31 D8
Moama 32 C3
Moapa 39 H6
Moate 10 C4
Moberly 40 F8
Mobile 43 K1
Mobile B. 43 K1
Mobridge 40 C4
Moçâmedes 29 H3
Mochudi 29 J5
Mococa 47 A6
Mocorito 44 B3
Mocuba 29 H7
Modane 12 D7
Modder → 29 K5
Módena, Italy 14 B4
Modena, U.S.A. 39 H7
Modesto 39 H3
Moe 32 C4
Moffat 10 F5
Mogadishu = Muqdisho 24 E3
Mogi das Cruzes 48 A7
Mogilev = Mahilyow 18 D7
Mogollon Rim 39 J8
Mohall 40 A4
Mohave, L. 39 J6
Mohawk → 42 D8
Moisie 37 C13
Moisie → 37 C13
Mojave 39 J4
Mojave Desert 39 J5
Mokau 31 H5
Mokpo 21 C7
Mol 11 C5
Mold 8 D4
Moldavia = Moldova ■ 17 A3
Molde 6 F10
Moldova ■ 17 A3
Mole → 9 F7
Mole Creek 32 D4
Molepolole 29 J5
Moline 40 E9
Mollendo 46 G4
Molong 32 B4
Molopo → 29 K4
Molotov = Perm 18 D10
Molucca Sea 23 E6
Moluccas = Maluku 23 E7
Mombasa 28 E7
Mona, Canal de la 45 D11
Mona Passage = Mona, Canal de la 45 D11
Monadhliath Mts. 10 D4
Monaghan 10 B5
Monaghan □ 10 B5
Monahans 41 K3
Monar, L. 10 D3
Monastir = Bitola 15 D9
Mönchengladbach 16 C3
Moncks Corner 43 J5
Monclova 44 B4
Moncton 37 D13
Moneague 44 a
Monessen 42 E6
Monett 41 G8
Moneymore 11 B5
Mongolia ■ 19 E10
Mongu 29 H4
Monifieth 10 E5
Monkira 32 C3
Monmouth, U.K. 9 F5
Monmouth, Ill., U.S.A. 40 E9
Monmouth, Oreg., U.S.A. 38 D2
Monmouthshire □ 9 F4
Mono L. 39 H4
Monona 40 D9
Monroe, Ga., U.S.A. 43 J4
Monroe, La., U.S.A. 41 J8
Monroe, Mich., U.S.A. 42 E4
Monroe, N.C., U.S.A. 43 H5
Monroe, Utah, U.S.A. 39 G7
Monroe, Wis., U.S.A. 40 D10
Monroe City 40 F9
Monrovia 26 G3
Mons 11 D3
Mont-de-Marsan 12 E3
Mont-Laurier 37 D12
Montana □ 38 C8
Montargis 12 C5
Montauban 12 D4
Montauk 42 E10
Montauk Pt. 42 E10
Montbéliard 12 C7
Montceau-les-Mines 12 C6
Monte-Carlo 13 D7
Monte Vista 39 H10
Montebello 44 a
Montego Bay 44 a
Montélimar 13 D6
Montemorelos 44 B5
Montenegro □ 15 C8
Monteria 46 B3
Monterey 39 H3
Monterrey 44 B4
Montes Claros 47 G10
Montesano 38 C2
Montevideo, Uruguay 48 C5
Montevideo, U.S.A. 40 C7
Montezuma 40 E8
Montgomery, Ala., U.S.A. 43 J2
Montgomery, W. Va., U.S.A. 42 F5
Montgomery City 40 F9
Monticello, Ark., U.S.A. 41 J9
Monticello, Fla., U.S.A. 43 K4
Monticello, Ind., U.S.A. 42 E2
Monticello, Ky., U.S.A. 42 G3
Monticello, Minn., U.S.A. 40 C8
Monticello, Miss., U.S.A. 41 K9
Monticello, Utah, U.S.A. 39 H9
Montluçon 12 C5
Montmagny 37 D12
Montpelier, Idaho, U.S.A. 38 E8
Montpelier, Vt., U.S.A. 42 C9
Montpellier 12 E5
Montréal 37 D12
Montreux 12 C7
Montrose, U.K. 10 E5
Montrose, U.S.A. 39 G10
Montserrat ■ 45 D12
Monza 12 D8
Moonie 32 A5
Moonie → 32 A4
Moora 30 G2
Moorcroft 40 C2
Moore → 30 F2
Moorefield 42 F6
Moorfoot Hills 10 F5
Moorhead 40 B6
Moose → 37 C11
Moose Jaw 36 C9
Moose Lake 40 B8
Moosehead L. 43 C11
Mooselookmeguntic L. 43 C10
Moosomin 36 C9
Moosonee 37 C11
Mopti 26 F5
Mora, Minn., U.S.A. 40 C8
Mora, N. Mex., U.S.A. 39 J11
Moradabad 25 C6
Moran, Kans., U.S.A. 41 G7
Moran, Wyo., U.S.A. 38 E8
Morant Bay 44 a
Morant Pt. 44 a
Moratuwa 25 G6
Morava →, Serbia, Yug. 15 C9
Morava →, Slovak Rep. 16 D8
Moravian Hts. = Českomoravská Vrchovina 16 D7

Moray Firth 10 D5
Morden 36 D10
Moreau → 40 C4
Morecambe 8 C5
Morecambe B. 8 C5
Moree 32 A4
Morehead City 43 H7
Morelia 44 D4
Morena, Sierra 13 C3
Moresby I. 36 C6
Moreton I. 32 A5
Morgan 32 B2
Morgan City 41 L9
Morganfield 42 G2
Morganton 43 H5
Morgantown 42 F6
Moriarty 39 J10
Morioka 22 E7
Morley 8 D6
Mornington 32 C4
Moro G. 23 C6
Morocco ■ 26 B4
Morogoro 28 F7
Morón 45 C9
Morón 45 C9
Morotai 23 D7
Morpeth 8 B6
Morrilton 41 H8
Morrinsville 31 G5
Morris, Ill., U.S.A. 42 E1
Morris, Minn., U.S.A. 40 C7
Morrison 40 E10
Morristown, Ariz., U.S.A. 39 K7
Morristown, Tenn., U.S.A. 43 G4
Morro Bay 39 J3
Mortlake 32 C3
Morton, Tex., U.S.A. 41 J3
Morton, Wash., U.S.A. 38 C2
Morundah 32 B4
Moruya 32 C5
Morven 32 A4
Morwell 32 C4
Moscow = Moskva 18 C4
Moscow 38 C5
Mosel → 12 A7
Moselle = Mosel → 12 A7
Moses Lake 38 C4
Mosgiel 33 L3
Moshi 28 E7
Moskva 18 C4
Mosquero 41 H3
Moss Vale 32 B5
Mosselbaai 29 L4
Mossendjo 28 E2
Mossoró 47 E11
Most 16 C6
Mostaganem 26 A6
Mostar 15 C7
Mosul = Al Mawşil 24 B3
Motherwell 10 F5
Motueka 33 J4
Motueka → 33 J4
Moulamein 32 B3
Moule à Chique, C. 45 f
Moulins 12 C5
Moulmein 25 D8
Moulouya, O. → 26 B5
Moultrie 43 K4
Moultrie, L. 43 J5
Mound City, Mo., U.S.A. 40 E7
Mound City, S. Dak., U.S.A. 40 C4
Moundsville 42 F5
Mount Airy 43 G5
Mount Barker 30 G2
Mount Burr 32 A3
Mount Carmel 42 F2
Mount Clemens 42 D4
Mount Darwin 29 H6
Mount Gambier 32 A3
Mount Hagen 34 H6
Mount Hope, N.S.W., Australia 32 B4
Mount Hope, S. Austral., Australia 32 B2
Mount Isa 30 E6
Mount Lofty Ra. 32 B2
Mount Magnet 30 F2
Mount Maunganui 31 G6
Mount Morgan 30 E9
Mount Pearl 37 D14
Mount Perry 32 A5
Mount Pleasant, Iowa, U.S.A. 40 E9
Mount Pleasant, Mich., U.S.A. 42 D3
Mount Pleasant, S.C., U.S.A. 43 J6
Mount Pleasant, Tenn., U.S.A. 43 H2
Mount Pleasant, Tex., U.S.A. 41 J7
Mount Pleasant, Utah, U.S.A. 38 G8
Mount Rainier Nat. Park 38 C3
Mount Shasta 38 F2
Mount Sterling, Ill., U.S.A. 40 F9
Mount Sterling, Ky., U.S.A. 42 F4
Mount Vernon, Ill., U.S.A. 40 F10
Mount Vernon, Ohio, U.S.A. 42 E4
Mount Vernon, Wash., U.S.A. 38 B2
Mountain Ash 9 F4
Mountain City, Nev., U.S.A. 38 F6
Mountain Grove 41 G8
Mountain Home, Ark., U.S.A. 41 G8
Mountain Home, Idaho, U.S.A. 38 E6
Mountain View 41 H8
Mountainair 39 J10
Mountmellick 10 C4
Mountrath 10 D4
Moura 46 D6
Mourne → 11 B4
Mourne Mts. 11 B5
Moven Atlas 26 B5
Moy → 10 B2
Moyale 28 D7
Mozambique ■ 29 H7
Mozambique Chan. 5 F11
Mu Us Shamo 20 C5
Muar 22 C2
Muck 10 E2
Muckadilla 32 A4
Mudanjiang 21 B7
Mudgee 32 B5
Mudgee Cr. → 32 A3
Mufulira 29 G5
Muine Bheag 10 D5
Mukden = Shenyang 21 B7
Mukomuko 22 E2
Mula 13 C5
Mulchén 48 D2
Mulde → 16 C6
Muleshoe 41 H3
Mulhacén 13 D4
Mülheim 16 C3
Mulhouse 12 C7
Mull 10 E3
Mull, Sound of 10 E3
Muller, Pegunungan 22 D4
Mullet Pen. 10 B1
Mullewa 30 F2
Mullingar 10 C4
Mullins 43 H6
Mullumbimby 32 A5
Multan 25 B6
Mulroy B. 10 A4
Mumbai 25 D6
Muna 23 F6
München 16 D6
Muncie 42 E3

Mundabbera 32 A5
Munday 41 J5
Münster, Ireland 10 D3
Munising 42 B2
Münster 16 C3
Muntok 22 E3
Muonio 6 E12
Muping 21 C7
Muqdisho 24 E3
Mur → 16 E8
Murat → 24 B3
Murchison → 30 F1
Murcia 13 D5
Murcia □ 13 D5
Murdo 40 D4
Mureş → 17 A2
Murfreesboro, N.C., U.S.A. 43 G7
Murfreesboro, Tenn., U.S.A. 43 H2
Murgon 32 A5
Müritz 16 B6
Murmansk 18 A4
Murom 18 C5
Muroran 22 D7
Muroto 22 G4
Murphy 38 E5
Murphys 39 H4
Murray, Ky., U.S.A. 43 G1
Murray, Utah, U.S.A. 38 F8
Murray → 32 B2
Murray, L. 43 H5
Murray Bridge 32 B2
Murrumbidgee → 32 B3
Murrumburrah 32 B4
Murrurundi 32 B5
Murtoa 32 C3
Murwillumbah 32 A5
Mürzzuschlag 16 E8
Mûsa, Gebel 27 C12
Musala 15 C10
Muscat = Masqat 24 C4
Muscatine 40 E9
Musgrave Ranges 30 F5
Musi → 22 E2
Muskeg → 36 B7
Muskegon 42 D2
Muskegon → 42 D2
Muskegon Heights 42 D2
Muskogee 41 H7
Musselburgh 10 F5
Musselshell → 38 C10
Mustang 25 C7
Mutare 29 H6
Muting 23 F10
Mutton L. 11 D2
Mwanza 28 E6
Mweelrea 10 C2
Mweru, L. 28 F5
My Tho 23 B3
Myanmar = Burma ■ 25 C8
Myeik Kyunzu 23 B1
Myingyan 25 C8
Myitkyina 25 C8
Mykolaiv 17 A4
Mymensingh 25 C8
Mynydd Du 9 F4
Myrtle Beach 43 J6
Myrtle Creek 38 E2
Myrtle Point 38 E1
Mysore 25 D6

N

Na Hearadh = Harris 10 D2
Naab → 16 D6
Naas 10 C5
Nabereznyye Chelny 18 D9
Naches 38 C3
Nacimiento L. 39 J3
Nacogdoches 41 K7
Nacozari 44 A3
Nadiad 25 D6
Nafud Desert = An Nafūd 24 C3
Naga 23 B6
Nagaland □ 25 C8
Nagano 22 E6
Nagaoka 22 E6
Nagasaki 22 G1
Nagaur 25 C6
Nagercoil 25 G6
Nagoya 22 F5
Nagpur 25 D7
Naguabo 45 d
Naha 22 G1
Nain 37 C13
Nairn 10 D5
Nairobi 28 E7
Najd 24 C3
Nakhodka 19 E14
Nakhon Ratchasima 23 B2
Nakhon Sawan 23 B2
Nakhon Si Thammarat 23 C1
Nakina 37 C11
Nakuru 28 E7
Nalchik 17 B6
Nam Co 20 C3
Nam Dinh 20 D5
Namacunde 29 H3
Namak, Daryācheh-ye 24 B4
Namaland 29 J3
Namangan 18 E8
Namapa 29 H7
Namber 23 E8
Nambour 32 A5
Nambucca Heads 32 B5
Namcha Barwa 20 D4
Namib Desert 29 J2
Namibe 29 H2
Namibia ■ 29 J3
Namlea 23 E7
Namoi → 32 B4
Nampa 38 E5
Namp'o 21 C7
Nampula 29 H7
Namrole 23 E7
Namse Shankou 25 C7
Namur 11 D4
Namutoni 29 H3
Nan 23 A2
Nanaimo 36 D7
Nanango 32 A5
Nanchang 21 D6
Nanchong 20 C5
Nancy 12 B7
Nanded 25 D6
Nandurbar 25 D6
Nandyal 25 D6
Nanga Parbat 25 B6
Nanjing 21 C6
Nanking = Nanjing 21 C6
Nanning 20 D5
Nanpara 25 C7
Nansen Sd. 4 A3
Nantes 12 C3
Nanticoke 42 E7
Nantong 21 C7
Nantucket I. 42 E10
Nantwich 8 D5
Nanuque 47 G10
Nanusa, Kepulauan 23 D7
Nanyang 21 C6
Napa 38 G2
Napanee 42 B7
Napier 31 H6
Naples = Nápoli 14 D6
Naples 43 N5
Napo → 46 D4
Napoleon, N. Dak., U.S.A. 40 B5
Napoleon, Ohio, U.S.A. 42 E3
Nápoli 14 D6
Nara 22 F4
Nara Visa 41 H3
Naracoorte 32 A3
Narayanganj 25 C8
Narbonne 12 E5
Nares Str. 4 B13
Narew → 16 B11
Narmada → 25 D6
Narodnaya 18 A10
Narooma 32 C5
Narrabri 32 B4
Narran → 32 A4
Narrandera 32 B4
Narromine 32 B4
Narvik 6 C11
Naryan-Mar 18 A9
Naseby 33 L3
Naser, Buheirat en 27 D12
Nashua, N.H., U.S.A. 42 D10
Nashville, Ark., U.S.A. 41 J8
Nashville, Ga., U.S.A. 43 K4
Nashville, Tenn., U.S.A. 43 G2
Nasik 25 D6
Nassau 45 B9
Nassau, B. 48 H3
Nasser, L. = Naser, Buheirat en 27 D12
Natal 47 E11
Natanz 24 B4
Natashquan 37 C13
Natashquan → 37 C13
Natchez 41 K9
Natchitoches 41 K8
Nathalia 32 C4
Natimuk 32 C3

Natuna Besar, Kepulauan 23 C2
Natuna Selatan, Kepulauan 23 C2
Naturaliste, C. 34 H5
Nauru ■ 34 H10
Navajo Reservoir 39 H10
Navan = An Uaimh 11 B5
Navarra □ 13 A5
Navasota 41 K6
Navojoa 44 B3
Navolato 44 C3
Nawabshah 25 C5
Naxçıvan 17 B6
Naze, The 9 F9
Ndjamena 27 F8
Ndola 29 G5
Neagh, Lough 11 B5
Near Is. 36 C1
Neath 9 F5
Nebine Cr. → 32 A4
Nebraska □ 40 E5
Nebraska City 40 E7
Necedah 40 C9
Neches → 41 K7
Neckar → 16 D4
Necochea 48 D5
Needles 39 J6
Needles, The 9 G6
Neenah 42 C1
Neepawa 36 C10
Nefyn 8 E3
Negele 24 D2
Negombo 25 G6
Negra, Pta. 46 E2
Negril 44 a
Negro →, Argentina 48 E4
Negro →, Brazil 46 D7
Negros 23 C6
Nei Monggol Zizhiqu □ 21 B6
Neijiang 20 D5
Neillsville 40 C9
Neilton 38 C2
Neiva 46 C3
Nejanilini L. 36 B10
Nekemte 28 D7
Nelson, Canada 36 D8
Nelson, N.Z. 33 J4
Nelson, U.K. 8 D5
Nelson, U.S.A. 39 J7
Nelson → 36 C10
Nelson, C. 32 C3
Nelspruit 29 K6
Neman → 18 D3
Nemunas = Neman → 18 D3
Nen Jiang → 21 B7
Nenagh 10 D3
Nene → 9 E8
Nenjiang 21 B7
Neosho 41 G7
Neosho → 41 H7
Nepal ■ 25 C7
Nephi 38 G8
Nephin 10 B2
Nerang 32 A5
Ness, L. 10 D4
Ness City 40 F5
Nesterov 18 E3
Netherlands ■ 11 C5
Netherlands Antilles ■ 45 E11
Nettilling L. 37 B12
Neuchâtel 12 C7
Neuchâtel, Lac de 12 C7
Neuse → 43 H7
Neusiedler See 16 E9
Nevada, Iowa, U.S.A. 40 D8
Nevada, Mo., U.S.A. 40 G7
Nevada □ 38 G5
Nevada, Sierra, Spain 13 D4
Nevada, Sierra, U.S.A. 38 G3
Nevada City 38 G3
Nevers 12 C5
Nevertire 32 B4
Nevinnomyssk 17 B6
New → 42 F5
Nevada, Iowa 40 D8
New Albany, Ind., U.S.A. 42 F3
New Albany, Miss., U.S.A. 41 H10
New Angledool 32 A4
New Baltimore 46 B7
New Bedford 42 E10
New Bern 43 H7
New Boston 41 J7
New Braunfels 41 L5
New Brighton 33 K4
New Britain, Papua N. G. 34 H7
New Britain, U.S.A. 42 E9
New Brunswick 42 E8
New Brunswick □ 37 D13
New Caledonia ■ 31 E12
New Castle, Ind., U.S.A. 42 F3
New Castle, Pa., U.S.A. 42 E5
New Delhi 25 C6
New England 40 B3
New England Ra. 32 B5
New Forest 9 G6
New Galloway 10 F4
New Georgia Is. 31 B7
New Glasgow 37 D13
New Guinea 34 H6
New Hampshire □ 42 D10
New Hampton 40 D8
New Haven 42 E9
New Hebrides = Vanuatu ■ 34 J8
New Iberia 41 K9
New Ireland 34 H7
New Jersey □ 42 E8
New Lexington 42 F4
New Liskeard 37 D12
New London, Conn., U.S.A. 42 E9
New London, Wis., U.S.A. 42 C1
New Madrid 41 G10
New Martinsville 42 F5
New Meadows 38 D5
New Mexico □ 39 J10
New Norfolk 32 D4
New Orleans 41 L9
New Philadelphia 42 E5
New Plymouth, N.Z. 31 H5
New Plymouth, U.S.A. 38 E5
New Providence 45 B9
New Quay 9 E3
New Radnor 9 E4
New Richmond 40 C8
New Roads 41 K9
New Rockford 40 B5
New Romney 9 G8
New Ross 10 D5
New Salem 40 B4
New Siberian Is. = Novosibirskiye Ostrova 19 B15
New Smyrna Beach 43 L5
New South Wales □ 32 B4
New Town 40 B3
New Ulm 40 C7
New Waterford 37 D13
New York 42 E9
New York □ 42 D8
New York Mts. 39 J6
New Zealand ■ 31 J6
Newala 28 G7
Newark, Del., U.S.A. 42 F8
Newark, N.J., U.S.A. 42 E8
Newark, N.Y., U.S.A. 42 D7
Newark, Ohio, U.S.A. 42 E4
Newark-on-Trent 8 D7
Newark-on-Trent 8 D7
Newberry, Mich., U.S.A. 42 B3
Newberry, S.C., U.S.A. 43 H5
Newbridge = Droichead Nua 10 C5
Newburgh 42 E8
Newbury 9 F6
Newburyport 43 D10
Newcastle, Australia 32 B5
Newcastle, Canada 37 D13
Newcastle Emlyn 9 E3

Newcastle-under-Lyme 8 D5
Newcastle-upon-Tyne 8 C6
Newcastle West 10 D2
Newell 40 C3
Newfoundland □ 37 C14
Newman 30 E2
Newmarket, Ireland 11 B5
Newmarket, U.K. 9 E8
Newnan 43 J3
Newport, Ireland 10 C2
Newport, Newp., U.K. 9 F5
Newport, I. of W., U.K. 9 G6
Newport, Ark., U.S.A. 41 H9
Newport, Ky., U.S.A. 42 F3
Newport, Oreg., U.S.A. 38 D1
Newport, R.I., U.S.A. 42 E10
Newport, Tenn., U.S.A. 43 H4
Newport, Vt., U.S.A. 42 C9
Newport, Wash., U.S.A. 38 B5
Newport Beach 39 K5
Newport News 42 G7
Newport Pagnell 9 E7
Newquay 9 G2
Newry 11 B5
Newton, Ill., U.S.A. 42 F1
Newton, Iowa, U.S.A. 40 E8
Newton, Kans., U.S.A. 40 F6
Newton, Mass., U.S.A. 42 D10
Newton, Miss., U.S.A. 41 J10
Newton, N.C., U.S.A. 43 H5
Newton, N.J., U.S.A. 42 E8
Newton Abbot 9 G4
Newton Aycliffe 8 C6
Newton Stewart 10 G4
Newtonhill 10 D6
Newtown 9 E4
Newtownabbey 11 B6
Newtownards 11 B6
Newtownstewart 11 B4
Nezperce 38 C5
Ngapara 33 L3
Ngoring Hu 20 C4
Nguigmi 27 F7
Nha Trang 23 B3
Niagara Falls, Canada 37 D12
Niagara Falls, U.S.A. 42 D6
Niamey 26 F6
Nias 22 D1
Nicaragua ■ 44 E7
Nicaragua, L. de 44 E7
Niceville 43 K2
Nicholasville 42 G3
Nicobar Is. 25 G8
Nicosia 17 B5
Nicoya, Pen. de 44 F7
Niedersachsen □ 16 B5
Niemen = Neman → 18 D3
Nieuw Nickerie 46 B7
Niğde 17 C5
Niger ■ 26 E7
Niger → 26 G7
Nigeria ■ 26 G7
Nightcaps 33 L2
Niigata 22 E6
Niihau 37 C12
Nijmegen 11 C5
Nikolayev = Mykolaiv 17 A4
Nikolayevsk-na-Amur 19 D15
Nikopol 17 A5
Niland 39 K6
Nile → 27 B12
Nîmes 13 E6
Nimmitabel 32 C4
Nindigully 32 A4
Ninepin Group 34 G6
Ningbo 21 D7
Ningjing Shan 20 D4
Ningxia Huizu Zizhiqu □ 20 C5
Niobrara 40 D5
Niobrara → 40 D5
Nipawin 36 C9
Nipigon 37 D11
Nipigon, L. 37 D11
Nipomo 39 J3
Niš 15 C9
Nisutlin → 36 B6
Nitra 16 D9
Nitra → 16 E9
Niuē 35 J11
Nivernais 12 C5
Nizamabad 25 D6
Nizhnevartovsk 18 C8
Nizhniy Novgorod 18 C5
Nizhniy Tagil 18 D10
Nízké Tatry 16 D9
Nizkeriya 17 C5
Nkongsamba 28 D1
Nobeoka 22 H2
Nobeoka 22 H2
Noblesville 42 E3
Nocona 41 J6
Nogales, Mexico 44 A2
Nogales, U.S.A. 39 L8
Noirmoutier, Î. de 12 C2
Nome 36 B3
Nong Khai 23 A2
Noranda = Rouyn-Noranda 37 D12
Nord-Ostsee-Kanal 16 A5
Nordfriesische Inseln 16 A5
Nordvik 19 B12
Norfolk, Nebr., U.S.A. 40 D6
Norfolk, Va., U.S.A. 42 G7
Norfolk □ 9 E9
Norfolk I. 34 K8
Norilsk 19 C9
Norman 41 H6
Norman Wells 36 B7
Normandie 12 B4
Normanton 30 D7
Norquinco 48 E2
Norrköping 6 G11
Norrland 6 F11
Norseman 30 G3
North, C. 37 D14
North Adams 42 D9
North Ayrshire □ 10 F4
North Battleford 36 C9
North Bay 37 D12
North Bend 38 E1
North Berwick 10 E6
North C. 31 F4
North Canadian → 41 H7
North Cape = North C. 31 F4
North Carolina □ 43 H6
North Cascades Nat. Park 38 B3
North Channel, Canada 42 B3
North Channel, U.K. 11 A6
North Charleston 43 J6
North Dakota □ 40 B5
North Down □ 11 B6
North Downs 9 F8
North East Lincolnshire □ 8 D7
North Esk → 10 E6
North Foreland 9 F9
North Frisian Is. = Nordfriesische Inseln 16 A5
North I. 31 H5
North Lanarkshire □ 10 F5
North Las Vegas 39 J6
North Little Rock 41 H8
North Loup → 40 E5
North Magnetic Pole 4 B2
North Minch 10 C3

North Myrtle Beach 43 J6
North Palisade 39 H4
North Platte 40 E4
North Platte → 40 E4
North Pole 4 A
North Pt. 45 g
North Ronaldsay 10 B6
North Saskatchewan → 36 C9
North Sea 3 B10
North Somerset □ 9 F5
North Sydney 37 D13
North Taranaki Bight 31 H5
North Thompson → 36 C8
North Truchas Pk. 39 J11
North Tyne → 8 B5
North Uist 10 D1
North Vernon 42 F3
North Wabasca L. 36 C8
North West C. 30 E1
North West Christmas I. Ridge 35 G11
North West Frontier □ 25 B6
North West Highlands 10 D4
North West River 37 C13
North Wildwood 42 F8
North York Moors 8 C7
North Yorkshire □ 8 C6
Northallerton 8 C6
Northam 30 G2
Northampton, U.K. 9 E7
Northampton, U.S.A. 42 D9
Northamptonshire □ 9 E7
Northern Ireland □ 11 B5
Northern Marianas ■ 34 F6
Northern Territory □ 30 D5
Northfield 40 C8
Northland □ 31 F4
Northome 40 B7
Northport, Ala., U.S.A. 43 J2
Northport, Wash., U.S.A. 38 B5
Northumberland □ 8 B6
Northumberland, C. 32 C3
Northumberland Str. 37 D13
Northwest Territories □ 36 B9
Northwood, Iowa, U.S.A. 40 D8
Northwood, N. Dak., U.S.A. 40 B6
Norton 40 F5
Norton Sd. 36 B3
Norwalk, Conn., U.S.A. 42 E9
Norwalk, Iowa, U.S.A. 40 E8
Norwalk, Ohio, U.S.A. 42 E4
Norway ■ 6 F11
Norway, Maine, U.S.A. 43 C10
Norway, Mich., U.S.A. 42 C2
Norway House 36 C10
Norwegian Sea 4 C8
Norwich, U.K. 9 E9
Norwich, Conn., U.S.A. 42 E9
Norwich, N.Y., U.S.A. 42 D8
Noss Hd. 10 C5
Nossob → 29 K4
Notre Dame B. 37 D14
Nottaway → 37 C12
Nottingham 8 E6
Nottingham I. 37 B12
Nottinghamshire □ 8 D7
Nottoway → 42 G7
Nouâdhibou 26 D2
Nouâdhibou, Ras 26 D2
Nouakchott 26 E2
Nouméa 31 F12
Nouvelle-Amsterdam, Î. 5 G13
Nova Friburgo 47 H10
Nova Iguaçu 48 A8
Nova Scotia □ 37 D13
Novara 12 D8
Novaya Zemlya 18 B7
Novgorod 18 C4
Novi Sad 15 B8
Novo Mesto 14 B6
Novocherkassk 17 B6
Novokuznetsk 18 D9
Novomoskovsk 18 D4
Novorossiysk 17 B6
Novosibirsk 18 D9
Novosibirskiye Ostrova 19 B15
Novotroitsk 18 D10
Nowata 41 G7
Nowra 32 B5
Nowy Sącz 16 D11
Nowy Tomyśl 16 B8
Noxen 42 E7
Noyon 12 B5
Nūbīya, Es Sahrâ en 27 D12
Nueces → 41 M6
Nueva Rosita 44 B4
Nuevitas 45 C9
Nuevo Laredo 44 B5
Nuevo León □ 44 C5
Nuk'alofa 31 E11
Nuku'alofa 31 E11
Nukulaelae 34 C10
Nukus 18 E7
Nullarbor Plain 30 G4
Numazu 22 F6
Nunap Isua 4 C5
Nunavut □ 4 B10
Nuneaton 9 E6
Nunivak I. 36 B3
Nürnberg 16 D6
Nuriootpa 32 B2
Nushki 25 B5
Nuweveldberge 29 L4
Nuyts Arch. 32 B1
Nyasa, L. 28 G6
Nyíregyháza 16 E11
Nylstroom 29 J5
Nyngan 32 B4
Nyoman = Neman → 18 D3
Nysa 16 C8
Nysa → 16 B7
Nyssa 38 E5

Ocean City, Md., U.S.A. 42 F8
Ocean City, N.J., U.S.A. 42 F8
Oceanside 39 K5
Ochil Hills 10 E5
Ocho Rios 44 a
Ocilla 43 K4
Ocmulgee → 43 K4
Oconee → 43 K4
Oconto Falls 42 C1
Odawara 22 F6
Odense 6 G10
Oder → 16 B7
Odesa = Odessa 17 A4
Odessa, Tex., U.S.A. 41 K3
Odessa, Wash., U.S.A. 38 C4
O'Donnell 41 J4
Odra = Oder → 16 B7
Oelrichs 40 D3
Oelwein 40 D9
Offa 26 G6
Offaly □ 10 C4
Offenbach 16 C5
Ogaden 24 D3
Ogasawara Gunto 34 E6
Ogbomosho 26 G6
Ogden 38 F7
Ogdensburg 42 C8
Ogeechee → 43 K5
Ogooué → = Ogowe → 28 E1
Ohakune 31 H5
Ohau, L. 33 L2
Ohio □ 42 E4
Ohio → 41 G10
Ohre → 16 C6
Ohridsko Jezero 15 D9
Oil City 42 E6
Oise → 12 B5
Ōita 22 G2
Ojai 39 J4
Ojos del Salado, Cerro 48 B3
Okanogan 38 B4
Okanogan → 38 B4
Okavango Delta 29 H4
Okayama 22 F3
Okazaki 22 F5
Okeechobee 43 M5
Okeechobee, L. 43 M5
Okefenokee Swamp 43 K4
Okehampton 9 G4
Okha 19 D15
Okhotsk, Sea of 19 D15
Okinawa-Jima 21 D7
Oklahoma □ 41 H6
Oklahoma City 41 H6
Okmulgee 41 H7
Okolona 41 J10
Oktyabrskiy Revolyutsii, Ostrov 19 B11
Ola 19 C16
Öland 6 G11
Olary 32 B3
Old Crow 36 B6
Old Town 43 C11
Oldbury 9 F5
Oldcastle 10 C4
Oldenburg 16 B5
Oldham 8 D5
Oléron, Î. d' 12 D3
Ólgiy 20 B4
Olhão 13 D2
Olímpia 46 A6
Olinda 47 E12
Olney, Ill., U.S.A. 42 F1
Olney, Tex., U.S.A. 41 J5
Olomouc 16 D8
Olsztyn 16 B11
Olt → 17 A2
Olton 41 H3
Olympia 38 C2
Olympic Mts. 38 C2
Olympic Nat. Park 38 C2
Olympus, Mt. = Olimbos, Óros 15 D10
Olympus, Mt. 38 C2
Omagh 11 B4
Omaha 40 E7
Omak 38 B4
Oman ■ 24 C4
Oman, G. of 24 C4
Omaruru 29 J3
Ombai, Selat 23 F6
Omdurmân 27 E12
Ometepec 44 D5
Ömuta 22 G2
Onaga 40 F6
Onalaska 40 D9
Onancock 43 G8
Onawa 40 D6
One Tree 32 B3
Onega, L. = Onezhskoye Ozero 7 E11
Onega → 18 B4
O'Neill 40 D5
Onekotan, Ostrov 19 E16
Oneonta 42 D8
Onezhskoye Ozero 7 E11
Ongarue 31 H5
Onitsha 26 G7
Onslow 30 E1
Onslow B. 43 H7
Ontario, Calif., U.S.A. 39 K5
Ontario, Oreg., U.S.A. 38 D5
Ontario □ 37 C11
Ontonagon 40 B10
Oodnadatta 32 A2
Ooldea 30 G5
Opala 28 E4
Opava 16 D8
Opelika 43 J3
Opelousas 41 K8
Opheim 38 B10
Opole 16 C8
Oporto = Porto 13 B1
Opotiki 31 H6
Opp 43 K2
Opunake 31 H4
Oracle 39 K8
Oradea 16 E11
Orai 25 C6
Öræfajökull 6 D5
Oral = Zhayyq → 18 E9
Oran 26 A5
Orange, France 13 D6
Orange, U.S.A. 41 K8
Orange, Va., U.S.A. 42 F6
Orange → 29 K3
Orange, C. 46 B8
Orange Grove 41 M6
Orangeburg 43 J5
Orchard City 39 G10
Ord → 30 C4
Ordos = Mu Us Shamo 20 C5
Örebro 6 G11
Oregon □ 38 E3
Oregon City 38 D2
Orel 18 D4
Orem 38 F8

Ocean City, Md. 42 F8
Ocean City, N.J. 42 F8
Ochil Hills 38 F6
...

Name	Page	Grid
Orenburg	18	D6
Orense = Ourense	13	A2
Orepuki	33	M1
Orford Ness	9	E9
Orhon Gol →	20	A5
Oriental, Cordillera	46	B4
Orinoco →	46	B6
Orissa □	25	D7
Oristano	14	E3
Orizaba	44	D5
Orizaba, Pico de	44	D5
Orkney Is.	10	B6
Orland	38	G2
Orlando	43	L5
Orléanais	12	C5
Orléans	12	C4
Ormara	24	C5
Ormoc	23	B4
Ormond	33	H5
Ormond Beach	43	L5
Örnsköldsvik	7	E7
Oro Valley	39	K8
Orofino	38	C5
Orono	43	C11
Oronsay	10	E2
Orogen Zizhiqi	21	A7
Oroville, Calif., U.S.A.	38	G3
Oroville, Wash., U.S.A.	38	B4
Orroroo	32	B2
Orsha	18	D4
Orsk	18	D10
Ortonville	40	C6
Oruimiyeh, Daryacheh-ye	24	B5
Oruro	46	G5
Orwell →	9	F9
Osage	40	D8
Osage →	40	F8
Osage City	40	F7
Ōsaka	22	F4
Osawatomie	40	F5
Osborne	40	F5
Osceola, Ark., U.S.A.	41	H10
Osceola, Iowa, U.S.A.	40	E8
Oscoda	42	C4
Osh	18	E8
Oshawa	37	D12
Oshkosh, Nebr., U.S.A.	40	E3
Oshkosh, Wis., U.S.A.	40	C10
Oshogbo	26	G6
Osijek	15	B8
Osipenko = Berdyansk	19	E6
Osizweni	29	K6
Oskaloosa	40	E8
Oskarshamn	7	F7
Oskemen	18	E9
Oslo	7	F6
Oslofjorden	7	F6
Osnabrück	16	B4
Osorno	48	E2
Ossa, Mt.	30	J8
Ossabaw I.	43	K5
Österdalälven	7	F6
Östersund	7	E6
Ostfriesische Inseln	16	B3
Ostrava	17	D10
Ostrów Wielkopolski	16	C8
Oswego	42	D7
Oswestry	8	E4
Otago □	33	L2
Otago Harbour	33	L3
Otaki	33	J5
Otaru	22	B7
Othello	38	C4
Otjiwarongo	29	J3
Otorohanga	33	H5
Otranto	15	D8
Otranto, Str. of	15	D8
Otsu	22	F4
Ottawa = Outaouais →	37	D12
Ottawa, Canada	37	D12
Ottawa, Ill., U.S.A.	40	E10
Ottawa, Kans., U.S.A.	40	F7
Ottawa Is.	37	C11
Otter St. Mary	9	G4
Ottumwa	40	E8
Otway, C.	32	C3
Ouachita →	41	K9
Ouachita Mts.	41	H8
Ouagadougou	26	F5
Ouarzazate	26	B4
Oubangi →	28	E3
Oudtshoorn	29	L4
Ouessant, Î. d'	11	C2
Oughterard	11	C2
Oujda	26	B5
Oulu	7	D9
Oulujärvi	7	E9
Oulujoki →	7	D9
Ouray	39	G10
Ourense	13	A2
Ouse →, E. Susx., U.K.	9	G8
Ouse →, N. Yorks., U.K.	8	D7
Outaouais →	37	D12
Outer Hebrides	10	D1
Outjo	29	J3
Ouyen	32	C3
Ovalau	33	C8
Overland Park	40	F7
Overton	39	H6
Oviedo	13	A3
Owaka	33	M2
Owatonna	40	C8
Owen Sound	30	B8
Owen Stanley Ra.	30	B8
Owens →	39	H5
Owensboro	42	G2
Owo	26	G7
Owosso	42	D3
Owyhee	38	F5
Owyhee →	38	E5
Owyhee, L.	38	E5
Ox Mts. = Slieve Gamph	11	B3
Oxford, N.Z.	33	K4
Oxford, U.K.	9	F6
Oxford, Miss., U.S.A.	41	H10
Oxford, N.C., U.S.A.	43	G6
Oxford, Ohio, U.S.A.	42	F3
Oxfordshire □	9	F6
Oxnard	39	J4
Oxus = Amudarya →	18	E6
Oyama	22	E6
Oykel →	10	D4
Oyo	26	G6
Ozark, Ala., U.S.A.	43	K3
Ozark, Ark., U.S.A.	41	H8
Ozark, Mo., U.S.A.	41	G8
Ozark Plateau	41	G9
Ozarks, L. of the	40	F8
Ozona	41	K4

P

Name	Page	Grid
Paamiut	37	B15
Paarl	29	L3
Pabbay	10	D1
Pacaraima, Sa.	46	C6
Pachuca	44	C5
Pacific-Antarctic Ridge	35	M16
Pacific Ocean	35	G14
Pacific Grove	38	H3
Padang	23	D2
Padangsidempuan	23	D1
Paderborn	16	C4
Padova = Pádova	14	B4
Padre I.	41	M6
Padstow	9	G3
Paducah, Ky., U.S.A.	42	G1
Paducah, Tex., U.S.A.	41	H4
Paeroa	33	G5
Pagadian	23	C4
Pago Pago	33	B13
Pagosa Springs	39	H10
Pahiatua	33	J5
Pahokee	43	M5
Pahrump	39	H6
Paignton	9	G4
Painted Desert	39	J8
Paintsville	42	G4
País Vasco □	13	A4
Paisley, U.K.	10	F4
Paisley, U.S.A.	38	E3
Pak Tam Chung	21	G11
Pakistan ■	24	C5
Pakokku	23	B2
Palacios	41	L6
Palagruža	32	C4
Palam	25	D6
Palanpur	25	C6
Palapye	29	J5
Palatka	43	L5
Palau ■	23	C5
Pee Dee →	43	J6
Palawan	23	C5
Palembang	23	D2
Palencia	13	A3
Palermo, Italy	14	E5
Palestine	41	K7
Palghat	25	D6
Pali	24	G8
Palikir	34	G7
Palk Strait	25	E6
Palm Bay	43	L5
Palm Beach	43	M6
Palm Coast	43	L5
Palm Springs	39	K5
Palma de Mallorca	13	C7
Palmas	46	E5
Palmdale	39	J4
Palmer	36	B5
Palmer Lake	40	F2
Palmer Land	6	E4
Palmerston	33	L3
Palmerston North	33	J4
Palmetto	43	M4
Palmira	46	C3
Palmyra Is.	35	G11
Palopo	23	D4
Palopo	23	J4
Palu	23	E6
Pamiers	12	E4
Pamir	18	F8
Pamlico →	43	H7
Pamlico Sd.	43	H8
Pampa	41	H4
Pampas	47	F3
Pamplona	13	A5
Pana	40	F10
Panaca	39	H6
Panaji	25	D6
Panamá	45	F9
Panamá ■	45	F9
Panama, G. de	45	F9
Panama Canal	45	F9
Panama City	43	K3
Panamint Range	39	H5
Panay	23	B4
Pančevo	15	B9
Panevėžys	7	F8
Pangkajene	23	D3
Pangkalpinang	23	D2
Pangnirtung	37	B13
Panguitch	39	H7
Panhandle	41	H4
Pantar	23	D4
Pantelleria	14	F4
Paola	40	F7
Paonia	39	G10
Papa Stour	10	A7
Papa Westray	10	B6
Papeete	35	J13
Papua New Guinea ■	34	H6
Pará = Belém	46	D5
Pará □	46	D4
Paracel Is.	23	B3
Parachilna	32	B2
Paradise	38	F3
Paradise Valley	38	F5
Paragould	41	G9
Paraguay ■	47	A5
Paraguay →	47	B5
Paraíba = João Pessoa	47	E12
Paraíba □	46	E11
Paramaribo	46	B7
Paraná	47	C4
Paraná □	47	A5
Paranaguá	47	B6
Parbhani	25	D6
Pardubice	16	C7
Parecis, Serra dos	46	F7
Parepare	23	D3
Paris, France	12	B5
Paris, Idaho, U.S.A.	38	E8
Paris, Ky., U.S.A.	42	F3
Paris, Tenn., U.S.A.	43	G1
Paris, Tex., U.S.A.	41	J7
Park City	41	G6
Park Falls	40	C9
Park Hills	41	G9
Park Rapids	40	B7
Park River	40	A6
Parker	39	J6
Parker Dam	39	J6
Parkersburg	42	F5
Parkston	40	D6
Parma, Italy	14	B4
Parma, Idaho, U.S.A.	38	E5
Parma, Ohio, U.S.A.	42	E5
Parnaíba →	47	D10
Paroo →	32	B3
Parowan	39	H7
Parrett →	9	F5
Parris I.	43	J5
Parry Is.	4	B2
Parry Sound	37	D12
Parsons	41	G7
Pasadena, Calif., U.S.A.	39	J4
Pasadena, Tex., U.S.A.	41	L7
Pascagoula	41	K10
Pascagoula →	41	K10
Pasco	38	C4
Pascua, I. de	35	K17
Pasni	24	C5
Paso Robles	39	J3
Passage West	11	E3
Passau	16	D7
Passo Fundo	47	B5
Pasto	46	C3
Patagonia, Argentina	48	F3
Patagonia, U.S.A.	39	L8
Patchewollock	32	C3
Patchogue	42	E9
Patea	33	H5
Paterson	42	E8
Petrified Forest Nat. Park	39	J9
Petrograd = Sankt-Peterburg	18	D4
Petropavl	18	D7
Petropavlovsk- Kamchatskiy	19	D17
Petrópolis	47	A7
Petrozavodsk	18	C4
Pforzheim	16	D5
Phan Thiet	23	B2
Pharr	41	M5
Phenix City	43	J3
Philadelphia, Miss., U.S.A.	41	J10
Philadelphia, Pa., U.S.A.	42	E8
Philip	40	C4
Philippi	42	F5
Philippines ■	23	B4
Philipsburg	38	C7
Phillip I.	32	C4
Phillips	40	C9
Phillipsburg	40	F5
Philomath	38	D2
Phnom Penh = Phnom Penh	23	B2
Phoenix	39	K7
Phoenix Is.	34	H10
Phra Nakhon Si Ayutthaya	23	B2

Name	Page	Grid
Peace River	36	C8
Peace River	12	D8
Peachtree City	43	J3
Peak District	8	D6
Peake Cr. →	32	A2
Peale, Mt.	39	G9
Pearl →	41	K10
Pearsall	41	L5
Pease →	41	H5
Peawanuck	37	C11
Pechora →	18	C6
Pecos	41	K3
Pecos →	41	L3
Pécs	16	E9
Pedder, L.	32	D4
Pedirka	32	A2
Peebles	10	F5
Peekskill	42	E9
Peel →	8	C3
Peel →, Australia	32	A2
Peel →, Canada	36	B6
Peel Sound	36	A10
Peera Peera Poolanna L.	32	A2
Pegasus Bay	33	K4
Pegu	25	D8
Pegu Yoma	25	D8
Peipus, L. = Chudskoye, Ozero	7	F9
Pekalongan	23	C2
Pekin	40	E10
Peking = Beijing	21	C6
Pelée, Mt.	44	c
Peleng	23	D4
Pella	40	E8
Pelly →	36	B6
Pelly Bay	37	B11
Peloponnese = Pelopónnisos □	15	F10
Pelopónnisos □	15	F10
Pelorus Sd.	33	J4
Pelotas	47	C5
Pelvoux, Massif du	12	D7
Pematangsiantar	23	C1
Pemba I.	28	F7
Pembina	40	A6
Pembroke, Canada	37	D12
Pembroke, U.K.	9	F3
Pembrokeshire □	9	F3
Pen-y-Ghent	8	C5
Penarth	9	F4
Penas, G. de	48	F2
Pend Oreille →	38	B5
Pend Oreille, L.	38	C5
Pendleton	38	D4
Peng Chau	21	G11
Penguin	32	D4
Penicuik	10	F5
Peninsular Malaysia □	23	C2
Penkridge	8	E5
Penmarch, Pte. de	11	B1
Penn Hills	42	E6
Penn Yan	42	D7
Pennines	8	C5
Pennington	39	H7
Pennsylvania □	42	E7
Penobscot →	43	C11
Penobscot B.	43	C11
Penola	32	C3
Penong	30	G5
Penrith, Australia	32	B5
Penrith, U.K.	8	C5
Penryn	9	G2
Pensacola	43	K2
Pensacola Mts.	6	E1
Penshurst	32	C3
Penticton	36	D8
Pentland Firth	10	C5
Pentland Hills	10	F5
Penza	18	D5
Penzance	9	G2
Peoria, Ariz., U.S.A.	39	K7
Peoria, Ill., U.S.A.	40	E10
Perabumulih	23	D2
Perdido, Mte.	13	A6
Perdu, Mt. = Perdido, Mte.	13	A6
Pereira	46	C3
Perham	40	B7
Péribonca →	37	D12
Périgueux	12	D4
Perm	18	D6
Pernambuco = Recife	47	E12
Pernatty Lagoon	32	B2
Perpendicular Pt.	32	B5
Perpignan	12	E5
Perry, Fla., U.S.A.	43	K4
Perry, Ga., U.S.A.	43	J4
Perry, Iowa, U.S.A.	40	E7
Perry, Okla., U.S.A.	41	G6
Perryton	41	G4
Perryville	41	G10
Persepolis	24	D4
Persian Gulf = Gulf, The	24	C4
Perth, Australia	30	G2
Perth, U.K.	10	E5
Perth & Kinross □	10	E5
Perth Amboy	42	E8
Peru ■	46	D4
Peru	42	E2
Peru Basin	35	J18
Peru-Chile Trench	35	K20
Perúgia	14	C5
Pervouralsk	18	D6
Pescara	14	C6
Peshawar	25	B6
Petah Tiqwa	47	D10
Petaling Jaya	23	D2
Petaluma	38	G2
Peter I. →	45	e
Peterborough, Australia	32	B2
Peterborough, Canada	37	D12
Peterborough, U.K.	9	E7
Peterculter	10	D6
Peterhead	10	D7
Peterlee	8	C6
Petersburg, Alaska, U.S.A.	36	C6
Petersburg, Va., U.S.A.	42	G7
Petersburg, W. Va., U.S.A.	42	F6
Petersfield	9	F7
Petit-Canal	44	a
Petit Piton	45	f
Petite Terre, Iles de la	44	b
Petitot →	44	b
Petitsikapau L.	37	C13
Peto	33	J4
Petone	33	J5
Petoskey	42	C3

Name	Page	Grid
Phuket	23	C1
Piacenza	12	D8
Pian Cr. →	32	B4
Picardie	12	B5
Picardy = Picardie	12	B5
Picayune	41	K10
Pichilemu	47	C2
Pickering, Vale of	8	C7
Pickwick L.	43	H1
Picton, Australia	32	B5
Picton, N.Z.	33	J5
Pidurutalagala	25	E7
Piedmont = Piemonte □	12	D7
Piedras Negras	44	B4
Piemonte □	12	D7
Pierre	40	C4
Piet Retief	29	K6
Pietermaritzburg	29	K6
Pietersburg	29	J5
Piggott	41	G9
Pikeville	42	G4
Pilcomayo →	48	B5
Pilibhit	25	C7
Pilica →	16	C10
Pilos	15	F9
Pima	39	K9
Pimba	32	B2
Pinar del Río	45	C8
Pincknevville	40	F10
Pindos Oros	15	E9
Pindus Mts. = Pindos Óros	15	E9
Pine Bluff	41	H9
Pine Bluffs	40	E2
Pine City	40	C8
Pine Point	36	B8
Pine Ridge	40	D3
Pine River	40	B7
Pinedale	38	E9
Pinetop	39	J9
Pineville	41	K8
Ping →	23	B2
Pingdingshan	21	C6
Pingdong	21	D7
Pingliang	20	C5
Pingtung	21	D7
Pinrang	23	D3
Pinsk	18	D3
Piotrków Trybunalski	16	C9
Pipestone	40	D6
Piqua	42	E3
Piracicaba	47	H9
Piraeus = Piraiévs	15	F10
Piraiévs	15	F10
Pisa	14	C4
Pishan	20	C2
Pit →	38	F2
Pitarpunga, L.	32	B3
Pitcairn I.	35	K14
Pitești	17	F13
Pitlochry	10	E5
Pittsburg, Kans., U.S.A.	41	G7
Pittsburg, Tex., U.S.A.	41	J7
Pittsburgh	42	E6
Pittsfield, Ill., U.S.A.	40	F9
Pittsfield, Maine, U.S.A.	43	C11
Pittsfield, Mass., U.S.A.	42	D9
Pittsworth	32	A5
Piura	46	E2
Placentia	37	D14
Placentia B.	37	D14
Placerville	38	G3
Placetas	45	C9
Plainfield	42	E8
Plains, Mont., U.S.A.	38	C6
Plains, Tex., U.S.A.	41	J3
Plainview, Nebr., U.S.A.	40	D6
Plainview, Tex., U.S.A.	41	H4
Plano	41	J6
Plant City	43	M4
Plaquemine	41	K9
Plata, Río de la	48	C5
Platte	40	D5
Platte →, Mo., U.S.A.	40	F7
Platte →, Nebr., U.S.A.	40	E7
Platteville	40	D9
Plattsburgh	42	C9
Plattsmouth	40	E7
Plauen	16	C6
Pleasanton	41	L5
Pleasantville	42	F8
Plenty, B. of	31	H14
Plentywood	40	A2
Plessisville	15	C11
Plevlja	16	B9
Płock	16	B9
Ploiești	15	B12
Plovdiv	15	C11
Plover Cove Res.	21	G11
Plummer	38	C5
Plymouth, U.K.	9	G3
Plymouth, Ind., U.S.A.	42	E2
Plymouth, N.C., U.S.A.	43	H7
Plymouth, Wis., U.S.A.	42	D2
Plynlimon = Pumlumon Fawr	9	E4
Plzeň	16	D6
Po →	14	B5
Pocahontas, Ark., U.S.A.	41	G9
Pocahontas, Iowa, U.S.A.	40	D7
Pocatello	38	E7
Pocomoke City	42	F8
Podgorica	15	C8
Pohnpei	34	G7
Point Hope	36	B3
Point L.	36	B8
Point Pleasant	42	F4
Pointe-à-Pitre	44	a
Pointe-Noire, Congo	28	E2
Poitiers	12	C4
Poitou	12	C3
Pojoaque	39	J11
Pokataroo	32	A4
Pokhara	25	C7
Pokrovsk = Engels	18	D5
Polacca	39	J8
Poland ■	16	C9
Polesye = Pripet Marshes	7	E8
Polotsk	18	D3
Poltava	19	E5
Polynesia	35	J11
Pomeroy, Ohio, U.S.A.	42	F4
Pomeroy, Wash., U.S.A.	38	C5
Pomona, Australia	32	A5
Pomona, U.S.A.	39	J5
Pompano Beach	43	M5
Pompeys Pillar	38	D10
Ponca	40	D6
Ponca City	41	G6
Ponce	45	d
Ponchatoula	41	K9
Pond Inlet	37	A12
Pondicherry	25	D7
Ponoka	36	C8
Ponta Grossa	47	B5
Pontarlier	12	C7
Pontchartrain L.	41	K10
Ponte Vedra	12	F4
Pontevedra	13	A1
Pontiac, Ill., U.S.A.	40	E10
Pontiac, Mich., U.S.A.	42	D4
Pontian Kechil	23	D2
Pontianak	23	D2
Pontine Is. = Ponziane, Ísole	14	D5
Pontypool	9	F4
Pontypridd	9	F4
Poole	9	G6
Poole □	9	G6

Name	Page	Grid
Pooncarie	32	B3
Poopelloe L.	32	B3
Poopó, L. de	46	G5
Popayán	46	C3
Popilta L.	32	B3
Popio L.	32	B3
Poplar	42	B2
Poplar Bluff	41	G9
Poplarville	41	K10
Popocatépetl, Volcán	44	D5
Porbandar	25	C5
Porcupine →	36	B5
Pori	7	E8
Port Alberni	36	D7
Port Allegany	42	E6
Port Allen	41	K9
Port Angeles	38	B2
Port Antonio	44	a
Port Aransas	41	M6
Port Arthur, Australia	30	J8
Port Arthur, U.S.A.	41	L8
Port-au-Prince	45	D10
Port Augusta	30	G6
Port Austin	42	C4
Port Blair	25	D8
Port Broughton	32	B2
Port-Cartier	37	C13
Port Chalmers	33	L3
Port Charlotte	43	M4
Port Chester	42	E9
Port Clinton	42	E4
Port Colborne	42	D7
Port Elgin	42	C6
Port Elizabeth	29	L5
Port Ellen	10	F2
Port Erin	8	C3
Port Fairy	32	C3
Port-Gentil	28	E1
Port Germein	32	B2
Port Gibson	41	K9
Port Glasgow	10	F4
Port Harcourt	26	H7
Port Hawkesbury	37	D13
Port Hedland	30	E2
Port Henry	42	C9
Port Hope Simpson	37	C14
Port Huron	42	D4
Port Jefferson	42	E9
Port Kenny	32	B1
Port Laoise	11	C4
Port Lavaca	41	L6
Port Lincoln	30	G6
Port Louis	29	J9
Port MacDonnell	32	C3
Port McNeill	36	C7
Port Macquarie	32	B5
Port Maria	44	a
Port Morant	44	a
Port Moresby	34	H6
Port Neches	41	L8
Port Nolloth	29	K3
Port of Spain	45	d
Port Orange	43	L5
Port Orford	38	E1
Port Pegasus	33	M1
Port Phillip B.	32	C3
Port Pirie	30	G6
Port St. Joe	43	L3
Port St. Lucie	43	M5
Port Shepstone	29	L6
Port Stanley = Stanley	48	G5
Port Sudan = Bûr Sûdân	27	E13
Port Sulphur	41	L10
Port Talbot	9	F4
Port Townsend	38	B2
Port Vila	34	J8
Port Wakefield	32	B2
Port Washington	42	D2
Portadown	11	B5
Portaferry	11	B6
Portage	40	D10
Portage La Prairie	36	D10
Portageville	41	G10
Portales	41	H3
Portarlington	11	C4
Porterville	39	H4
Porthcawl	9	F4
Porthill	38	B5
Porthmadog	8	E3
Portile de Fier	15	B10
Portishead	9	F5
Portknockie	10	D6
Portland, N.S.W., Australia	32	B3
Portland, Vic., Australia	32	C3
Portland, Maine, U.S.A.	37	D12
Portland, Mich., U.S.A.	42	D3
Portland, Oreg., U.S.A.	38	D2
Portland, Tex., U.S.A.	41	M6
Portland, I. of	9	G5
Portland B.	32	C3
Portland Bight	44	a
Portland Bill	9	G5
Portland Pt.	44	a
Portmadoc = Porthmadog	8	E3
Portmore	44	a
Porto	13	B1
Pôrto Alegre	48	C6
Porto-Novo	26	G6
Porto-Vecchio	12	F8
Porto Velho	46	E6
Portola	38	G3
Portoviejo	46	D2
Portpatrick	10	G3
Portree	10	D2
Portrush	11	A5
Portsmouth, U.K.	9	G6
Portsmouth, N.H., U.S.A.	43	D10
Portsmouth, Ohio, U.S.A.	42	F4
Portsmouth, Va., U.S.A.	42	G7
Portsmouth, U.K.	9	G6
Portstewart	11	A5
Portugal ■	13	C1
Portumna	11	C3
Posadas	47	B5
Possum Kingdom L.	41	J5
Post	41	J4
Post Falls	38	C5
Postmasburg	29	K4
Potchefstroom	29	K5
Poteau	41	H7
Poteet	41	L5
Potenza	14	D6
Poteriteri, L.	33	M1
Potgietersrus	29	J5
Potomac →	42	G7
Potosí	46	G5
Potsdam, Germany	16	B6
Potsdam, U.S.A.	42	C8
Pottstown	42	E8
Pottsville	42	E7
Poughkeepsie	42	E9
Poulaphouca Res.	11	C5
Poulsbo	38	C2
Poulton-le-Fylde	8	D5
Poverty B.	31	H14
Póvoa de Varzim	13	B1
Powassan	42	B7
Powder →	38	D10
Powell	38	D9
Powell, L.	39	H8
Powell River	36	D7
Powers	42	C2
Powys □	9	E4
Poyang Hu	21	D6
Poza Rica	44	C5
Poznań	16	B8
Prado	46	G11
Prague = Praha	16	C7
Praha	16	C7
Prairie City	38	D4
Prairie Dog Town Fork →	41	H5
Prata	46	G10
Prato	14	C4
Pratt	41	G5
Prattville	43	J2
Praya	23	D3

Name	Page	Grid
Prentice	40	C9
Québec	37	D12
Québec □	37	C13
Prescott Valley	39	J7
Prescott, Ariz., U.S.A.	39	J7
Prescott, Ark., U.S.A.	41	J8
Preservation Inlet	33	M1
Presho	40	D4
Presidente Prudente	47	H8
Presidio	41	L2
Prespansko Jezero	15	D9
Presque Isle	43	B12
Prestatyn	8	D4
Presteigne	9	E5
Preston, U.K.	8	D5
Preston, Idaho, U.S.A.	38	E8
Preston, Minn., U.S.A.	40	D8
Prestonsburg	42	G4
Prestwick	10	F4
Pretoria	29	K5
Pribilof Is.	36	C2
Price	38	G8
Prichard	43	K1
Prieska	29	K4
Priest L.	38	B5
Priest River	38	B5
Prime Seal I.	32	D4
Prince Albert	36	C9
Prince Albert Pen.	36	A8
Prince Albert Sd.	36	A8
Prince Charles I.	37	B12
Prince Charles Mts.	6	D6
Prince Edward I. □	37	D13
Prince Edward Is.	5	G11
Prince George	36	C7
Prince of Wales I., Canada	36	A10
Prince of Wales I., U.S.A.	36	C6
Prince Patrick I.	6	B1
Prince Rupert	36	C6
Princeton, Ill., U.S.A.	40	E10
Princeton, Ind., U.S.A.	42	F2
Princeton, Ky., U.S.A.	42	G2
Princeton, Mo., U.S.A.	40	E8
Princeton, W. Va., U.S.A.	42	G5
Principe, I. de	5	D10
Prineville	38	D3
Priozersk	18	C4
Pripet →	17	C16
Pripet Marshes	7	E9
Pripyat Marshes = Pripet Marshes	7	E9
Pripyats →	17	C16
Prishtinë	15	C9
Privas	12	D6
Prizren	15	C9
Prodolinggo	23	D3
Progreso	44	C7
Prokopyevsk	18	D9
Prosser	38	C4
Proston	32	A5
Provence	12	E6
Providence, Ky., U.S.A.	42	G2
Providence, R.I., U.S.A.	42	E10
Providencia, I. de	45	E8
Provins	12	B5
Provo	38	F8
Prudhoe Bay	36	A5
Pryor	41	G7
Prypyat →	17	C16
Pskov	18	D3
Puebla	44	D5
Pueblo	40	F2
Puerca, Pta.	45	d
Puerco →	39	J10
Puerto Barrios	44	D7
Puerto Cabezas	45	E8
Puerto Cortés	44	D7
Puerto La Cruz	46	A6
Puerto Plata	45	D10
Puerto Princesa	23	C3
Puerto Rico □	45	d
Puffin I.	11	E1
Puget Sound	38	C2
Pukaki, L.	33	L3
Pukapuka	35	J11
Pukekohe	33	G5
Pulaski, Tenn., U.S.A.	43	H2
Pulaski, Va., U.S.A.	42	G5
Pullman	38	C5
Pulog, Mt.	23	B4
Pumlumon Fawr	9	E4
Pune	25	D6
Punjab □, India	25	D6
Punjab □, Pakistan	25	D6
Punta Arenas	48	G2
Punta Gorda	43	M4
Punto Fijo	46	A4
Punxsatawney	42	E6
Purbeck, Isle of	9	G5
Purcell	41	H6
Puri	25	E7
Purus →	46	D6
Pusan	21	C7
Putao	25	C8
Putaruru	33	H5
Puttalam	25	E6
Putumayo →	46	D5
Puy-de-Dôme	12	D5
Puyallup	38	C2
Pwllheli	8	E3
Pyapon	25	D8
P'yŏngyang	21	C7
Pyote	41	K3
Pyramid L.	38	F4
Pyrénées	12	E4

Q

Name	Page	Grid
Qaanaaq	6	B3
Qahremänshahr = Bakhtärän	24	B3
Qaidam Pendi	20	C4
Qamdo	20	C4
Qandahär	24	D4
Qaraghandy	18	E8
Qaraghan He →	20	C3
Qarshi	18	F7
Qattâra, Munkhafed el	27	C11
Qattâra Depression = Qattâra, Munkhafed el	27	C11
Qazvin	24	B4
Qena	27	C12
Qeqertarsuaq, Greenland	6	B5
Qeqertarsuaq, Greenland	37	B14
Qeshm	24	C4
Qian Gorlo	21	B7
Qianshan	20	B6
Qi'ao	21	G10
Qi'ao Dao	21	G10
Qian Shan	20	C5
Qilian Shan	20	C4
Qingdao	21	C7
Qinghai □	20	C4
Qinghai Hu	20	C5
Qinhuangdao	21	C6
Qinzhou	20	D5
Qiqihar	21	B7
Qitai	20	B3
Qom	24	B4
Qoraqalpoghistan □	18	E6
Qostanay	18	D7
Quang Ngai	23	B2
Quanzhou	21	D6
Quaqtaq	37	B13
Quartzsite	39	K6

R

Name	Page	Grid
Raahe	7	E8
Raasay	10	D2
Raasay, Sd. of	10	D2
Raba	23	D3
Rabat	26	B4
Rabaul	34	H7
Race, C.	37	D14
Rach Gia	23	B2
Racine	42	D2
Radcliff	42	G3
Radford	42	G5
Radnor Forest	9	E4
Radstock, C.	32	B1
Rae	36	B8
Rae Isthmus	37	B11
Raetihi	33	H5
Ragged Pt.	45	g
Raglan	33	G5
Ragusa	14	F6
Raichur	25	D6
Railton	32	D4
Rainbow Lake	36	C8
Rainier	38	C2
Rainier, Mt.	38	C3
Rainy L.	36	D10
Raipur	25	C7
Rajahmundry	25	D7
Rajang →	23	D3
Rajapalaiyam	25	E6
Rajasthan □	25	C6
Rajkot	25	C6
Rakaia	33	K4
Rakaia →	33	K4
Raleigh	43	H6
Rame Hd.	32	C4
Râmnicu Vâlcea	15	B11
Ramona	39	K5
Ramore I.	42	B6
Rampur	25	C7
Ramsey	8	C3
Rancagua	47	C2
Ranchi	25	C7
Randalstown	11	B5
Randolph, Utah, U.S.A.	38	F8
Randolph, Vt., U.S.A.	42	C9
Ranganu B.	33	G4
Rangeley	42	C10
Rangitaiki →	33	K4
Rangitata →	33	K3
Rangoon	25	D8
Rankin	41	K4
Rankin Inlet	36	B10
Rankins Springs	32	B4
Rannoch, L.	10	E4
Rannoch Moor	10	E4
Rantemario	23	D3
Rantoul	40	E10
Rapa	35	K13
Rapid City	40	C3
Rapid River	42	C2
Rapti →	25	C7
Raraku	35	K12
Rarotonga	35	K12
Ra's al Khaymah	24	C4
Rasht	24	B3
Rat Islands	36	C1
Rat Luirc	11	D3
Rathdrum	11	D5
Rathkeale	11	D3
Rathlin I.	11	A5
Rathmelton	11	A4
Raton	41	G2
Rattray Hd.	10	D7
Raukumara Ra.	33	H6
Raurkela	25	C7
Ravenna, Italy	14	B5
Ravenna, U.S.A.	40	E5
Ravenswood	42	F5
Rawalpindi	25	B6
Rawene	33	F4
Rawlins	38	F10
Rawson	48	F3
Ray, C.	37	D14
Rayleigh	9	F8
Rayville	41	J9
Razgrad	15	C12
Ré, Î. de	12	C3
Reading, U.K.	9	F7
Reading, U.S.A.	42	E8
Reay Forest	10	C4
Rebun-Tō	22	B7
Recife	47	E12
Red →, N. Dak., U.S.A.	40	A6
Red →, La., U.S.A.	41	K9
Red Bluff	38	F2
Red Bluff L.	41	K3
Red Cliffs	32	B3
Red Deer	36	C8
Red Lake	36	C10
Red Lodge	38	D9
Red Oak	40	E7
Red Rock, L.	40	E8
Red Wing	40	C8
Redcar	8	C6
Redcar & Cleveland □	8	C7
Redcliffe	32	A5
Redding	38	F2
Redditch	9	E6
Redfield	40	C5
Redon	11	C5
Redruth	9	G2
Redwood City	39	H2
Redwood Falls	40	C7

Name	Page	Grid
Redwood Nat. Park	38	F1
Reed City	42	D3
Reedley	39	H4
Reedsburg	40	D9
Reedsport	38	E1
Reefton	33	K3
Reese →	38	F5
Refugio	41	L6
Regensburg	16	D6
Réggio di Calábria	14	E6
Réggio nell'Emília	14	B4
Regina	36	C9
Rehoboth	29	J3
Reichenbach	16	C6
Reidsville	43	G6
Reigate	9	F7
Reims	12	B6
Reindeer L.	36	C9
Reinga, C.	30	H13
Remarkable, Mt.	32	B2
Remeshk	24	C4
Renfrewshire □	10	F4
Renmark	32	B3
Rennell	31	C11
Rennes	11	B8
Reno	38	G4
Rensselaer	42	E2
Renton	38	C2
Republic, Mo., U.S.A.	41	G8
Republic, Wash., U.S.A.	38	B4
Republican →	40	F6
Repulse Bay	37	B11
Resistencia	47	B5
Resolution I., Canada	37	B13
Resolution I., N.Z.	33	L1
Retford	8	D7
Réthímnon	15	G11
Réunion ■	5	F12
Reval = Tallinn	18	D3
Revelstoke	36	C8
Rexburg	38	E8
Rey Malabo	28	B1
Reykjavík	6	B1
Reynosa	44	B5
Rhayader	9	E4
Rhein →	16	C3
Rheine	16	B3
Rhineland-Pfalz □	16	D3
Rhin = Rhein →	16	C3
Rhine = Rhein →	16	C3
Rhineland-Palatinate = Rheinland-Pfalz □	16	D3
Rhinelander	40	C10
Rhinns Pt.	10	F2
Rhode Island □	42	E10
Rhodopi Planina	15	D11
Rhön	16	C5
Rhondda	9	F4
Rhondda Cynon Taff □	9	F4
Rhum	10	E2
Rhyl	8	D4
Riau, Kepulauan	23	C2
Ribble →	8	D5
Ribeirão Prêto	47	H9
Riccarton	33	K4
Rice Lake	40	C9
Richards Bay	29	K6
Richardson Lakes	42	C10
Richey	38	C11
Richfield	39	G8
Richland, Ga., U.S.A.	43	J3
Richland, Wash., U.S.A.	38	C4
Richland Center	40	D9
Richlands	42	G5
Richmond, N.Z.	33	J4
Richmond, Calif., U.S.A.	38	H2
Richmond, Ind., U.S.A.	42	F3
Richmond, Ky., U.S.A.	42	G3
Richmond, Mo., U.S.A.	40	F8
Richmond, Va., U.S.A.	42	G7
Richmond, Utah, U.S.A.	38	F8
Richmond Ra.	32	A5
Richwood	42	F5
Ridgecrest	39	J5
Ridgeland	43	J5
Ridgway	42	E6
Ridgway	38	G10
Rifle	38	G10
Rigby	38	E8
Riggins	38	D5
Rigolet	37	C14
Rijeka	16	F7
Riley	38	E4
Rimini	14	B5
Rimouski	37	D13
Rio Branco	46	E5
Río Cuarto	47	C4
Rio de Janeiro	47	H10
Rio Gallegos	48	G3
Rio Grande = Grande, Rio →	41	N6
Río Grande, Brazil	48	C6
Río Grande, Nic.	45	E8
Rio Grande City	41	M5
Rio Grande do Norte □	47	E11
Rio Rancho	39	J10
Riobamba	46	D3
Ripley, Tenn., U.S.A.	41	H10
Ripley, W. Va., U.S.A.	42	F5
Ripon, U.K.	8	C6
Ripon, U.S.A.	42	D1
Riverdale	38	H2
Riverhead	42	E9
Riverton, N.Z.	33	M2
Riverton, U.S.A.	38	E9
Rivière-du-Loup	37	D13
Rivière-Pilote	44	c
Rivière-Salée	44	c
Riyadh = Ar Riyâd	24	C3
Road Town	45	e
Roan Plateau	38	G9
Roanne	12	C6
Roanoke, Ala., U.S.A.	43	J3
Roanoke, Va., U.S.A.	42	G6
Roanoke →	43	H7
Roanoke I.	43	H8
Roanoke Rapids	43	G7
Robbins I.	32	D4
Robert Lee	41	K4
Robertson	29	L3
Robinson →	30	D6
Robinvale	32	B3
Robson, Mt.	36	C8
Robstown	41	M6
Roca, C. da	13	C1
Rocha	47	C6
Rochdale	8	D5
Rochefort	12	D3
Rochelle	40	E10
Rochester, U.K.	9	F8
Rochester, Ind., U.S.A.	42	E2
Rochester, Minn., U.S.A.	40	C8
Rochester, N.H., U.S.A.	43	D10
Rochester, N.Y., U.S.A.	42	D7
Rock →	36	B7
Rock Hill	43	H5
Rock Island	40	E9
Rock Rapids	40	D6
Rock Sound	45	C9
Rock Springs, Mont., U.S.A.	38	C10
Rock Springs, Wyo., U.S.A.	38	F9

Name	Page	Grid
Rock Valley	40	D6
Rockford	41	K6
Rockhampton	30	E9
Rockingham	43	H6
Rockland, Idaho, U.S.A.	38	E7
Rockland, Maine, U.S.A.	43	C11
Rockland, Mich., U.S.A.	40	B10
Rockport, Mo., U.S.A.	40	E7
Rockport, Tex., U.S.A.	41	M6
Rocksprings	41	K4
Rockville	42	F7
Rockwall	41	J6
Rockwell City	40	D7
Rockwood, Maine, U.S.A.	43	C11
Rockwood, Tenn., U.S.A.	43	H3
Rocky Ford	40	F3
Rocky Mount	43	H7
Rocky Mountain Nat. Park	38	F11
Rocky Mts.	4	C5
Rodney, C.	33	G5
Rodez	12	D5
Rodriguez	5	F13
Roe →	11	A5
Roes Welcome Sd.	37	B11
Rogers	41	G7
Rogers City	42	C4
Rogue →	38	E1
Rojo, C.	44	C5
Rolla	41	G9
Roma, Australia	30	F8
Roma, Italy	14	D5
Roma, N.Y., U.S.A.	42	D8
Romain C.	43	J6
Romaine →	37	C13
Romania ■	17	F12
Romans-sur-Isère	12	D6
Rome = Roma	14	D5
Rome, Ga., U.S.A.	43	H3
Rome, N.Y., U.S.A.	42	D8
Romney	42	F6
Romney Marsh	9	F8
Romorantin-Lanthenay	12	C4
Romsey	9	F6
Rona	10	D3
Ronda	13	D3
Rondônia □	46	F6
Rong, I. la	36	C9
Ronne Ice Shelf	6	E4
Ronse	10	D3
Roof Butte	39	H9
Roosevelt →	46	E6
Roosevelt I.	6	E16
Roraima □	46	C6
Roraima, Mt.	46	B6
Røros	7	E6
Rosario, Argentina	47	C4
Rosario, Mexico	44	C3
Roscommon	11	C3
Roscommon □	11	C3
Roscrea	11	D4
Rose Blanche	37	D14
Roseau, Domin.	45	D12
Roseau, U.S.A.	40	A7
Roseberry	32	D4
Rosebud, S. Dak., U.S.A.	40	D4
Rosebud, Tex., U.S.A.	41	K6
Roseburg	38	E2
Rosemary	41	K7
Rosenberg	41	L7
Rosenheim	16	E6
Rosetown	36	C9
Roseville	38	G3
Rosewood	32	A5
Ross, N.Z.	33	K3
Ross Ice Shelf	6	F16
Ross L.	38	B3
Ross River	36	B6
Ross Sea	6	E15
Rosscarbery	11	E2
Rosses, The	11	A3
Rosslare	11	A3
Rosslare Harbour	11	D5
Rosso	26	E2
Rossosh	19	D6
Rostock	16	A6
Rostov	19	E6
Roswell, Ga., U.S.A.	43	H3
Roswell, N. Mex., U.S.A.	41	J2
Rotan	41	J4
Rother →	9	G8
Rotherham	8	D6
Rothes	10	D5
Rothesay	10	F3
Roti	23	D4
Rotorua	33	H6
Rotorua, L.	31	H14
Rotterdam	16	C3
Rotuma	34	J9
Roubaix	12	A5
Rouen	12	B4
Round Mountain	38	G5
Round Rock	41	K6
Rousay	10	B5
Roussillon	12	E5
Rouyn-Noranda	37	D12
Rovaniemi	7	D9
Rovno = Rivne	17	C14
Rowena	32	A4
Roxas	23	B4
Roxboro	43	G6
Royal Canal	11	C4
Royal Leamington Spa	9	E6
Royal Tunbridge Wells	9	F8
Royston	9	E7
Rtishchevo	18	D5
Ruahine Ra.	33	H6
Ruapehu	33	H5
Ruapuke I.	33	M2
Rub' al Khali	24	D3
Rugby, U.K.	9	E6
Rugby, U.S.A.	40	A5
Rügen	16	A6
Ruhr →	16	C4
Ruidoso	39	K11
Rum = Rhum	10	E2
Rum Jungle	30	D5
Rumania = Romania ■	17	F12
Rumford	42	C10
Runanga	33	K3
Runaway, C.	31	H14
Runcorn	8	D5
Ruoqiang	20	C3
Rupat	23	C2
Rush	11	C5
Rushden	9	E7
Rushville, Ill., U.S.A.	40	E9
Rushville, Nebr., U.S.A.	40	D3
Russell	40	F5
Russellville, Ala., U.S.A.	43	H2
Russellville, Ark., U.S.A.	41	H8
Russellville, Ky., U.S.A.	42	G2
Russia ■	19	C11
St. Martins	45	g

Name	Page	Grid
Rustenburg	29	K5
Ruston	41	J8
Ruteng	23	D4
Rutland	42	D9
Rutland □	9	E7
Rutland Water	9	E7
Ruwenzori	28	D5
Rwanda ■	28	E5
Ryan, L.	10	G3
Rybinsk	18	D4
Ryde	9	G6
Rye	9	G8
Rye →	8	C7
Rye Bay	9	G8
Rye Patch Reservoir	38	F4
Ryegate	38	C9
Ryōtsu	22	E6
Ryukyu Is. = Ryūkyū-rettō	21	D7
Ryūkyū-rettō	21	D7
Rzeszów	7	G8

S

Name	Page	Grid
Saale →	16	C5
Saar →	12	B7
Saarbrücken	16	D3
Sabadell	13	B7
Sabah □	23	C3
Sabinal	41	L5
Sabinas	44	B4
Sabinas Hidalgo	44	B4
Sabine →	41	L8
Sabine Pass	41	L8
Sable, C.	37	D13
Sable I.	37	D14
Sac City	40	D7
Sachsen □	16	C6
Sachsen-Anhalt □	16	C6
Saco, Maine, U.S.A.	43	D10
Saco, Mont., U.S.A.	38	B10
Sacramento	38	G3
Sacramento →	38	G3
Sacramento Mts.	39	K11
Safford	39	K9
Saffron Walden	9	E8
Safi	26	B4
Saga	22	G2
Sagar	25	C6
Saginaw	42	D4
Saginaw B.	42	D4
Sagua la Grande	45	C8
Saguache	39	G10
Saguaro Nat. Park	39	K8
Sahara	26	D6
Saharanpur	25	C6
Saharien, Atlas	26	B6
Sahuarita	39	L8
Sai Kung	21	G11
Sa'idābād	24	C4
Saigon = Thanh Pho Ho Chi Minh	23	B2
St. Abb's Head	10	F6
St. Albans, U.K.	9	F7
St. Albans, Vt., U.S.A.	42	C9
St. Albans, W. Va., U.S.A.	42	F5
St. Alban's Head	9	G5
St. Andrews	10	E6
St. Ann's Bay	44	a
St. Anthony, Canada	37	C14
St. Anthony, U.S.A.	38	E8
St. Arnaud	32	C3
St-Augustin-Saguenay	37	C14
St-Barthélemy	45	D12
St. Austell	9	G3
St-Brieuc	12	B2
St. Catharines	42	D7
St. Catherine's Pt.	9	G6
St. Charles, Ill., U.S.A.	42	E1
St. Charles, Mo., U.S.A.	40	F9
St. Christopher-Nevis = St. Kitts & Nevis ■	45	D12
St. Cloud, Fla., U.S.A.	43	L5
St. Cloud, Minn., U.S.A.	40	C7
St. Croix	45	d
St. Croix →	40	C8
St. Croix Falls	40	C8
St. David's	9	F2
St. David's Head	9	F2
St-Denis	5	F12
St. Elias, Mt.	36	B5
St. Elias Mts.	36	B5
St-Dizier	12	B6
St-Flour	12	D5
St. Francis	40	F4
St. Francis →	41	H9
St. Francisville	41	K9
St-Gaudens	12	E4
St. George, Australia	32	A4
St. George, Utah, U.S.A.	43	J5
St. George's	45	E12
St. George's Basin	32	B5
St. George's Channel	11	E6
St-Gilles	12	E6
St. Gotthard P. = San Gottardo, P. del	16	E5
St. Helena, Atl. Oc.	5	E9
St. Helena B.	29	L3
St. Helens, Australia	30	J8
St. Helens, U.K.	8	D5
St. Helens, Mt.	38	C2
St. Helier	11	B9
St-Hyacinthe	37	D12
St. Ignace	42	C3
St. Ives	9	G2
St. James	40	D7
St-Jean, L.	37	D12
St-Jérôme	42	C8
St. John, Canada	37	D13
St. John →	43	C11
St. John's, Antigua	45	D12
St. John's, Canada	37	D14
St. Johns, Ariz., U.S.A.	39	J9
St. Johns, Mich., U.S.A.	42	D3
St. Johns →	43	L5
St. Johnsbury	42	C9
St. Joseph, La., U.S.A.	41	K9
St. Joseph, Mo., U.S.A.	40	F7
St. Joseph →	42	F2
St. Joseph, L.	37	C10
St. Kitts & Nevis ■	45	D12
St. Lawrence →	37	D13
St. Lawrence, Gulf of	37	D13
St. Lawrence I.	36	B2
St-Louis, Senegal	26	E2
St. Louis, U.S.A.	40	F9
St. Lucia ■	45	f
St. Lucia, L.	29	K6
St. Magnus B.	10	A7
St-Malo	11	B8
St-Marc	45	C10
St. Maries	38	C5
St-Martin	45	C7
St. Martins	45	g

Name	Pg	Ref
St. Mary Pk.	32	B2
St. Marys, Australia	32	D4
St. Mary's, Corn., U.K.	9	H1
St. Mary's, Orkney, U.K.	10	C6
St. Marys, Ga., U.S.A.	43	K5
St. Matthew I.	36	B2
St-Nazaire	12	C2
St. Neots	9	E7
St-Omer	12	A5
St. Paul, Minn., U.S.A.	40	C8
St. Paul, Nebr., U.S.A.	40	E6
St. Paul, I.	5	F13
St. Peter	40	C8
St. Peter Port	9	H5
St. Petersburg = Sankt-Peterburg	18	D4
St. Petersburg	43	M4
St-Pierre	44	c
St-Pierre et Miquelon □	37	D14
St-Quentin	12	B5
St. Regis	38	C6
St. Simons Island	43	K5
St. Simons I.	45	e
St-Tropez	12	E7
St. Vincent, G.	30	G6
St. Vincent & the Grenadines ■	45	E12
Ste-Anne	44	b
Ste. Genevieve	40	G9
Ste-Marie	44	c
Ste-Rose	44	b
Saintes	12	D3
Saintes, I. des	44	b
Saintfield	11	B6
Saintonge	12	D3
Saipan	36	F6
Sakakawea, L.	40	B4
Sakarya	17	B4
Sakata	22	D6
Sakha □	19	C13
Sakhalin	19	D15
Sala	7	F7
Sala-y-Gómez	35	K17
Salado →, Argentina	48	C4
Salado →, Mexico	41	M5
Salālah	24	D4
Salamanca, Spain	13	B3
Salamanca, U.S.A.	42	D6
Salayar	23	D4
Salcombe	9	G4
Saldanha	29	L3
Sale, Australia	30	H8
Sale, U.K.	8	D5
Salekhard	18	C7
Salem, India	25	D6
Salem, Ill., U.S.A.	42	F1
Salem, Ind., U.S.A.	42	F2
Salem, Mass., U.S.A.	42	D10
Salem, Mo., U.S.A.	41	G9
Salem, Ohio, U.S.A.	42	E5
Salem, Oreg., U.S.A.	38	D2
Salem, S. Dak., U.S.A.	40	D6
Salem, Va., U.S.A.	42	G5
Salerno	14	D6
Salford	8	D5
Salina, Kans., U.S.A.	40	F6
Salina, Utah, U.S.A.	39	G8
Salina Cruz	44	D5
Salinas	39	H3
Salinas Grandes	48	C3
Saline →, Ark., U.S.A.	41	J8
Saline →, Kans., U.S.A.	40	F6
Salisbury, U.K.	9	F6
Salisbury, Md., U.S.A.	42	F8
Salisbury, N.C., U.S.A.	43	H5
Salisbury Plain	9	F6
Saliq	41	H7
Salisaw	37	B12
Salmon	38	D7
Salmon →	38	D5
Salmon Arm	38	C8
Salmon River Mts.	38	D6
Salome	39	K7
Salon-de-Provence	12	E6
Salonica = Thessaloníki	15	D10
Salt →	39	K7
Salt Lake City	38	F8
Salta	48	A3
Saltash	9	G3
Saltburn by the Sea	8	C7
Saltcoats	10	F4
Saltee Is.	11	D5
Saltillo	44	B4
Salton Sea	39	K6
Saluda →	43	J5
Salvador	46	F6
Salvador, L.	41	L9
Salween →	25	D8
Salzburg	16	E7
Salzgitter	16	B6
Sam Rayburn Reservoir	41	K7
Samar	23	B4
Samara	18	D6
Samarinda	23	D3
Samarkand = Samarqand	18	F7
Samarqand	18	F7
Samoa ■	35	C16
Sámos	15	F12
Samsun	17	B8
Samut Prakan	23	B2
San Agustín, C.	23	C4
San Ambrosio	35	K20
San Andreas	38	G3
San Andrés Mts.	39	K10
San Andrés Tuxtla	44	D5
San Angelo	41	K4
San Antonio, N. Mex., U.S.A.	39	K10
San Antonio, Tex., U.S.A.	41	L5
San Antonio →	41	L6
San Augustine	41	K7
San Benito	41	M6
San Bernardino	39	K5
San Bernardino Str.	23	B4
San Blas, C.	43	L3
San Carlos, Phil.	23	B4
San Carlos, U.S.A.	39	K8
San Carlos I.	39	K8
San Clemente	39	K5
San Clemente I.	39	K4
San Cristóbal, Solomon Is.	31	C11
San Cristóbal, Venezuela	46	B4
San Cristóbal de la Casas	44	D6
San Diego, Calif., U.S.A.	39	K5
San Diego, Tex., U.S.A.	41	M5
San Félix	35	K20
San Francisco	39	H2
San Francisco →	39	K9
San Francisco de Macorís	45	D10
San Gottardo, P. del	12	C8
San Joaquín →	39	H3
San Jorí	15	F11
San Jorge, G.	48	F3
San Jose, Costa Rica	45	F8
San Jose, Phil.	23	B4
San Jose, U.S.A.	39	H3
San Juan, Argentina	48	C3
San Juan →, Argentina	48	C3
San Juan →, Dom. Rep.	45	D10
San Juan →, Puerto Rico	45	D11
San Juan →, U.S.A.	39	H8
San Juan Mts.	39	H10
San Luis, Ariz., U.S.A.	39	K6
San Luis, Colo., U.S.A.	39	H11
San Luis Obispo	39	J3
San Luis Potosí	44	C4
San Manuel	39	K8
San Marcos	41	L6
San Marino	14	C5
San Marino ■	14	C5
San Matías, G.	48	E4
San Miguel, El Salv.	44	E7
San Miguel, U.S.A.	39	J3
San Miguel →	46	F6
San Miguel de Tucumán	48	B3
San Nicolas I.	39	K4
San Pedro de las Colonias	44	B4
San Pedro de Macorís	45	D11
San Pedro Sula	44	D7
San Rafael, Calif., U.S.A.	38	H2
San Rafael, N. Mex., U.S.A.	39	J10
San Remo	12	E7
San Saba	41	K5
San Salvador	44	E7
San Salvador de Jujuy	48	A3
San Salvador I.	45	C10
San Sebastián = Donostia-San Sebastián	13	A5
San Simon	39	K9
Sana'	24	D3
Sanaga →	28	D1
Sanandaj	24	B3
Sancti Spíritus	45	C9
Sancy, Puy de	12	D5
Sand Hills	40	D4
Sand Springs	41	G6
Sandakan	23	C3
Sanday	10	B6
Sanders	39	J9
Sandersville	43	J4
Sandpoint	38	B5
Sandray	10	E1
Sandringham	8	E8
Sandusky, Mich., U.S.A.	42	D4
Sandusky, Ohio, U.S.A.	42	E4
Sandy C.	30	D6
Sandy Cr. →	38	F9
Sandy L.	36	C10
Sanford, Fla., U.S.A.	43	L5
Sanford, Maine, U.S.A.	43	D10
Sanford, N.C., U.S.A.	43	H6
Sanford →	36	B5
Sanford, Mt.	36	B5
Sanger	39	H4
Sanghe, Pulau	23	C4
Sangli	25	D6
Sangre de Cristo Mts.	41	G2
Sanirajak	37	B11
Sankt Gallen	16	E5
Sankt Moritz	12	C8
Sankt-Peterburg	18	D4
Sankuru →	28	E4
Sanliurfa	17	C5
Sanmenxia	21	C6
Sanming	21	D6
Sanquhar	10	F5
Santa Ana, El Salv.	44	E7
Santa Ana, U.S.A.	39	K5
Santa Barbara	39	K4
Santa Catalina, Gulf of	39	K5
Santa Catalina I.	39	K4
Santa Clara, Cuba	45	C9
Santa Clara, U.S.A.	39	H2
Santa Coloma de Gramenet	13	B7
Santa Cruz, Bolivia	46	G6
Santa Cruz, U.S.A.	39	H2
Santa Cruz I.	39	K4
Santa Cruz de Tenerife	26	C1
Santa Fe, Argentina	48	C4
Santa Fe, U.S.A.	39	J11
Santa Inés, I.	48	G2
Santa Isabel = Rey Malabo	28	D1
Santa Isabel	31	B10
Santa Lucia Range	39	J3
Santa María, Brazil	48	B6
Santa María	39	J3
Santa Maria →	44	A3
Santa Marta, Sierra Nevada de	46	A4
Santa Monica	39	K4
Santa Rita	41	H2
Santa Rosa, N. Mex., U.S.A.	41	H2
Santa Rosa, Calif., U.S.A.	38	G2
Santa Rosa, Fla., U.S.A.	43	K2
Santa Rosa Range	38	F5
Santander	13	A4
Santaquin	38	G8
Santarém, Brazil	47	D8
Santarém, Portugal	13	C1
Santee →	43	J6
Santiago	48	C2
Santiago de Compostela	13	A1
Santiago de Cuba	45	D10
Santiago de los Cabelleros	45	D10
Santiago del Estero	48	B4
Santo André	48	A7
Santo Domingo	45	D11
Santo Domingo Pueblo	39	J10
Santorini = Thira	15	F11
Sanxiang	21	G10
São Bernardo do Campo	48	A7
São Francisco →	47	F11
São José do Rio Prêto	48	A7
São Lourenço	48	A6
São Paulo	48	A7
São Paulo, I.	2	D8
São Roque, C. de	47	E11
São Tomé & Príncipe ■	5	D10
Saône →	12	C6
Sapele	26	G7
Sapporo	22	B7
Saragossa = Zaragoza	13	B5
Sarajevo	15	C8
Saran, Gunung	23	D3
Saranac Lake	42	D8
Sarangani B.	23	C4
Sarangarh	25	D7
Saransk	18	D5
Sarapul	18	D6
Sarasota	43	M4
Saratoga Springs	42	D9
Saratov	18	D5
Sarawak □	23	C3
Sardegna □	14	D3
Sardinia = Sardegna □	14	D3
Sargasso Sea	35	D20
Sargodha	24	B9
Sark	9	H5
Sarlat-la-Canéda	12	D4
Sarnia	42	D3
Sarreguemines	12	B7
Sarthe →	12	C3
Saskatchewan □	36	C9
Saskatchewan →	36	C9
Saskatoon	36	C9
Sasovo	18	D5
Sássari	14	D3
Sasschitz	16	A7
Satka	18	D6
Satmala Hills	25	D6
Satna	25	C7
Satpura Ra.	25	D6
Satu Mare	17	E10
Satun	23	C2
Saudi Arabia ■	24	C3
Saugerties	42	D9
Sauk Centre	40	C7
Sauk Rapids	40	C7
Sault Ste. Marie, Canada	37	D11
Sault Ste. Marie, U.S.A.	37	D11
Saumur	12	C3
Saunders, C.	33	L3
Savá	15	B9
Savage	40	B2
Savage River	32	D4
Savanna-la-Mar	44	D6
Savannah, Ga., U.S.A.	43	J5
Savannah, Mo., U.S.A.	40	F7
Savannah, Tenn., U.S.A.	43	H1
Savannah →	43	J5
Savannakhet	23	B2
Savoie □	12	D7
Savona	12	D8
Sawu	23	D4
Sawu Sea	23	D4
Saxmundham	9	E9
Saxony = Sachsen □	16	C7
Sayan, Zapadnyy	19	D10
Saydā	17	D5
Sayhut	24	D4
Saynshand	21	B6
Sayre, Okla., U.S.A.	41	H5
Sayre, Pa., U.S.A.	42	E7
Scafell Pike	8	C4
Scalloway	10	A7
Scalpay	10	D3
Scandinavia	7	E6
Scapa Flow	10	C5
Scarba	10	E3
Scarborough	8	C7
Scarp	10	C1
Scebeli, Wabi →	24	E3
Schaffhausen	12	C8
Schefferville	37	C13
Schelde →	16	C2
Schell Creek Ra.	38	G6
Schenectady	42	D9
Schleswig	16	A4
Schleswig-Holstein □	16	A4
Schœlcher	44	c
Schouten I.	32	D4
Schurz	38	G4
Schwaben □	16	D6
Schwarzwald	16	D5
Schwerin	16	B6
Schwyz	12	C8
Scilly, Isles of	9	H1
Scioto →	42	F4
Scobey	40	A2
Scone	32	B5
Scotia	38	F1
Scotland □	10	E5
Scott City	40	F4
Scottish Borders □	10	F6
Scottsbluff	40	E3
Scottsboro	43	H2
Scottsburg	42	F3
Scottsdale, Australia	32	D4
Scottsdale, U.S.A.	39	K8
Scottville	42	D2
Scranton	42	E8
Scunthorpe	8	D7
Seaford, U.K.	9	G8
Seaford, U.S.A.	42	F8
Seaforth, L.	10	D2
Seagraves	41	J3
Seaham	8	C6
Seal →	36	C10
Sealy	41	L6
Searchlight	39	J6
Searcy	41	H9
Seascale	8	C4
Seaside, Calif., U.S.A.	39	H3
Seaside, Oreg., U.S.A.	38	C2
Seaspray	32	D4
Seattle	38	C2
Sebastián Vizcaíno, B.	44	B2
Sebastopol = Sevastopol	42	F2
Sebewaing	42	D4
Sebring	43	M5
Sebuku, Teluk	23	C3
Secretary I.	33	L1
Security-Widefield	40	F2
Sedalia	40	F8
Sedan, France	12	B6
Sedan, U.S.A.	41	G6
Seddon	33	J5
Seddonville	33	J4
Sedley	42	G7
Sedro Woolley	38	B2
Segovia	13	B3
Séguéla	26	G4
Seguin	41	L6
Seil	10	E3
Seiling	41	G5
Seine →	12	B4
Sekondi-Takoradi	26	H5
Selby, U.K.	8	D6
Selby, U.S.A.	40	C4
Selden	40	F4
Selenge Mörön →	20	A5
Selkirk, Canada	36	C10
Selkirk, U.K.	10	F6
Selkirk Mts.	36	C8
Selma, Ala., U.S.A.	43	J2
Selma, Calif., U.S.A.	39	H4
Selma, N.C., U.S.A.	43	H6
Selmer	43	H1
Selsey Bill	9	G7
Selu	23	D4
Selvas	46	E5
Selwyn L.	36	B9
Selwyn Mts.	36	B6
Semarang	23	D3
Semey	18	D9
Seminole, Okla., U.S.A.	41	H6
Seminole, Tex., U.S.A.	41	J3
Seminole Draw →	41	J3
Semporna	23	C3
Semnan	24	B4
Sena Madureira	46	E5
Senatobia	41	H10
Sendai	22	D7
Seneca	43	H4
Seneca Falls	42	D7
Seneca L.	42	D7
Senegal ■	26	E2
Senegal →	26	E2
Senja	6	B9
Senlis	12	B5
Sens	12	B5
Seoul = Sŏul	21	C7
Sept-Îles	37	C13
Sequim	38	B2
Sequoia Nat. Park	39	H4
Seram	23	D4
Seram Sea	23	D4
Serbia ■	15	C9
Serdobsk	18	D5
Seremban	23	C2
Serov	18	D7
Serowe	29	J5
Serpukhov	18	D4
Serua	23	D5
Sète	12	E5
Settat	26	B4
Settle	8	C5
Settlement Pt.	43	M6
Setúbal	13	C1
Seul, Lac	36	C10
Sevastopol	18	E4
Sevenoaks	9	F8
Severn →, Canada	37	C11
Severn →, U.K.	9	F5
Severnaya Zemlya	19	B10
Severodvinsk	18	C4
Sevier →	39	G7
Sevier Desert	38	G7
Sevier L.	38	G7
Sevilla	13	D2
Seville = Sevilla	13	D2
Seward, Alaska, U.S.A.	36	B5
Seward, Nebr., U.S.A.	40	E6
Seward Peninsula	36	B3
Seychelles ■	5	E12
Seymour, Australia	32	D4
Seymour, Ind., U.S.A.	42	F3
Seymour, Tex., U.S.A.	41	J5
Sfax	26	B7
Sha Tau Kok	21	F11
Sha Tin	21	G11
Shaanxi □	21	C5
Shaba = Katanga □	28	F4
Shache	20	C2
Shaftesbury	9	F5
Shahjahanpur	25	C7
Shajing	21	F10
Shakhty	17	A7
Shaki	26	G6
Shaluli Shan	20	C4
Shām, Bādiyat ash	24	B3
Shamo = Gobi	21	B5
Shamokin	42	H4
Shan □	25	C5
Shandong □	21	C6
Shanghai	21	C7
Shangqiu	21	C6
Shangrao	21	D6
Shangshui	21	C6
Shannon, Mouth of the	11	D2
Shannon →, Ireland	11	D2
Shannon →, N.Z.	33	J5
Shantou	21	D6
Shanxi □	21	C6
Shaoguan	21	D6
Shaoxing	21	D7
Shaoyang	21	D6
Shap	8	C5
Shapinsay	10	B6
Shaqrā'	24	C3
Sharjah = Ash Shāriqah	24	C4
Shark B.	30	F1
Sharon	42	E5
Sharon Springs	40	F4
Sharya	18	D5
Shashi	21	C6
Shasta, Mt.	38	F2
Shasta L.	38	F2
Shatt al'Arab →	24	C3
Shawano	42	C1
Shawinigan	37	D12
Shawnee	41	H6
Shcherbakov = Rybinsk	18	D4
Shebele = Scebeli, Wabi →	24	E3
Sheberghan	24	B5
Sheboygan	42	D2
Sheelin, L.	11	C4
Sheep Haven	11	A4
Sheerness	9	F8
Sheffield, U.K.	8	D6
Sheffield, U.S.A.	43	H2
Shekou	21	G10
Shelby, Mich., U.S.A.	42	D2
Shelby, Miss., U.S.A.	41	J9
Shelby, Mont., U.S.A.	38	B8
Shelby, N.C., U.S.A.	43	H5
Shelbyville, Ill., U.S.A.	40	F10
Shelbyville, Ky., U.S.A.	42	F3
Shelbyville, Tenn., U.S.A.	43	H2
Sheldon	40	D7
Shelikhova, Zaliv	19	D16
Shellharbour	32	B5
Shelton	38	C2
Shenandoah, Iowa, U.S.A.	40	E7
Shenandoah, Pa., U.S.A.	42	E7
Shenandoah, Va., U.S.A.	42	F6
Shenandoah →	42	F6
Shenandoah Nat. Park	42	F6
Shenyang	21	B7
Shenzhen	21	F10
Shenzhen Shuiku	21	G10
Shenzhen Wan	21	G10
Sheppey, Isle of	9	F8
Shepton Mallet	9	F5
Sherborne	9	G5
Sherbrooke	37	D12
Sheridan, Ark., U.S.A.	41	H8
Sheridan, Wyo., U.S.A.	38	D10
Sherman	41	J6
Sherwood Forest	8	D6
Shetland □	10	A7
Shetland Is.	10	A7
Sheung Shui	21	F11
Sheyenne →	40	B6
Shiel, L.	10	C3
Shihezi	20	B3
Shijiazhuang	21	C6
Shikarpur	24	C5
Shikoku □	22	G3
Shiliguri	25	C7
Shillelagh	11	D5
Shimoga	25	D6
Shimonoseki	22	G2
Shin, L.	10	C4
Shiping	20	D5
Shippensburg	42	E7
Shiquanhe	20	C2
Shiraz	24	C4
Shire →	29	H7
Shivpuri	25	C6
Shiyan	21	C6
Shizuoka	22	F6
Shkodër	15	C8
Sholapur = Solapur	25	D6
Shoshone	38	E6
Shoshone L.	38	D8
Shoshone Mts.	38	G5
Shoshong	29	J5
Show Low	39	J9
Shreveport	41	J8
Shrewsbury	9	E5
Shropshire □	9	E5
Shuangliao	21	B7
Shuangyashan	21	B8
Shule	20	C2
Shwebo	25	C8
Shymkent	18	E8
Si Kiang = Xi Jiang →	21	D6
Sialkot	24	B9
Siam = Thailand ■	23	B2
Sian = Xi'an	21	C5
Šiauliai	7	H12
Sibenik	14	C7
Siberia	4	C14
Siberut	23	D1
Sibi	24	C5
Sibiu	17	F11
Sibolga	23	C1
Sibu	23	C3
Sibuyan Sea	23	B4
Siccus →	32	B2
Sichuan □	20	C5
Sicilia □	14	F6
Sicily = Sicilia □	14	F6
Sidi-bel-Abbès	26	A5
Sidlaw Hills	10	E5
Sidmouth	9	G4
Sidney, Mont., U.S.A.	40	B2
Sidney, N.Y., U.S.A.	42	D8
Sidney, Nebr., U.S.A.	40	E3
Sidney, Ohio, U.S.A.	42	E3
Sidney Lanier, L.	43	H4
Sidon = Saydā	17	D5
Siedlce	17	B11
Siegen	16	C4
Siena	14	C4
Sierra Blanca	39	L11
Sierra Blanca Peak	39	K11
Sierra Leone ■	26	G3
Sierra Nevada, Spain	13	D4
Sierra Nevada, U.S.A.	38	G3
Sierra Vista	39	L8
Sikasso	26	F4
Sikeston	41	G10
Sikhote Alin, Khrebet	19	E14
Sikkim □	25	C7
Silesia = Śląsk	16	C8
Siling Co	20	C3
Silloth	8	C4
Siloam Springs	41	G7
Silsbee	41	K7
Silver City	39	K9
Silver L.	38	E4
Silverton, Colo., U.S.A.	39	H10
Silverton, Tex., U.S.A.	41	H4
Silvies →	38	E4
Simbirsk	18	D5
Simeulue	23	C1
Simferopol	18	E4
Simi Valley	39	J4
Simplonpass	12	C8
Simpson Pen.	37	B11
Sinai, Mt. = Mûsa, Gebel	27	C12
Sinclair	38	F10
Sind = Sind □	24	C5
Sind □	24	C5
Singapore ■	23	C2
Singaraja	23	D3
Singkawang	23	C2
Singleton	32	B5
Sinkiang Uighur = Xinjiang Uygur Zizhiqu □	20	C3
Sinton	41	L6
Sion	12	C7
Sioux City	40	D6
Sioux Falls	40	D6
Sioux Lookout	36	C10
Siping	21	B7
Siracusa	14	F6
Siret →	17	F14
Sisak	14	B7
Sisseton	40	C6
Sīstān, Daryācheh-ye	24	B4
Sisters	38	D3
Sitges	13	B6
Sittard	11	D12
Sittingbourne	9	F8
Sittwe	25	C8
Siwa	27	C11
Six Cross Roads	45	g
Sixmilebridge	11	D3
Själland	7	E8
Skagerrak	7	E8
Skagway	36	C6
Skeena →	36	C6
Skegness	8	D8
Skellefteälv →	6	D12
Skerries, The	8	D3
Skiathos	15	E10
Skibbereen	11	E2
Skiddaw	8	C4
Skien	7	G9
Skikda	26	A7
Skipton	8	D5
Skopje	15	C9
Skowhegan	43	C11
Skull	11	E2
Skye	10	D2
Skykomish	38	C3
Slaney →	11	D5
Śląsk	16	C8
Slatina	15	B11
Slaton	41	J4
Slave →	36	B8
Slave Coast	26	G6
Slave Lake	36	C8
Sleaford	8	D7
Sleat, Sd. of	10	D3
Sleeper Is.	37	C11
Sleepy Eye	40	C7
Slidell	41	K10
Slieve Aughty	11	C3
Slieve Bloom	11	C4
Slieve Donard	11	B6
Slieve Gamph	11	B3
Slieve Gullion	11	B5
Slieve Mish	11	D2
Slievenamon	11	D4
Sligo	11	B3
Sligo □	11	B3
Sligo B.	11	B3
Slough	9	F7
Slough □	9	F7
Slovak Rep. = Slovakia ■	16	D9
Slovakia ■	16	D9
Slovenia ■	14	B6
Slovenské Rudohorie	17	D10
Slovyansk	17	A5
Slyne Hd.	11	C1
Smallwood Res.	37	C13
Smederevo	15	B9
Smerwick Harbour	11	D1
Smith Center	40	F5
Smithfield, N.C., U.S.A.	43	H6
Smithfield, Utah, U.S.A.	38	F8
Smiths Falls	42	C8
Smithton	32	D4
Smithville	41	K6
Smoky →	36	C8
Smoky Hill →	40	F6
Smoky Hills	40	F5
Smolensk	18	D4
Smyrna = İzmir	17	C2
Smyrna	43	J3
Snaefell	8	C3
Snake →	38	C4
Snake I.	32	D4
Snake River Plain	38	E7
Snizort, L.	10	D2
Snøhetta	7	F9
Snow Hill	42	F8
Snowdon	8	D3
Snowshoe Pk.	38	B6
Snowtown	32	B2
Snowy →	32	D4
Snowy Mts.	32	C4
Snyder, Okla., U.S.A.	41	H5
Snyder, Tex., U.S.A.	41	J4
Sobral	47	D11
Soc Trang	23	C2
Socastee	43	J6
Sochi	17	B6
Société, Is. de la	35	J12
Society Is. = Société, Is. de la	35	J12
Socorro, N. Mex., U.S.A.	39	K10
Socorro, Tex., U.S.A.	39	L10
Socotra	24	D4
Soda L.	39	J5
Soda Springs	38	E8
Soddy-Daisy	43	H3
Söderhamn	7	F11
Sofia = Sofiya	15	C10
Sofiya	15	C10
Sognefjorden	7	F9
Sohâg	27	C12
Soissons	12	B5
Sŏkcho	21	C7
Sokhumi = Sukhumi	17	B6
Soko Islands	21	G10
Sokoto	26	F7
Solapur	25	D6
Soldotna	36	B4
Soledad	39	H3
Solent, The	9	G6
Solihull	9	E6
Solikamsk	18	D6
Solimões = Amazonas →	47	D9
Solingen	16	C3
Solomon, N. Fork →	40	F5
Solomon, S. Fork →	40	F5
Solomon Is. ■	31	B10
Solomon Sea	30	B9
Solon	21	B7
Solon Springs	40	B9
Solothurn	12	C7
Solway Firth	8	C4
Somali Rep. ■	24	F4
Somalia = Somali Rep. ■	24	F4
Sombrerete	44	C4
Somerset, Ky., U.S.A.	42	G3
Somerset, Pa., U.S.A.	42	E6
Somerset □	9	F5
Somerset I.	36	A10
Somerton	39	K6
Somme →	12	A4
Songhua Jiang →	21	B8
Songhua Hu	21	C7
Songpan	20	C5
Sonora, Calif., U.S.A.	38	H3
Sonora, Tex., U.S.A.	41	K4
Sonora →	44	B2
Sonoran Desert	39	K6
Sonsonate	44	E7
Sopot	16	A9
Soria	13	B4
Sorong	23	D5
Soroti	28	D6
Sorsele	6	D11
Sørøya	6	A12
Sosnowiec	16	C9
Souris →	40	A5
Soufrière, Guadeloupe	44	b
Soufrière, St. Lucia	44	f
Soufrière Bay	44	f
Sŏul	21	C7
Sousse	26	A7
South Africa ■	29	L4
South Australia □	30	G6
South Ayrshire □	10	F4
South Baldy	39	J10
South Bend	42	E2
South Boston	42	G6
South Carolina □	43	J5
South Charleston	42	F5
South China Sea	23	B3
South Dakota □	40	C4
South Downs	9	G7
South East C.	32	D4
South Esk →	10	E6
South Foreland	9	F9
South Fork Grand →	40	C3
South Georgia	2	G9
South Gloucestershire □	9	F5
South Honshu Ridge	34	E6
South I.	33	L3
South Korea ■	21	C7
South Lake Tahoe	38	G4
South Lanarkshire □	10	F5
South Loup →	40	E5
South Magnetic Pole	5	C18
South Milwaukee	42	D2
South Molton	9	F4
South Nahanni →	36	B7
South Orkney Is.	5	C18
South Pittsburg	43	H3
South Platte →	40	E4
South Pole	5	E
South Portland	43	D10
South Pt.	45	g
South Ronaldsay	10	C6
South Saskatchewan →	36	C9
South Shetland Is.	5	C18
South Shields	8	C6
South Sioux City	40	D6
South Taranaki Bight	33	H5
South Tyne →	8	C5
South Uist	10	D1
South West C.	32	D4
South Yorkshire □	8	D6
Southampton, U.K.	9	G6
Southampton, U.S.A.	42	E9
Southampton I.	37	B11
Southaven	41	H9
Southbridge	33	K4
Southend-on-Sea	9	F8
Southern Alps	33	K3
Southern Indian L.	36	C10
Southern Ocean	5	C6
Southern Pines	43	H6
Southern Uplands	10	F5
Southport, Australia	32	A5
Southport, U.K.	8	D4
Southport, U.S.A.	43	J6
Southwest C.	33	M1
Southwest Nat. Park	32	D4
Southwold	9	E9
Soweto	29	K5
Spain ■	13	B4
Spalding, Australia	32	B2
Spalding, U.K.	8	E7
Spanish Fork	38	F8
Spanish Town, Br. Virgin Is.	45	e
Spanish Town, Jamaica	44	a
Sparks	38	G4
Sparta, Mich., U.S.A.	42	D3
Sparta, Wis., U.S.A.	40	D9
Spartanburg	43	H5
Spearfish	40	C3
Spearman	41	G4
Speightstown	45	g
Spencer, Idaho, U.S.A.	38	D7
Spencer, Nebr., U.S.A.	40	D5
Spencer, C.	32	C2
Spencer G.	32	B2
Spennymoor	8	C6
Sperrin Mts.	11	B5
Spey →	10	D5
Spitzbergen = Svalbard	4	B8
Split	14	C7
Spokane	38	C5
Spooner	40	C9
Spratly Is.	23	C3
Spray	38	D4
Spree →	16	B7
Springdale	41	G7
Springerville	39	J9
Springfield, N.Z.	33	K3
Springfield, Colo., U.S.A.	41	G3
Springfield, Ill., U.S.A.	40	F10
Springfield, Mass., U.S.A.	42	D9
Springfield, Mo., U.S.A.	41	G8
Springfield, Ohio, U.S.A.	42	F4
Springfield, Oreg., U.S.A.	38	D2
Springfield, Tenn., U.S.A.	43	G2
Springfield, Vt., U.S.A.	42	D9
Springhill	41	J8
Springs	29	K5
Spur	41	J4
Spurn Hd.	8	D8
Sri Lanka ■	25	E7
Srebrenica	15	B8
Sredinnyy Khrebet	19	D16
Srednekolymsk	19	C16
Srepok →	23	B2
Srinagar	25	B6
Stade	16	B5
Stafford, U.K.	8	E5
Stafford, U.S.A.	41	G5
Staffordshire □	8	E5
Staines	9	F7
Stalingrad = Volgograd	18	E5
Stalino = Donetsk	17	A5
Stalinogorsk = Novomoskovsk	18	D5
Stalybridge	8	D5
Stamford, U.K.	9	E7
Stamford, Conn., U.S.A.	42	E9
Stamford, Tex., U.S.A.	41	J5
Standish	42	D4
Stanford	38	C8
Stanley, China	21	G11
Stanley, Falk. Is.	48	G5
Stanley, Idaho, U.S.A.	38	D6
Stanley, N. Dak., U.S.A.	40	A3
Stanovoy Khrebet	19	D13
Stanthorpe	32	A5
Stanton	41	J4
Staples	40	B7
Stara Planina	15	C10
Stara Zagora	15	C11
Starbuck I.	35	H12
Start Pt.	9	G4
State College	42	E7
Statesboro	43	J5
Statesville	43	H5
Staunton, Ill., U.S.A.	40	F10
Staunton, Va., U.S.A.	42	F6
Stavanger	7	G8
Staveley	8	D6
Stavropol	17	A6
Stawell	32	D3
Stayton	38	D2
Steamboat Springs	38	F10
Steelton	42	E7
Steens Mt.	38	E4
Steiermark □	16	E8
Steinkjer	6	D10
Stephenville, Canada	37	D14
Stephenville, U.S.A.	41	J5
Sterling, Colo., U.S.A.	40	E3
Sterling, Ill., U.S.A.	40	E10
Sterling, Kans., U.S.A.	40	F5
Sterling City	41	K4
Sterling Heights	42	D4
Sterlitamak	18	D6
Stettin = Szczecin	16	B8
Stettler	36	C8
Steubenville	42	E5
Stevenage	9	F7
Stevens Point	42	C1
Stewart →	36	B6
Stewart, I.	48	G2
Stewart I.	33	M1
Stigler	41	H7
Stikine →	36	C6
Stillwater, N.Z.	33	K3
Stillwater, Minn., U.S.A.	40	C8
Stillwater, Okla., U.S.A.	41	G6
Stillwater Range	38	G4
Stilwell	41	H7
Stirling	10	E5
Stirling □	10	E4
Stockerau	16	D8
Stockholm	7	G11
Stockport	8	D5
Stocksbridge	8	D6
Stockton, Calif., U.S.A.	39	H3
Stockton, Mo., U.S.A.	41	G8
Stockton-on-Tees	8	C6
Stockton Plateau	41	K3
Stoke-on-Trent	8	D5
Stokes Pt.	32	D3
Stone	8	E5
Stonehaven	10	E6
Stora Lulevatten	6	C11
Storavan	6	D11
Storm B.	32	D4
Storm Lake	40	D7
Stornoway	10	C2
Storsjön	6	E10
Storuman	6	D11
Stour →, Dorset, U.K.	9	G6
Stour →, Kent, U.K.	9	F9
Stour →, Suffolk, U.K.	9	F9
Stourbridge	9	E5
Stowmarket	9	E9
Strabane	11	B4
Stralsund	16	A7
Stranraer	10	G4
Strasbourg	12	B7
Stratford, N.Z.	33	H5
Stratford, U.S.A.	41	G3
Stratford-upon-Avon	9	E6
Strath Spey	10	D5
Strathalbyn	32	C2
Strathaven	10	F4
Strathmore	10	E5
Strathpeffer	10	D4
Strathroy	42	D3
Strathy Pt.	10	C4
Straubing	16	D7
Streaky B.	32	B1
Streaky Bay	32	B1
Streator	40	E10
Strömboli	14	E6
Stromeferry	10	D3
Stromness	10	C5
Stromsburg	40	E6
Strömstad	7	G9
Strömsund	6	E10
Stronsay	10	B6
Stroud	9	F5
Stroud Road	32	B5
Strzelecki Cr. →	32	A2
Stuart, Fla., U.S.A.	43	M5
Stuart, Nebr., U.S.A.	40	D5
Stuart Ra.	32	A1
Sturgeon Bay	42	C2
Sturgis, Mich., U.S.A.	42	E3
Sturgis, S. Dak., U.S.A.	40	C3
Stuttgart, Germany	16	D5
Stuttgart, U.S.A.	41	H9
Styria = Steiermark □	16	E8
Subotica	15	A8
Suceava	17	E14
Suchou = Suzhou	21	C7
Süchow = Xuzhou	21	C6
Sucre	46	G5
Sudan ■	27	E11
Sudan	41	J3
Sudbury, Canada	37	D11
Sudbury, U.K.	9	E8
Sudeten Mts. = Sudety	16	C8
Sudety	16	C8
Suez = El Suweis	27	C12
Suffolk	42	G7
Suffolk □	9	E9
Şuḩār	24	C4
Suihua	21	B7
Suir →	11	D4
Sukabumi	23	D2
Sukhumi = Sokhumi	17	B6
Sukkur	24	C5
Sulaiman Range	24	C5
Sulawesi □	23	D4
Sulawesi Sea = Celebes Sea	23	C4
Sullana	46	D2
Sullivan, Ill., U.S.A.	40	F10
Sullivan, Ind., U.S.A.	42	F2
Sullivan, Mo., U.S.A.	40	F9
Sulphur, La., U.S.A.	41	K8
Sulphur, Okla., U.S.A.	41	H6
Sulphur Springs	41	J7
Sulu Arch.	23	C4
Sulu Sea	23	C4
Sumatera □	23	C2
Sumatra = Sumatera □	23	C2
Sumba	23	D3
Sumba, Selat	23	D3
Sumbawa	23	D3
Sumburgh Hd.	10	B7
Sumenep	23	D3
Summer L.	38	E3
Summerside	37	D13
Summersville	42	F5
Summerville, Ga., U.S.A.	43	H3
Summerville, S.C., U.S.A.	43	J5
Summit Peak	39	H10
Sumqayit	17	B8
Sumter	43	J5
Sun City	39	K7
Sun City Center	43	M4
Sun Lakes	39	K8
Sun Valley	38	D6
Sunbury, Australia	32	C3
Sunbury, U.S.A.	42	E7
Sunburst	38	B8
Sunda Str. = Sunda, Selat	23	D2
Sunda, Selat	23	D2
Sundance	40	C2
Sunderland	8	C6
Sundsvall	7	E11
Sungaipenuh	23	D2
Sunnyside	38	C3
Sunnyvale	38	H2
Superior, Ariz., U.S.A.	39	K8
Superior, Mont., U.S.A.	38	C6
Superior, Nebr., U.S.A.	40	E5
Superior, Wis., U.S.A.	40	B8
Superior, L.	37	D11
Supiori	23	D5
Sūr, Pt.	39	H3
Surabaya	23	D3
Surakarta	23	D3
Surat, Australia	32	A4
Surat, India	25	D6
Surat Thani	23	C1
Surgut	18	C8
Surigao	23	C4
Suriname ■	47	C7
Surinam = Suriname ■	47	C7
Surrey □	9	F7
Surt, Khalij	28	B3
Susquehanna →	42	F7
Sussex, E. □	9	G8
Sussex, W. □	9	G7
Sutherland, S. Africa	29	L4
Sutherland, U.S.A.	40	E4
Sutherland Falls	33	L1
Sutlej →	24	C8
Sutton, Nebr., U.S.A.	40	E6
Sutton, W. Va., U.S.A.	42	F5
Sutton →	37	C11
Sutton Coldfield	9	E6
Sutton in Ashfield	8	D6
Suva	31	D14
Suwarrow Is.	35	J11
Svalbard	4	B8
Svealand	7	G10
Sverdlovsk = Yekaterinburg	18	D7
Swabian Alps = Schwäbische Alb	16	D5
Swakopmund	29	J2
Swan Hill	32	C3
Swan Hills	36	C8
Swan River	36	C9
Swanage	9	G6
Swansea, Australia	32	D4
Swansea, U.K.	9	F4
Swaziland ■	29	K6
Sweden ■	7	F11
Sweet Home	38	D2
Sweetwater, Tenn., U.S.A.	43	H3
Sweetwater, Tex., U.S.A.	41	J4
Sweetwater →	38	E10
Swellendam	29	L4
Swift Current	36	C9
Swilly, L.	11	A4
Swindon	9	F6
Swords	11	C5
Switzerland ■	12	C8
Sydney, Australia	32	B5
Sydney, Canada	37	D13
Sydprøven = Alluitsup Paa	4	C5
Syktyvkar	18	C6
Sylacauga	43	J2
Sylvania	43	J5
Sylvester	43	K4
Syracuse, Kans., U.S.A.	41	G4
Syracuse, N.Y., U.S.A.	42	D7
Syracuse, Nebr., U.S.A.	40	E6
Syrdarya →	18	E7
Syria ■	24	B3
Syrian Desert = Shām, Bādiyat ash	24	B3
Syzran	18	D5
Szczecin	16	B8
Szczecinek	16	B8
Szechwan = Sichuan □	20	C5
Szeged	17	E10
Székesfehérvár	16	E10
Szekszárd	16	E9
Szolnok	17	E10
Szombathely	16	E9

T

Name	Pg	Ref
Tabas	24	B4
Table Mt.	29	L3
Table Rock L.	41	G8
Tabora	28	F6
Tabriz	24	B3
Tabuaeran	35	G12
Tabūk	24	C2
Tacheng	20	B3
Tacloban	23	B4
Tacna	46	G4
Tacoma	38	C2
Tacuarembó	48	C5
Tademaït, Plateau du	26	C6
Tadzhikistan = Tajikistan ■	18	F8
Taegu	21	C7
Taejon	21	C7
Taft	39	J4
Taganrog	17	A6
Tagus = Tejo →	13	C1
Tahan, Gunung	23	C2
Tahat	26	D7
Tahiti	35	J13
Tahlequah	41	H7
Tahoe, L.	38	G3
Tahoe City	38	G3
Tahoka	41	J4
Tahoua	26	F7
Tai Au Mun	21	G11
Tai Lam Chung	21	G10
Tai Mo Shan	21	G10
Tai O	21	G10
Tai Pang Wan	21	F11
Tai Po	21	G11
Taibei = T'aipei	21	D7
Taichung = T'aichung	21	D7
Taiden = Taejon	21	C7
Taihape	33	H5
Tailem Bend	32	C2
Taimyr Peninsula = Taymyr, Poluostrov	19	B11
Tain	10	D4
Taínaron, Ákra	15	F10
Taipa	21	G10
T'aipei	21	D7
Taiping	23	C2
Taitao, Pen. de	48	F2
T'aitung	21	D7
Taiwan ■	21	D7
Taiyuan	21	C6
Ta'izz	24	D3
Tajikistan ■	18	F8
Tajo = Tejo →	13	C1
Tak	23	B1
Takaka	33	J4
Takamatsu	22	G4
Takaoka	22	E5
Takapuna	33	G5
Takla Makan = Taklamakan Shamo	20	C3
Taklamakan Shamo	20	C3
Talaud, Kepulauan	23	C4
Talbragar →	32	B4
Talca	48	D2
Talcahuano	48	D2
Talladega	43	J2
Tallahassee	43	K3
Tallangatta	32	C4
Tallinn	7	G12
Tallulah	41	J9
Taloyoak	36	B10
Talwood	32	A4
Talyawalka Cr. →	32	B3
Tama	40	E8
Tamale	26	G5
Tamanrasset	26	D7
Tamar →	9	G3
Tambov	18	D5
Tampa	43	M4
Tampa B.	43	M4
Tampere	7	F12
Tampico	44	C5
Tamworth, Australia	32	B5
Tamworth, U.K.	9	E6
Tana →, Kenya	28	E8
Tana →, Norway	6	A13
Tanami Desert	30	D5
Tananarive = Antananarivo	29	H9
Tandil	48	D5
Tandragee	11	B5
Taneatua	33	H6
Tanga	28	F7
Tanganyika, L.	28	F5
Tangier = Tanger	26	A4
Tangshan	21	C6
Tanimbar, Kepulauan	23	D5
Tanjungkarang Telukbetung	23	D2
Tanjungpandan	23	D2
Tanjungredeb	23	C3
Tanta	27	B12
Tanunda	32	B2
Tanzania ■	28	F6
Taos	39	H11
Tapachula	44	E6
Tapajós →	47	D8
Tapuaenuku	33	K4
Tara	18	D8
Tarabagatay, Khrebet	18	E9
Tarābulus, Lebanon	17	D5
Tarābulus, Libya	28	B2
Tarakan	23	C3
Taranaki, Mt.	33	H5
Taranto	14	D7
Taranto, G. di	14	D7
Tarbat Ness	10	D5
Tarbela Dam	24	B9
Tarbert, Arg. & Bute, U.K.	10	F3
Tarbert, W. Isles, U.K.	10	D2
Tarbes	12	E4
Tarcoola	32	B1
Taree	32	B5
Târgovişte	15	B11
Târgu-Jiu	15	B10
Târgu Mureş	17	E12
Tarim Basin = Tarim Pendi	20	B3
Tarim He →	20	C3
Tarim Pendi	20	B3
Tarn →	12	E4
Tarnów	16	C11
Taroom	32	A4
Tarpon Springs	43	L4
Tarragona	13	B6
Tarraleah	32	D4
Tartu	7	G13
Tartus	17	D5
Tashi Chho Dzong = Thimphu	25	C7
Tashkent = Toshkent	18	E8
Tasikmalaya	23	D2
Tasman B.	33	J4
Tasman Mts.	33	J4
Tasman Pen.	32	D4
Tasman Sea	31	E10
Tasmania □	32	D4
Tassili n'Ajjer	26	C7
Tatarsk	18	D8
Tatra = Tatry	16	D11
Tatry	16	D11
Tatum	41	J3
Tat'ung = Datong	21	B6
Taumarunui	33	H5
Taunggyi	25	C8
Taunton, U.K.	9	F4
Taunton, U.S.A.	42	E10
Taunus	16	C5
Taupo	33	H6
Taupo, L.	33	H5
Tauranga	33	G6
Tauranga Harb.	33	G6
Taurus Mts. = Toros Dağları	17	C5
Tavda	18	D7
Tavistock	9	G3
Tavoy	23	B1
Taw →	9	F4
Tawas City	42	C4
Tawau	23	C3
Tay →	10	E5
Tay, Firth of	10	E6
Tay, L.	10	E4
Taylor, Nebr., U.S.A.	40	E5
Taylor, Tex., U.S.A.	41	K6
Taylor, Mt.	39	J10
Taylorville	40	F10
Tayport	10	E6
Taymyr, Poluostrov	19	B11
Taz →	18	C8
Tbilisi	17	F7
Tchad = Chad ■	27	F8
Te Anau, L.	33	L1
Te Aroha	33	G5
Te Awamutu	33	H5
Te Kuiti	33	H5
Te Puke	33	G6
Te Waewae B.	33	M1
Tecumseh, Mich., U.S.A.	42	D4
Tecumseh, Okla., U.S.A.	41	H6
Tees →	8	C6
Tees B.	8	C6
Tegal	23	D2
Tegucigalpa	44	E7
Tehachapi	39	J4
Tehachapi Mts.	39	J4
Tehrān	24	B4
Tehuantepec	44	D5
Tehuantepec, G. de	44	D5
Tehuantepec, Istmo de	44	D6
Teifi →	9	E3
Teign →	9	G4
Teignmouth	9	G4
Tejo →	13	C1
Tekamah	40	E6
Tekapo, L.	33	K3
Tekoa	38	C5
Tela	44	D7
Telegraph Creek	36	C6
Teles Pires →	46	E7
Telescope Pk.	39	H5
Tell City	42	G2
Telluride	39	H10
Teluk Intan	23	C2
Tema	26	G6
Temecula	39	K5
Temirtau	18	D8
Temora	32	B4
Tempe	39	K8
Temple	41	K6
Templemore	11	D4
Temuco	48	D2
Temuka	33	L3
Ten Degree Channel	25	E8
Tenaha	41	K7
Tenby	9	F3
Tenerife	26	C1
Tennant Creek	30	D5
Tennessee □	43	H2
Tennessee →	42	G1
Tenterden	9	F8
Teófilo Otoni	47	G10
Tepic	44	C4
Teplice	16	C7
Téramo	14	C5
Terang	32	C3
Teresina	47	E11
Teridgerie Cr. →	32	B4
Termez = Termiz	18	F7
Termiz	18	F7
Térmoli	14	C6
Ternate	23	C4
Terni	14	C5
Ternopil	17	D13
Terowie	32	B2
Terrace	36	C7
Terre Haute	42	F2
Terrebonne B.	41	L9
Terry	40	B2
Teruel	13	B5
Teslin	36	B6
Test →	9	F6
Tetbury	9	F5
Tete	29	H6
Teton →	38	C8
Tétouan	26	A4
Tetovo	15	C9
Teutoburger Wald	16	B5
Tevere →	14	C5
Teviot →	10	F6
Tewantin	32	A5
Tewkesbury	9	F5
Texarkana, Ark., U.S.A.	41	J8
Texarkana, Tex., U.S.A.	41	J7
Texas □	41	K5
Texas City	41	L7
Texel	11	A5
Texoma, L.	41	J6
Tezpur	25	C8
Thabana Ntlenyana	29	K5
Thabazimbi	29	J5
Thailand ■	23	B2
Thailand, G. of	23	C2
Thallon	32	A4
Thames →	9	F8
Thames	33	G5
Thames Estuary	9	F8
Thane	25	D6
Thanet, Isle of	9	F9
Thanh Hoa	20	D5
Thanh Pho Ho Chi Minh	23	B2
Thar Desert	24	C8
Thargomindah	32	A3
Thásos	15	D11
Thatcher, Ariz., U.S.A.	39	K9
Thatcher, Colo., U.S.A.	41	G2
Thaton	25	D8
The Alberga →	32	A1
The Coorong	32	C2
The Crane	45	g
The Dalles	38	D3
The Frome →	32	A2
The Hague = 's-Gravenhage	11	B4
The Hamilton →	32	A2
The Macumba →	32	A2
The Neales →	32	A2
The Pas	36	C9
The Rock	32	C4
The Salt L.	32	A3
The Stevenson →	32	A2
The Warburton →	32	A2
The Woodlands	41	K7
Thedford	40	E4
Theebine	32	A5
Theodore	30	E8
Theodore Roosevelt Nat. Memorial Park	40	B3
Theodore Roosevelt Res.	39	K8
Thermaïkós Kólpos	15	D10
Thermopolis	38	E9
Thessalon	42	B3
Thessaloníki	15	D10
Thetford	9	E8
Thetford Mines	37	D12
Thevenard	32	B1
Thibodaux	41	L9
Thief River Falls	40	A6
Thiers	12	D5
Thimphu	25	C7
Thionville	12	B7
Thira	15	F11
Thirsk	8	C6
Thistle I.	32	C2
Thomaston	43	J3
Thomasville, Ala., U.S.A.	43	K2
Thomasville, Ga., U.S.A.	43	K4
Thomasville, N.C., U.S.A.	43	H5
Thompson	36	C10